250 SONGS BY

STOMPIN' TOM CONNORS

I sing and write songs
About the people and the country I live in.
And if that's not True Country Music,
Then I don't know what is.

- Stompin' Tom Connors.

CROWN-VETCH MUSIC

Copyright © & Published by Crown-Vetch Music (Division of Stompin' Tom Ltd.)
Box 129 Georgetown, Ont. Can. L7G 4T1

First Published 2005

Printed and bound in Canada by Webcom, on acid-free paper.

Library and Archives Canada Cataloguing in Publication

Connors, Stompin' Tom, 1936-
250 songs by Stompin' Tom Connors.

Lyrics with chord symbols.
Includes discography and 3000 Year Calendar.
ISBN 0-9738171-0-0

1. Songs, English--Texts.   2. Popular music--Canada--Texts.
I. Title.   II. Title: Two hundred and fifty songs by Stompin' Tom Connors.

M1679.18.C74T97 2005   782.42164'0268   C2005-903744-X

3000 Year Calendar by Tom C. Connors ©1978 by Everdate.
Liaison and Coordinator - Tom Connors Jr.
Cover design, sketches & format - Michael Dunlop
Photos - Stompin' Tom collection

Visit Stompin' Tom's website at www.stompintom.com

─────── INTRODUCTION ───────

Well, finally folks, HERE IT IS! The One Book that so many Stompin' Tom fans have been waiting for. The Book that contains All the Words and Chords to practically every song I have either personally written, co-written, or traditionally arranged as well as recorded over the last 40 years.

I say 'practically every song' because I may have missed one or two that I recorded on the now obsolete 45 rpm singles in Timmins, Ont. when I was first getting started.

Nevertheless, I think this book with over 250 songs is probably, up until now, the most extensive song collection ever compiled on any one song writing artist, and they're all under the one cover. It took quite a while but I'm finally glad it's done. The many people who have written me over the years, asking for song lyrics, will also be glad it's done, no doubt. From now on, when ever they play an album, all they have to do is pick up the book and sing right along, whether the song is a well known one or not. And of course the chords are there also for anyone who sings and plays an instrument and wants to have a little fun. That's what a lot of these songs were written for; Having Fun. So Let's Party!

Although, to date, there have been some 48 or 49 Stompin' Tom Albums released, either on vinyl or CD, a lot of them were either 'cover songs' of other artists which are now obsolete, or they were 'compilations' of my songs which were selected from the 22 Albums I now present to you in this book.

Also, along with the 250 or more songs contained in this book, there are 23 songs written by other Canadian artists which are included on the 22 albums. These are great songs which I recorded over the years because of how well they seemed to fit into my singing style and repertoire. You'll find these songs together with their writers listed in another place under the heading of "acknowledgement".

It has been supposed that I probably would have written and recorded a few more albums of songs by now if I had not returned my 6 Junos and retired for 10 years or so in protest of the Americanization of our Canadian Music Industry. And while the whole meaning of what I did seems to have fallen on deaf ears, I did what I believed I had to do at the time, and in retrospect, I would have done it all over again. But that's another story and it's already dealt with in my autobiographies. For those, along with my CD's and other Stompin' Tom Information and Memorabilia, you may wish to visit my son Tommy's Website where it is all available at: *www.stompintom.com* and I hope you all enjoy the Song Book.

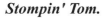

Stompin' Tom.

SOME BIOGRAPHICAL INFORMATION

Thomas Charles Connors, O.C., LL.D., Litt.D., alias "STOMPIN' TOM", singer, songwriter, musician and author, was born in Saint John, N.B., Canada, on Feb. 9th, 1936. He spent his earliest years hitch-hiking with his unwed mother until placed in care of the Children's Aid and was later adopted from the St. Patrick's Orphanage of Saint John by the Aylward family of Skinner's Pond, P.E.I.

With a formal education of only grade 9 he began to travel Canada and North America by way of hitch-hiking and riding freight-trains, always writing songs, playing guitar and singing for his keep. The jobs he did were always of short duration and between the age of 15 and 28 he was a merchant seaman, farm-hand, lumberjack, tobacco primer, truck driver, tire & rubber factory worker, house painter, grave-digger and many other jobs, far too numerous to mention.

His professional career as a full time entertainer began in 1964 with a 14 month booking at the Maple Leaf Hotel in Timmins, Ontario, with regular daily broadcasts on local C.K.G.B. radio, where he also committed his first two songs to tape and sent them to Quality Records in Toronto to be 'custom pressed' into a 45 rpm vinyl single recording. The songs were: "Movin' On to Rouyn" and "Carolyne".

Since writing his first song, "Reversing Falls Darling", at age 11, he has written literally hundreds of songs; at one time losing 994 of them when he lost an old battered suitcase in a flop-house somewhere in Toronto. The songs, nevertheless, kept on coming and so did the records. To date he has released 48 albums. And all the words and chords of the songs he wrote for 22 of them will be found here in this book. The total over 250. In 1995, Tom wrote the first half of his autobiography, "Before the Fame", which immediately became a No.1 Best Seller. And the second half, entitled, "The Connors Tone" in the year 2000 stayed for some time in the No.5 spot. Other books authored by Stompin' Tom are: "Stompin' Tom Song Folio" 1970; "Stompin' Tom, Story & Song" 1975; and 3 children's books in the 1990's. Tom was co-founder of Boot Records and Morning Music Publishing in 1971, and the founder of ACT Records in 1986. He has guest starred on many T.V. talk and musical variety shows, starred in his own C.B.C. T.V. weekly series, "Stompin' Tom's Canada", 1974-75; And has been the subject of 2 films, "This is Stompin' Tom", 1972; and "Across This Land With Stompin', Tom", a feature length movie, in 1973.

Tom was named Officer of the Order of Canada and received his medal in 1996; his first Honorary Doctorate of Laws (LL.D.) he received in 1993 from the University of St. Thomas in Fredericton, N.B., and his second LL.D. was conferred by the University of Toronto in the year 2000. His Honorary Doctorate of Literature (Litt.D.) came from the University of P.E.I. in 2002, the same year he received Her Majesty, Queen Elizabeth II's Golden Jubilee Medal while attending a special dinner in her honour at Rideau Hall in Ottawa.

On Nov. 2nd, 1973, Tom and his wife, Lena, were the first couple to ever be married on National Television in Canada. This occurred on the C.B.C.'s Elwood Glover Show, "Luncheon Date". And from 1970 to '75 Tom won 6 Juno Awards for Male Country Singer of the Year and for Best Album of the Year in 1973. In 1978 he returned his Junos and retired from performing in protest against awards given to expatriate Canadians. After 11 years of seeing no improvement in this regard and after continued insistence on the part of his fans that he should make a 'come back', he signed a record deal with Capitol Records

(EMI of Canada) and finally began touring again in the summer of 1990. He then won 3 East Coast Music Awards for Best Male Country Artist of '91 and '96 and Best Entertainer of the Year for 1991, and during this time initiated the "Stompin' Tom Award" which was named after him and presented yearly by the East Coast Music Assn. to the 'unsung heros' who inspired the present day performers of Atlantic Canada. Since 1996 Tom has refused to allow his name to stand for nomination in any of the award programs, including but not limited to, the Junos and the Canadian Country Music Association. (He may change his mind only when and if they become more 'Canadian'.)

Other awards Tom has received include the Periodical Marketers of Canada's Leadership Award, 1993; SOCAN's National Achievement Award, 1999; and the Governor General's Performing Arts Award for Lifetime Achievement in the year 2000. He has frequently been given the Key and/or Honorary Citizenship of Canadian cities and continues to enjoy great popularity and attendance throughout Canada on his yearly Concert Tours. While being honoured with his doctorate at the University of Toronto convocation, 2000, the eulogy contained this line: "His songs have given voice to the common people of Canada in a way unmatched by any other performer of his generation". While playing a concert in Toronto's Massey Hall in 2000, Tom auctioned off his "Stompin' Board" (the piece of plywood he stomps on to prevent stagefloor damage) for a cool $14,000. It is now considered to be the most valuable piece of battered plywood in the world. Proceeds were donated to the needy and homeless people of Toronto. Is it any wonder how this one time drifter has found a special place in the hearts of so many Canadians? In the recent C.B.C. T.V. nation-wide poll to find the "Greatest Canadian" of all time, out of the Top 100 we find that Stompin' Tom's name pops up as number 13. Is there any more to come? Stay tuned.

"This Song Ain't Over Yet".

SONG REFERENCE INSTRUCTIONS

1. The SONGS in this Book are ALPHABETICALLY LISTED in the CONTENTS which also contains the PAGE NUMBER WHERE THE SONG CAN BE FOUND.

2. EACH SONG on the Pages of this Book has an ALBUM NUMBER and a SONG NUMBER which tells you How To LOCATE the SONG AND THE ALBUM in the "DISCOGRAPHY".

3. The "DISCOGRAPHY" at the Back of this Book contains the TITLES of the 22 ALBUMS from which all Songs are taken.

4. EACH ALBUM & EACH SONG in the "DISCOGRAPHY' is Plainly NUMBERED.

5. EACH NUMBERED SONG in the "DISCOGRAPHY" also has a PAGE NUMBER which tells you the PAGE in the Book WHERE THE SONG CAN BE FOUND.

THE REFERENCE WORKS BOTH WAYS

CONTENTS

THE SONGS OF STOMPIN' TOM

(In Alphabetical Order)

6

CONTENTS

CONTENTS

CONTENTS

C.D. 17, SNG. 08

ALBERTA ROSE.

By T.C.Connors & G.Lepine
©1991 CROWN VETCH MUSIC
(SOCAN) All rights reserved.

1.

G.
Alberta means so much to me everytime I play
                                        D7.
        G.
My old guitar, a melody, a song.
                G7.   C.
And Rose, I know you're waiting out Alberta way
    D7.   G.
For me to come back home and settle down.

Chorus.
    C.   G.
Alberta Rose, I miss you;
        D7.   G.
The ranch, the rolling foothills far away.
G7.   C.
And the songs of old Alberta,
    G.   D7.   G.
I sing them every day.
D7.   G.
Rose, I'm coming home to stay.

2.

(First three lines spoken)
    G.
Rose, I hear your name tonight
            D7.
As Alberta lures my soul
                                            G.
On the westerlies that whisper in my window.
                    G7.   C.
You're home alone and waiting for that sunny day;
            D7.   G.
Well, Darling tell your heart I'm on my way.

(Repeat Chorus and tag last line)

C.D. 01, SNG. 06
C.D. 05, SNG. 08

ALGOMA CENTRAL #69.

By T.C.Connors
©1967 CROWN VETCH MUSIC
(SOCAN) All rights reserved.

1.

E.
She's on a bar-hoppin' spree
        A.
Back in Sault Ste. Marie
    B7.   E.
Because of me she's now a fallen star.
                        E7.
She could have been true
        A.
But I left her in the "Soo"
        B7.   E.
And I travelled north upon the A.C.R.

Chorus.
        B7.
But if it's go home or be a roamer,
A.   E.
I've made up my mind.
        B7.
So take me home tonight Algoma Central
            E.
Sixty-Nine.

2.

I was workin' one day
When I heard this fella say,
He met my girl while drinkin' at the bar.
Though we fought between us two,
Still he swore that it was true,
Now I curse that day I rode the A.C.R.

Repeat Chorus.

3.

Though it might be in vain,
Here I wait for the train;
I hope it's not too late to right the wrongs.
When she rolls around the bend
We'll be southbound again,
Come on old A.C.R. wheels, move along.

Repeat First Verse Before Repeating
Chorus... End.

C.D. 19, SNG. 13 **ALL NIGHT CAFE BLUES.** By T.C.Connors & G.Lepine

1

A.   E7.
Juke Box playing low,
A.   E7.
I close the door behind me slow
        D.   E7.   A.   E7.
I can smell burning onions from the kitchen
        A.   E7.
There's a pretty girl, but just like me
A.   E7.
She's as tired as can be
        D.   E7.   A.
She's a waitress in this All Night Cafe.

2.

A.   E7.
Truck drivers coming in,
A.   E7.
Two old geezers playin' Gin
        D.   E7.   A.   E7.
It's a hangout for the lonely after midnight.
        A.   E7.
They all come here to hang around
        A.   E7.
And since my baby left this town
        D.   E7.   A.
I'm a regular in this All Night Cafe.

CHORUS...
D.   A.
I've got these "All Night Cafe Blues"
D.   E7.
Listening to old winos and sad news
        A.   E7.
In my coffee, there's a spike,
A.   E7.
Outside, three motor bikes
D.
Just a-hummin' along to these
        E7.   A.
"All Night Cafe Blues."

3.

Now, the owner? He don't care,
Just as long as he gets his share
Of the dirty cups of coffee and the doughnuts;
In the washroom, there's a fight,
Two women of the night;
Old juke-box, whine these
"All Night Cafe Blues".

Repeat Chorus and end.

C.D. 19, SNG. 02 **AL SASS & DEE JOHN.** By T.C.Connors & G.Lepine

1

A.
He was born right on the border
    D.
Of Alberta - Sas-katch-ew-an
    E7.
Albert Sass was never fast
                        A.
But he always wore a gun

T'was the year of eighteen-ninety-two,
    D.
On a soggy' afternoon
    E7.
When Fast Dee John came blasting in
                    A.
To the Big Brown Bull Saloon.

2.

As Al Sass sat upon a rickety chair
By the picture of the Big Brown Bull
With a blushing blonde there upon his knee,
He poured their glasses full

But Fast Dee John said "That's my gal,
And I'm gonna gun you down"
And when Albert Sass came off that chair
You could only hear one sound.

3.

Because Al Sass couldn't move too fast,
We only saw one gun pulled
And Fast Dee John had five 'squirts' gone
When down came the Big Brown Bull
Pull after pull, he kept shootin' the Bull
'Cause Fast Dee John was fast
But when his gun went dry
He started lookin' shy,
Like he wanted to kiss Al Sass

4.

But Al Sass drew and then Dee John knew
That 'shootin' the bull' don't pay
And he got flushed real fast, there, when
Albert Sass just blew Dee John away.

Now, I'll tell you why and I'll tell you how
And I'll tell you the truth at last
Why Fast Dee John kept shootin' the Bull
And why he never got to shoot Al Sass.

5.

Dee John, at last, was twice as fast
As half-fast Al Sass was fast
And half-fast Al Sass was half as fast
As Fast Dee John at last.
Dee John was fast, but his blast at last
Passed fast past Albert Sass,
But half-fast Al Sass's half-fast blast
Blasted Fast Dee John at last.

6.

And when all was past we could see Al Sass
Leave town with the Blushing Blonde
And the West still sings of that Water-Gun King
And the water that flushed Dee John
Katch-ew-an, Katch-ew-an, Catch you on?
Catch you on? Do you catch on?

C.D. 04, SNG. 09   **AN ORPHAN'S CHRISTMAS.**

By T.C.Connors
©1970 CROWN VETCH MUSIC
(SOCAN) All rights reserved.

Chorus,

A.   A7.   D.
'Twas only An Orphan's Christmas,
    E7.   A.
But a Christmas I'll never forget.

Recitation: 1.

A.   A7.
It was Christmas time at the Orphan's Home
        D.
When the matron came to all of us and said:
    E7.
Santa Claus will be coming to the orphanage

this year

                              A.
And he's gonna bring each boy a new sled.
                              A7.
She said he'd have some left over this year
        D.
After visiting all the other kids' homes,
        E7.
Then he'd stop and see us

And give us a present a-piece,
                    A.
A sled of our very own.

2.

We'd all heard the stories about Santa Claus
With his bag full of gifts and toys galore
But he always only brought them
To kids with parents
And he never came to the orphanage before.
We'd faithfully done up our chores every day
And my job was making the beds
And I think I done pretty well
For a seven-year-old
Expecting a shiny new sled.

3.

Well, Christmas morning came
And the kids all lined up
And I arrived, the very last one.
'Cause the matron had told me
I couldn't go down
Until my beds were all properly done.
And when my turn came to meet Santa Claus
I can still remember those words that he said
"And that's all the presents I have for this
year, kids."
And I turned away hanging my head.

Repeat Chorus.

C.D. 02, SNG. 12
C.D. 05, SNG. 13

AROUND THE BAY AND BACK AGAIN.

By T.C.Connors
©1969 CROWN VETCH MUSIC
(SOCAN) All rights reserved.

Chorus.

  C.   G7.
Ferry man, Ferry man,
                 C.
Have you seen my Mary Ann?

In my search for her I've been
  F.   C.   G7.   C.
Around the Bay and Back Again.
  F.   C.   G7.   C.
Around the Bay and Back Again.

1.

C.
From Espanola to Manitoulin,
                G7.
Across the channel I'm bound:

I heard a story in Tobermory
               C.
That my baby's in Owen Sound.

I was close behind her but I couldn't find her,
  C7.   F.
So to Meaford I'm away;
                   C.
Down to Collingwood, that's where I stood
  D7.   G7.
At the bottom of the Georgian Bay.

Repeat Chorus.

2.

From Wasaga to Penetanguishene,
North to Parry Sound,
There's thirty thousands of lakes and islands
And where can she be found?
From Britt, my baby never hit French River;
In Sudbury they say,
She took a ferry to Tobermory
Across the Georgian Bay.

Repeat Chorus.

3.

From Espanola to Manitoulin,
Across the channel I'm bound:
Another story in Tobermory
Said to try old Hepworth town.
I was close behind her but I couldn't find her,
So l guess I'll have to stay
Without my lovely, on Lonely Island,
In the middle of the Georgian Bay.

Repeat Chorus.

C.D. 12, SNG. 05
C.D. 21, SNG. 11

BACK YARDIN'.

By T.C.Connors
©1975 CROWN VETCH MUSIC
(SOCAN) All rights reserved.

Chorus:

  D.
Back Yardin', Back Yardin',
                   A7.
That's a chit-chat party in the garden.

Just a Barbecue with a friend or two

Where you don't give a (Beg your pardon);
      D.
That's Back Yardin'.

1.

D
I may go broke on a business deal
                  A7.
So I phoned up uncle Lou.

He said, "When I'm Back Yardin', boy,
              D.
I don't care what you do."

Chorus:

2.

Well, I'm on the phone tryin' to get a loan
And I called up cousin Fred.
He said, "When I'm Back Yardin', boy,
You might as well be dead."

Chorus:

3.

Well, I had to phone my rich aunt Joan.
Would you like to buy some shares?
She said, "When I'm Back Yardin', boy,
I mind my own affairs,"

Chorus:

4.

Oh, brother Clyde, I can't survive
If I don't get some loot.
He said, "When I'm Back Yardin', brother,
I just don't give a hoot.

Chorus:

5.

Now, don't you know that business deal
Came through for me at last.
And I say, "This old 'Back Yardin' stuff
Is really quite the 'gas'."

Omit Chorus:

6.

And everybody's on the phone,
My relatives wantin' 'dough'.
I say, "It's too bad I'm Back Yardin, friends,
But there's one place you can go

Repeat Chorus Twice and Fade.

C.D. 17, SNG. 14 **BALLINAFAD BALL, THE** By T.C.Connors
©1992 CROWN VETCH MUSIC
(SOCAN) All rights reserved.

1.

A.
If you should go to Ontario,
E7.   A.
To the town of Ballinafad

At the general store they can tell you more
B7.   E7.
About the phone-call they once had.
D.   A.
When they heard the man say, "Tell the band,

From Nashville I did call."

And "Hold on tight, I'll be there tonight
E7.   A.
To play the ball at the Ballinafad Hall."

2.

Now, the word got around from town to town
Till a thousand tickets were sold;
To see the "star" with the "great big car"
From "Nashville", they were told.
And the local band got a great big hand
When they walked into the hall.
But the crowd looked high and low for that guy
Who made the telephone call.

3.

Then through the door with a rush and a roar
Came Sam, the furnace man.
With a fiddle case and a big red face,
And he jumped up on the stand.
"I'll have to state, I'm a little bit late,
But I hope you got my call"?

With an old straw hat, he grinned like a cat
When he bounced that fiddle like a ball

4.

Now, about that 'car' with the 'Nashville Star'
The band was never told.
But after the 'pause' and the 'one for the cause',
The mystery did unfold.
From the general store they knew the score
When Sam walked in the hall,
That he couldn't have been in Nashville when
He made that telephone call.

5.

Now, Sam took a bow as he laughed out loud
And he said, "I'll have you know,
There's a little place called "Nashville" here
In old Ontario."
"And there my truck got stuck in the muck
And I thought I'd better call,"
And tell the band I'll be on hand
When they play the Ballinafad Ball.

ENDING: Same Melody as the last four lines.

Said Sam, "My truck got stuck in the muck,
But tonight I'm tellin' you all,
Ah jis' cum' down f'om Nashveel town
Ta play da Bal'nafad Ball."

"Y'all cum' back now, hear?"

Use Southern U.S. accent on last two lines.)

C.D. 02, SNG. 09

BATTLE OF DESPAIR.

By T.C.Connors
©1968 CROWN VETCH MUSIC
(SOCAN) All rights reserved.

1.

D.   G.
Oh, we know the battle's coming
        D.
But the world don't seem to care,
            A7.
But they'll be sorry if this battle
        D.
Is the Battle of Despair.

When people fall a-crying

With their faces in the mud,

There'll be wailin', there'll be shriekin',
        A7.   D.
When the rivers run with blood.

Chorus: l.
        A7.
When the sun, the moon, the stars go black,
        D.
We'll know it's judgement day.
        E7.
And will the world be willing then
                    A7.
To get on its knees and pray?
                D.
They'll be wishin' they had bibles

'Stead of rifles in their hands

And the fear of God will till the sod
        A7.   D.
In the heart of every man.

2.

There'll be nothin' but disaster,
There'll be gnashing of the teeth;
And the heavens will be opened
To the wicked world beneath.
Then we'll hear the mighty trumpet
Sounding off throughout the land;
Non-believers will believe it
When the hour is at hand.

Chorus 2.

We'll see the blessed Savior
With the army that he brings.
He's the Splendor of the Nations,
He's the King of all the kings.
He will wear the Crown of Heaven,
Sittin' on the Judgement Seat,
And the Battle of Armageddon
Will be over and complete.

3.

Then the bodies upon bodies
In the shambles of the earth,
They'll be called to life again
To find out what their soul is worth.
Come all ye who have been faithful
To thy God whom you adore,
But burn all ye who evil be, in hell forever more.

Chorus 3.

The Battle of Despair, it may be this one to come.
What will be will have to be
But let us pray this ain't the one.
Take the Bible, not the rifle,
Never kill just bend the knee.
And if we lose or win the battle we'll still live
eternally.

C.D. 17, SNG. 07

BELIEVE IN YOUR COUNTRY.

By T.C.Connors
©1990 CROWN VETCH MUSIC
(SOCAN) All rights reserved.

1.

A.   D.
Good-bye Jim and Jackie, Good-bye John and May;
E7.   A.
We hate to see you leaving, bound for the U.S.A.

But if you don't Believe Your Country
A7.   D.
Should come before yourself,
        E7.
You can better serve your country
                    A.
By living some where else.

2.

I know the times are changing;
Factories closing down.
But if you'd stay and help us,
We can turn these things around.
But if you don't Believe Your Country
Should come before yourself.
You can better serve your country
By living somewhere else.

3.

And while our politicians
Divide our precious land,
We speak in French and English
But they still don't understand
That if you don't Believe Your Country
Should come before yourself,
You can better serve your country
By living somewhere else.

4.

In a land that's short on heroes,
They 'trade' our jobs away;
And we don't need no 'zeroes'
To come and help us save the day.
So if you don't Believe Your Country
Should come before yourself.
You can better serve your country
By living somewhere else.

5.

And if you should find your 'heaven'
Where Stars & Stripes are flown,
You'll learn to stand more proudly
Than you ever did back home.
And they'll tell you that your country
Must come before yourself,
Or you'll have to serve your country
By living somewhere else.

6.

So good-bye Jim and Jackie,
Good-bye John and May;
We hope that you'll be happy living in the U.S.A.
'Cause if you don't Believe Your Country
should come before yourself,
You can better serve your country
By living somewhere else.

REPEAT LAST FOUR LINES AND FINISH.

C.D. 03, SNG. 03   **BEN, IN THE PEN.**   By T.C.Connors

Chorus:.
  A.   D.
They call me Ben, here in, the Pen,
  A.   E7.
Where you take the guff and you suffer.
  A.   D.
But I'll be free when I'm fifty-three
  E7.   A.
And I bet I'll be a whole lot tougher.
  E7.   A.
I bet I'll be a whole lot tougher.

1.
  A.   D.
When I was a lad I was really bad,
  A.   E7.
it wasn't smart to be good.
  A.   D.
I beat up my dog and I choked my frog
  E7.   D.
And I acted just as mean as I could.

2.
I hit all the girls and put gum in their curls
'Cause I liked to hear them cry and plea.
I'd punch little boys and steal all their toys
Cause I knew they weren't smarter than me.

Chorus:

3.
When I was sixteen I was really mean;
I could scrap at the toss of a coin.
I was leader of a gang of rough rangy-tangs
And you had to be a good thief to join.

4.
Yeah, we had the black jackets and the
motor-bikes
And we forced all the girls to skip school.
And the cops, they'd all try to sympathize
When we told them how our parents were so
cruel.

Chorus:

5.
When I turned twenty-one I had to have a gun
'Cause I planned me a robbery one day.
And my girlfriend said that she'd rather
be dead
Than to hang around with a guy like me.

6.
So I granted her wish and dumped her in with
the fish
And then I went to meet Frank.
That's the same day I shot and killed me that
cop;
He didn't want to let me into the bank.

Repeat Chorus with the following last lines

I hope I'll be a whole lot tougher.
Ah, what's the use. I guess I ain't a very good
bluffer.
Yeah, back to that hammer, man, back to the
hammer........

BENNY, THE BUM.

1.

D.
If a man staggers by and he gives you the eye
          A7.
And he calls you his very best chum.

If he hands you a line, then begs for a dime,
               D.
You've just met old Benny, the Bum.
  A7.   D.
Oh, Benny, the Bum, you can't afford rum,
                  A7.
No, and you ain't got no place to go.

So you spend your time with a bottle of wine
             D.
In a flop-house way down on Skid Row.

2.
From where do you hail? Maybe just out of jail,
Or what new strange lands have you seen?
Your clothes are all tar from a railway box-car
And your blue-molded tie is now green.
Oh, Benny, the Bum, why should you be glum
When your brand new pair shoes are a-glow?

Though one shoe is brown and the other one's black
You're in style way down here on Skid Row.

3.
Now, the cop on this beat, he's about seven feet,
And he just won't leave Benny alone;
'Cause he thinks it's fun to see Benny run
And his wine bottle smash on the stones.
But who'd ever dream that Benny was seen
With the girl of his dreams, long ago.
Then God bid her "Come"
To leave Benny the Bum
To live in memories down on Skid Row.

(Sing Next Four Lines to Same Melody as Last Four Lines.)

Oh, Benny, The Bum, he can't afford rum.
And he ain't got no place to go.
So he spends his time with a bottle of wine
In a flop-house way down on Skid Row.

BIBLES AND RIFLES.

1.
G.   D7.
In this world of warring nations,
      C.   G.
Through man's eternal strife
      D7.   G.
We've come to see the writing on the wall.

And the house that is divided
C.
Is found to be our own
      D7.   G.
And above the battle cry the children call.

Chorus:
  C.   G.
Bibles and Rifles we cherish.
  D7.   G.
Bibles and Rifles we own.
  C.   G.
How will we fight over bibles
        D7.   G.
If we leave rifles alone?

2.
The wisdom of the children,
We claim we taught them well.
We trained the light of truth upon their minds.
But if they follow satan, believing God is dead
Then who will say the blind have led the blind.
Chorus:

Should the light of understanding
Through the window of each soul
Shine within each heart His Holy Name;
Would this world of warring nations
Be humbled on that day
In wonder while the earth goes up in flames.

Repeat Chorus and finish with this Tag Line.

When will we leave them alone?

BIG AND FRIENDLY WAITER JOHN.

By T.C.Connors
©1975 CROWN VETCH MUSIC
(SOCAN) All rights reserved.

1.

A.   A7.
When there ain't no end to the money you spend
  D.
I'm your friendly Waiter John.
  E7.
It ain't my job to listen to you sob,
                A.
But money, heh, heh, turns me on.
             A7.
You can sit right here and drink your beer
  D.
While you wonder where your woman's gone.
  E7.
And if your tips are high there ain't a nicer guy
             A.
Than Big and Friendly Waiter John.

2.

There ain't another man that can understand
Like Big and Friendly Waiter John.
I'm known to be a man of sympathy
'Least up until your money's gone.
So drink away all your cares and pay,
And forget about your run-away blonde.
Lean on the bar and have a big cigar
With Big and Friendly Waiter John.

3.

When you fall apart with a broken heart
Come to friendly Waiter John.
He'll pour your beer for you and lend an ear
And a shoulder to cry upon.
He'll dry your eyes for you and sympathize
Till all your troubles are gone.
So pull out your dough and let the big tips flow
To Big and Friendly Waiter John.

4.

Now everything has a price, even sound advice
From Big and Friendly Waiter John.
When I serve booze I kind o' pick up news
About lots of things that's been goin' on.
Might even be you could find out from me
Who stole your sweet Yvonne.
But for news to flash you gotta drop the cash
To Big and Friendly Waiter John.

5.

Yeah, that's a good old sot, and thanks a lot
From your Friendly Waiter John.
Here's enough to grab yourself a taxi cab,
But the rest of your money's gone.
You spent your load, now hit the road toad
And stop all this carryin' on.
You lost your gal like all your money, Pal,
To your Big and Friendly Waiter John.

C.D. 05, SNG. 01
C.D. 06, SNG. 02
C.D. 20, SNG. 14

BIG JOE MUFFERAW.

Refrain:

E7.   D.   A.
Heave Hi, Heave Hi Ho. The best man in Ottawa
     E7.   A.
was Mufferaw Joe. Mufferaw Joe.

Chorus:

  A.   D.
Big Joe Mufferaw paddled into Mattawa
  A.   E7.
All the way from Ottawa in just one day.

Hey, Hey.
  A.   D.
On the River Ottawa the best man we ever saw
    A.   E7.
Was Big Joe Mufferaw the old folks say.
       A.   E7.
Come and listen and I'll tell you what the old
   A.
folks say.

1.

 A.   D.
They say Big Joe had an old pet frog
 A.   E7.
Bigger than a horse and he barked like a dog.
   A.
And the only thing quicker
   D.
Than a train upon a track
  A.   E7.   A.
Was Big Joe ridin' on the bull frog's back.

2.

They say Big Joe used to get real wet
From cuttin' down timber and workin' up a sweat.
And everyone'll tell you 'round Carleton Place
The Mississippi dripped off of Big Joe's face.

3.

Now Joe had to portage
From the Gatineau down
To see a little girl he had in Kemptville town.
He was back and forth so many times
To see that gal
The path he wore became the Rideau Canal.
Repeat Refrain and Chorus:

4.

Now, they say Big Joe put out a forest fire
Half way between Renfrew and old Arnprior.
He was fifty miles away
Down around Smiths Falls
But he drowned out the fire with five spit-balls.

5.

Now, he jumped in the Calabogie Lake real fast
And he swam both ways
To catch a cross-eyed bass.
But he threw it on the ground
And said I can't eat that,
So he covered it over with Mount Saint Pat.

6.

Now, they say Big Joe drank a bucket of gin
Then he beat the livin' tar
Out of twenty-nine men.
And high on the ceiling of a Pembroke pub
There's twenty-nine bootmarks
And they're signed with love.

Repeat Refrain and Chorus and End with
Refrain. Then Fade by Repeating
"Big Joe Mufferaw, Big Joe Mufferaw...........

C.D., SNG.
To Be Recorded

BIRTH OF THE TEXAS GULPH MINE.
aka Birth of the New Dragon Mine.

By T.C.Connors & M.Martin

Refrain.

C.   Am.
Nineteen-sixty-four was the time
          C.   G7.   C.
For the Birth of the Texas Gulph Mine.

1.

C.   G7.   C.
In Timmins, that great northern place of renown
                          D7.   G7.
The Hollinger Mine was about to close down.
          C.
Twas enough to strike fear

In the hearts of the bold,
                              G7.   C.
Wondering just what their future would hold.
                              Am.
Nobody knew it was time
          C.   G7.   C.
For the Birth of the Texas Gulph Mine.

2.

But a 'copter flew daily from Timmins, they say;
To land in Kidd Township, just 12 miles away.
Still no one paid heed
As they walked down the streets
Engrossed with the problems
They'd soon have to meet.
Then just a few heard it was time
For the Birth of the Texas Gulph Mine.

3.

There was a mere handfull
Who found out the score
That Texas Gulph Sulphur
Had struck some good ore.
Together they staked every claim to be found;
'Tis said, some made millions
For holding good ground.
Yes, somebody knew it was time
For the Birth of the Texas Gulph Mine.

4.

At last it leaked out,
"There's a big copper find",
And the people of Timmins
Went out of their minds.
The well beaten path to the stock broker's door
Was trodden by thousands
Never seen there before.
Now everyone knew it was time
For the Birth of the Texas Gulph Mine.

5.

From Reid to Karskallen, then eastward to Tech,
The bush filled with stakers
Who daily would trek.
And the moose had to hide themselves
Most of the day
While claim-stakers rushed in
To make the bush pay.
All the papers proclaimed it was time
For the Birth of the Texas Gulph Mine.

6.

To Timmins came people
From south, east and west;
From thousands of miles they all came to invest.
Some mortgaged their homes
Just to try out their luck;
A few struck it rich while the others got stuck.
But the hopes of the north made a climb
Because of the Texas Gulph Mine.

7.

So nobody's worried, the future looks bright
For a smelter in Timmins,
They all joined the fight.
A smelter with lots of rich ore to refine
Has brought a new life to the "Old Porcupine".
And the eyes of the world have inclined,
Well fixed on the Texas Gulph Mine.
They're all watching the Texas Gulph Mine.

C.D. 02, SNG. 08   **BLACK DONNELLY'S MASSACRE, THE**

By T.C.Connors

Chorus
> A7.
The Black Donnellys ride.
> G.   D.
Their killers by their side.
> A7.   D.
Down the Roman Line till the end of time.

1.
> D.   G.
Back in eighteen hundred and forty some
> A7.   D.
To Lucan, Ontario, a man did come.
>   G.
A man who pushed his weight around,
>   A7.
And his wife Johannah
>   D.
Could slap the devil down.

2.
With seven sons who fought as well,
They opened up wide the gates of Hell;
And they fired up the land for miles around,
The Black Donnellys from Lucan town.

3.
With every glance that a Donnelly gave,
Came the sound of shovels diggin' your grave:
And many a club there came a-crashin' down,
Upon the heads of the men around Lucan town.

4.
Down the old Roman Line the further you went,
The folks got tougher and meaner bent,
And then the Black Donnellys for their abode,
They lived away down at the end of the road.

REPEAT CHORUS:

5.
Now old Jim Donnelly killed a man one day.
And everybody thought
That old Jim had run away,
But Jim was home and quite concealed,
In Johannah's old dress
Where he still plowed the field.

6.
But he served his time so the story goes,
He then came back again to cheat his foes;
With seven sons he robbed and burned,
Till the whole town knew
That old Jim had returned.

7.
They started up a coach-line from Lucan down,
With daily trips on in to London town;
And to destroy their competitors route,
They cut the tongues of all his horses out.

8.
Then eighteen men
With their clubs in their arms,
They marched on over to the Donnelly's barn;
But a Donnelly boy could fight like ten.
And they sure put a licken
On those eighteen men.

REPEAT CHORUS:

9.
They poisoned cattle now by the score,
They burned down buildings more and more,
They horse-whipped men
Just to make them say,
That they wouldn't appear in court next day.

10.
And every sheriff that the town could find,
They met the Black Donnellys
And then resigned,
For thirty-three years with their clubs in hand
The Black Donnellys had ruled the land.

11.
Then there came one man into Lucan town,
He was hired to cut all the Donnellys down,
A fearless man of a mighty frame,
And James Carol was that mans name.

12.
They made him the sheriff
And they followed through.
And formed his secret Vigilante crew,
In the old Swamp School House in winter time.
They planned their fatal night of crime.

REPEAT CHORUS:

13.
In eighteen-eighty, on that February night,
As "Old Granny" had foretold,
It was a terrible sight;
Old Jim and Johannah and Tom their son,
And Bridget were slaughtered,
They axed every one.

14.
Then the thirty drunks left
With the house all a-flame,
Hell-bent for more Black Donnelly game,
And from out of the fire and into the cold,
Ran that young Connor boy just eleven years old.

15.
Then the gun shots rang
And they ripped into J⟨
And another Black Donne⟨⟩
And so the "Grim Reaper had c⟨⟩
And the other three Donnellys
Then wandered away.

16
Now the Vigilantes they got away free,
From the law, but they all died mysteriously,
So one word of caution
To those who would hate,
At the end of your road
The Black Donnellys wait.

Repeat Chorus.

22 / C.D. 1

C.D. 22, SNG. 03 **BLACK VELVET BAND.** By T.C.Connors (Trad. Arr.)

First Verse/Chorus
   A.
Her eyes, they shone like the diamonds.
                   E7.
You'd think she was Queen of the Land.
      A.
With her hair flung over her shoulders fair,
 E7.   A.
Tied up with a Black Velvet Band.

2nd Verse.
As I was walking in Belfast,
Not meaning to do any wrong.
I met with a frolicsome damsel there
As she came tripping along.

3rd Verse.
A watch she had stole from a stranger;
She slipped it right into my hand.
On the very first day that we met, Bad Luck
Was wearing a Black Velvet Band.

Repeat 1st Verse.

4th Verse.
In the morning, before judge and jury,
Quite shaken, I had to appear
With a gentleman claiming his watch, I knew
The verdict, it would be severe.

5th Verse.
For seven long years of hard labour
They sent me to Van Dieman's Land.
Far away from my friends and relations, there
I paid for the Black Velvet Band.

Repeat 1st Verse.

6th Verse.
So come all ye jolly young fellows,
You'd better come listen to me.
Whenever you ramble in Belfast
Beware of this pretty colleen.

Repeat 1st Verse Twice, Ending with any of
these Optional Lines;
(She's known as the Black Velvet Band),
(They call her the Black Velvet Band), or
(Beware of the Black Velvet Band).

BLUE BERETS.

By T.C.Connors

1.

G.
Yes, we are the Blue Berets,
    C.   G.
We're up and on our way,
    D7.   G.
With another U.N. flag to be unfurled.

Till the factions are at bay
    C.   G.
And Peace is on its way,
    D7.   G.
We'll display our Blue Berets around the world.

Chorus
  G7.   C.
For we are the Blue Berets
      G.
And though we're far away
      C.   D7.
Tell our family and our friends who come to call;
      G.
If you count the lonely days
      C.   G.
You'll see your Blue Berets
        D7.   G.
Marching home again to say "We love you all".

2.

Yes, we are the Blue Berets
And we're always proud to say,
We shall stand between the mighty and the frail.
And where children cannot play
Because war is in their way,
We shall send our Blue Berets in without fail.

Repeat Chorus

3.

Yes, we are the Blue Berets,
We're marching on our way,
Where the bullets fly and rockets madly hurl.
Where hungers never cease
And mothers cry for peace,
We try to bring some hope to an ugly world.

Repeat Chorus

BLUE MISERY.

By T.C.Connors

1.

C.
You think you're O.K.,

But how can you be?
           G7.
When you've got a heart full
    C.
Of Blue Misery.

2.

   C.
The nights are so long

With no company;
         G7.
Where love is a shadow
      C.
In my memory.

Chorus
  C.   G7.
I wrote a letter;
              C.
I wrote quite a few.
           G7.
If I had your address
           C.
I'd send them to you.

But you'll never know

What has happened to me.
        G7.
I'm left with a lifetime
        C.
Of Blue Misery.

Repeat Chorus:

C.D. 12, SNG. 04

BLUE NOSE.

By T.C.Connors
©1975 CROWN VETCH MUSIC
(SOCAN) All rights reserved.

Chorus.
A.   A7.
My father was a "Blue Nose"
D.
And his dad, through and through;
E7.
My mother, she's a "Blue Nose"
A.
And her mother's mother, too.
A7.
We live in Nova Scotia
D.
Where the sea and sky are blue;
E7.
And when they call us "Blue Nose",
A.
We're gall-dang proud they do,

1.
A.   A7.
From Sydney, through to Yarmouth town,
D.
And all points in between,
E7.
It's just a magic picture book,
A.
The like you never seen.
A7.
And the pioneer who settled here
D.
And gave this land a name,
E7.
If he was called a "Blue Nose",
A.
I want to be called the same.
A7.   D.
For we turned the wheels of industry

Before the days of oil,

When the Nova Scotia miners
B7.   E7.
Gave the world their precious coal.
A.
And we built the fastest sailing ship
A7.   D.
That ever sailed the sea;
E7.
And if that was called, "Blue Nose",
A.
That's good enough for me.

Repeat Chorus

2.
Now, you might work in Halifax
Or make Cape Breton steel,
But there's a bond between us all,
We understand and feel.
And the world has seen our brothers
Who went off to fight the war,
And if they were called "Blue Nose",
Could we be something more?
Down where the sea-foods are the finest,
always Grade "A", Number One;
And the orchards of Annapolis,
They're the second best to none.
We love you, Nova Scotia,
May you stand forever proud.
And when they call you "Blue Nose",
Just smile and take a bow.

Repeat Chorus

C.D. 08, SNG. 04

BLUE SPELL.

By T.C.Connors
©1972 CROWN VETCH MUSIC
(SOCAN) All rights reserved.

Chorus:
G7.   C.
It's the Blue Spell all right,
G.
Creepin' into my house tonight,
D7.   G.
With only loneliness to foretell.
G7.   C.
It's the Blue Spell alright,
G.
Creepin' into my heart tonight.
G7.   C.   D7.   G.
But don't get smart with my heart, Blue Spell.

1.
G7. C.
Here I am, Oh here I am,
G.
You doggone lonesome blues.
A7.   D7.   A7.   D7.
But I won't be disappointed in love on account of you.
G.
I know I won't be cheated

'Cause I know my love too well;
G7.   C.   D7.   G.
So don't get smart with my heart, Blue Spell.

Repeat Chorus and Verse as required.

BONNIE BELINDA.

1.

A.   A7.   D.   A.
I met her up north in old Ontario
   E7.
Where beams of moonlight
     A.
Make wild roses grow.
    A7.   D.   A.
Sweeter than flowers that make people stare,
   E7.   A.
My Bonnie Belinda, so fair.

Chorus:
     D.   A.   E7.
Bonnie Belinda, the heavens are blue.
            A.
Bonnie Belinda, the stars shine on you.
A7.   D.   A.   E7.
My purest of maidens, I'll always dream of
           A.
Sweet Bonnie Belinda, my love.

2.

I left the old homestead in young days of yore,
Explaining to Bonnie, my love wasn't sure.
She told me she loved me,
Her eyes filled with tears;
Oh, Bonnie Belinda, my dear.

Repeat Chorus

3.

Then one sunny day
Found me heading back home
To plead with Belinda, to make her my own.
My friends came to meet me;
At the station they said,
"Bonnie Belinda is dead."

Repeat Chorus

4.

I went to her grave and I fell on my knees;
"My tears are too late, but Darling please
Forgive me, I love you,
You're my one only prayer,
My Bonnie Belinda, so fair."

Repeat Chorus

BRAND NEW LOVE AFFAIR.

1.

 G.   D7.
As an old flame tonight goes fading from sight
             G.
A new kind of love fills the air

And while dancing with you
   D7.
The old becomes new
                 G.
And I'm ready for A Brand New Love Affair.

2.

 G.
So if you hold me tight
    D7.
'Till the mood is just right
               G.
Those warm tender kisses we'll share
                D7.
And as old lovers learn, new love returns

                        G.
And I'm ready for A Brand New Love Affair.

CHORUS.
D7.   G.
Just as the old year fades into the new
A7.   D7.
Love reappears here and there
          G.   D7.
And as I waltz with you the old becomes new
                   G.
And I'm ready for A Brand New Love Affair.

3.

There's an old love tonight fading from sight
And a new kind of love fills the air
And while dancing with you
The old becomes new
And I'm ready for A Brand New Love Affair.

4.
So just hold me tight till the mood is just right
And those warm tender kisses we'll share
And as old fires die, new fires rise
And I'm ready for A Brand New Love Affair.

CHORUS.
Just as the old year fades into the new
Love reappears here and there
And as I waltz with you, the old becomes new
And I'm ready for A Brand New Love Affair.

TAG.
And as old fires die, new fires rise
And I'm ready for A Brand New Love Affair.
I'm ready for A Brand New Love Affair.

C.D. 07, SNG. 02 **BRIDGE CAME TUMBLIN' DOWN.** By T.C.Connors

1.
C. G7. C.   G7. C.
Nineteen scarlet roses, the Chaplan spread around,
     G7. C.
In the waters of Burrard Inlet,
    G7. C.
In old Vancouver town;
          C7.
Where the Bridge Came Tumblin' Down.
    F.
When the Bridge Came Tumblin' Down,
 C.
nineteen men were drowned,
  G7.
In June of Nineteen Fifty-Eight
 F.   C.
In old Vancouver town.

2.
There were seventy-nine men workin'
To build this brand new bridge
To span the Second Narrows
And connect up with the ridge,
When a big wind hit the bridge.
And the Bridge Came Tumblin' Down
And nineteen men were drowned.
And the medical corps couldn't be too sure
About the rest of the men they found.

3.
In among the twisted girders, one man realized
How last night he'd been dreaming
And saw before his eyes
The big wind on the rise.
And the Bridge Came Tumblin' Down
And nineteen steel-men drowned.
He foresaw the fright of the darkest night
In old Vancouver town.

4.
With frog-men in the water,
By the cutting torch's glow,
Then fought to save the steel-men
From certain death below,
And pain we'll never know.
When the Bridge Came Tumblin' Down
And nineteen men were drowned,
And sixty more that came ashore
Were thankful they were found.

5.
It often makes you wonder,
In strength, who has the edge,
The longest steel-beam structure,
That spans the highest ridge,
Or the men that built the bridge.
For the Bridge Came Tumblin' Down
And nineteen men were drowned,
But the rest of the men came back again
To lay the new beams down.

6.
Now, if you're ever crossing
This mighty bridge sublime
And nineteen scarlet roses
Pass before your mind,
Remember and be kind.
For the Bridge Came Tumblin' Down,
And nineteen men were drowned,
So you could ride to the other side
Of old Vancouver town.

Repeat Last Two Lines Slowly and Finish.....

C.D. 19, SNG. 09

BROKEN WINGS.

By T.C.Connors & G.Lepine

1.

D.
When that "Big Wheel" strolls around, man,
    G.
Do you dread it?
     A7.
When the work-place gets you down, boy,
    D.
Do you let it?

And do you think your boss
    G.
Is just a jolly old Santa Claus?
      A7.
Well, there's a 'clause' in Murphy's Law, says
   D.
"Just forget it."

Chorus:
 G.   D.
This old world is so unforgivin'
  A7.   D.
It's a wonder how a good man keeps on livin'.
  G.
No matter what you try,
  D.
You can work and laugh or cry,
  A7.   D.
But you won't fly them Broken Wings to heaven.
(Repeat this line.)

2.
Do you bring your pay-check home
Or do you bank it?
Or does your wife hang up the phone
Because you drank it?
And does your old dog bite
When you sleep with him at night?
Or does he cuddle up real tight
There in the blanket?

Repeat Chorus

3.
Does the phone call say
There's someone at the station?
And your mother-in-law, she's here
For a long vacation?
And man, does she look mad;
She's found out you've been bad,
And she's got no time
For 'simple' conversation.

Repeat Chorus... End.

C.D. 16, SNG. 04

BROWN EYES FOR THE BLUES.

By T.C.Connors

1.
C.   C7.   F.
I've got the Blues instead of Brown Eyes;
     C.   G7.
I couldn't wait, I had to choose.
       C.   C7.   F.
And now I just can't tell my Blue Eyes,
    C.   G7.   C.
How I've traded Brown Eyes For The Blues.

2.
C.   C7.   F.
I've got the Blues instead of Brown Eyes,
      C.   G7.
And when my heart received the news;
    C.   C7.   F.
I just knew that night with Blue Eyes,
  C.   G7.   C.
I had traded Brown Eyes For The Blues.

Chorus
C. C7. F.   C.
I never measured the lure of pleasure,
     D7.   G7.
I never measured all I had to lose.
       C.   C7.   F.
And I got the Blues instead of Brown Eyes
    C.   G7.   C.
When I traded Brown Eyes For The Blues.

Repeat Verses 1 & 2 and End with Chorus

C.D. 03, SNG. 01
C.D. 06, SNG. 12

BUD THE SPUD.

By T.C.Connors

Chorus:
    E.   A.   E.
It's Bud The Spud, from the bright red mud
                    B7.
Rollin' down the highway, smilin'

The spuds are big on the back of Bud's rig,
                       E.
They're from Prince Edward Island.
    B7.   E.
They're from Prince Edward Island.

Verse No .1 (Spoken)
         E.   E7.
Now from Charlottetown or from Summerside
   A.
They load him down for the big long ride.
   B7.
He jumps in the cab
                E.
And he's off with the pride Sabagoes.
                   E7.
He's gotta catch the boat to make Tormentine,
   A.
Then he hits up that old New Brunswick line.
    B7.
Through Montreal he comes just a-flyin'
               E.
With another big load of potatoes.

(Repeat Chorus)

(Extra Line Spoken/Optional
Now the Ontario Provincial Police don't
think much of Bud.

Verse No.2 (Spoken)

Yeah, the cops have been lookin'
For the son-of-a-gun
That's been rippin' the tar off the Four-O-One;
They know the name on the truck
Shines up in the sun, "Green Gables".
But he hits Toronto and it's seven o'clock
When he backs 'er up agin' the terminal dock
And the boys gather 'round just to hear him talk
About another big load of potatoes.

(Repeat Chorus)

Verse No.3 (Spoken)

Now I know a lot of people from east to west
That like the spuds from the Island best
'Cause they'll stand up to the hardest test;
right on the table.
So when you see that big truck a-rollin' by,
Wave your hand or kinda wink your eye,
'Cause that's Bud The Spud from old P.E.I.
With another big load of potatoes.

Last Chorus:
      E.   A.   E.
It's Bud The Spud from the bright red mud
                      B7.
Rollin' down the highway smilin'

(Slow Down and Speak Next Two Lines)

Because he's got another big load

Of the best doggone potatoes that's ever been
growed, (Resume Singing)
                           E.
And they're from Prince Edward Island.
    B7.   E.
They're from Prince Edward Island.

BUG SONG, THE By T.C.Connors

1.

Chorus:
A. E7. A.   D.   E7.
Bugs, Bugs, Bugs. If I had them all in jugs,

I'd dig, dig, dig, 'til a big, big hole

Was dug, dug, dug, dug, dug.
E7.   A.
And that would be the end of the Bug Song.

(Repeat Last Line.)

Verses Spoken......... 1.
A.   A7.
Now when the good old holidays roll around
    D.
I'm the kind of a guy that likes to be found
E7.   A.
Just takin' it easy and layin' around. Doin' nothin'.
         A7.
But I take my chair and I sit on the lawn
    D.
And just when all my cares are gone
      E7.
About a million bugs start carryin' on,
    A.
And I'm cussin'.

2.
Some caterpillar from up some tree
Decides, as far as he can see,
There's nothin' to do but to fall on me.
The damn worm.
And a dirty old fly, just makin' it clear,
That he ain't had a bath for over a year,
So he's takin' one now in my glass of beer
To lose germs.

Chorus:
3.
Well, I try to sleep when I get the chance
But you just can't trust them cursed ants;

They're never satisfied
'Til they're in your pants, and you're crawlin'
With a spider web right across the face,
I'm lookin' around for a better place,
'Til a couple of hornets take up the chase,
And I'm howlin'.

4.
I hit for the house and I hold my breath
'Til I find some stuff in the medicine chest
For the welts I got on the spot, you guessed,
where I'm sittin'.
And the wife gets mad 'cause I forgot
To get stuff for the fleas our kitten caught
Off some old dog on the neighbour's lot;
And she's rippin'.

Chorus
5.
Well, I chased that moth
From the middle drawer
That chewed the clothes I used to wore.
And I jammed my thumb
In the bedroom door, tryin' to catch 'im.
And I'm sure the mosquitoes
All know their skill,
'Cause one pried up my window sill,
And he limped through the air
With a broken drill; and I'm scratchin'.

6.
Now you might think I'm a little bit rough
'Cause I don't take to that 'nature' stuff;
But I think I've just about had enough
Of them bugs.
Now, your back yard might be okay,
But I'm goin' down to buy some spray,
'Cause my little place is walkin' away
With them bugs.

Repeat Chorus and Fade with
"I'm gonna dig, dig, dig, dig, dig?...etc.

BUS TOUR TO NASHVILLE. By T.C.Connors

1.

E.   B7.   E.
There's a big bus goin' to Nashville,
A.   E.
Leavin' at a quarter to nine.

I've got a baby called Bashful,

    Gb7.   B7.
And we're gonna make it on time.
E.   E7.
Down to the Horseshoe Tavern,
A.   E.
You'll see Bashful and me.

A.   E.
We'll board the bus in Toronto
B7.   E.
For Nashville, Tennessee.

Chorus:
E7.   A.   E.
Here we are on the big bus rollin',
E7.   A.   B7.
Play guitar, get everybody goin'
        E.   E7.
To the Grand Ole Opry in Nashville;
A.   E.
We're on a weekend spree,
        A.   E.
When the chartered bus comes a-rollin' us
B7.   E.
Into Nashville, Tennessee.

Repeat Chorus:

2.
There's a big bus goin' to Nashville,
Down the freeway, center lane;
And I'm gonna take my Bashful
To the Country Hall of Fame.
We're gonna meet all the singing stars
At the Grand Ole Opry door;
And I've got a feelin' Bashful
Won't be that way no more.

Repeat Chorus Twice and finish.

C.D. 15, SNG. 09
C.D. 18, SNG. 08

CANADA DAY, UP CANADA WAY.

By T.C.Connors
©1988 CROWN VETCH MUSIC
(SOCAN) All rights reserved.

CHORUS
    C.   G7.
O CANADA: Standing tall together.
        C.   C7.   F.   C.
We raise our hands and hail our flag,
        F.   G7.   C.
The Maple Leaf Forever.

1.
    C.
It's Canada Day, up Canada Way,
        F.   C.
On the first day of July;

And we're shoutin' "Hurray" up CanadaWay,
                D7.   G7.
When the Maple Leaf flies high.
        C.
When silver jets, from east to west,
    F.   C.
Go streaming through our sky,
        F.   C.
We'll be shoutin' Hurray! up Canada Way,
        G7.   C.
When the great parade goes by.

Chorus:
2.
It's Canada Day, up Canada Way,
On the coast of Labrador;
And we're shoutin' Hurray! up Canada Way,

On the wide Pacific shore.
People everywhere have a song to share
On Canada's Holiday.
From Pelee Island in the sunny south,
To the North Pole, far away.

Chorus:
3.
It's Canada Day, up Canada Way,
When the long cold winter's done;
And we're shoutin' Hurray! up Canada Way,
For the great days yet to come.
Where maple trees grow maple leaves
When the northern sun is high;
We're Canadians and we're born again
On the first day of July.

Chorus:
4.
It's Canada Day, up Canada Way,
From the Lakes to the Prairies wide;
And we're shoutin' Hurray! up Canada Way,
On the St. Lawrence River side.
People everywhere have a song to share
On Canada's Holiday.
From Pelee Island in the sunny south
To the North Pole far away.

Chorus:

C.D. 01, SNG. 12

CAROLYNE.

By T.C.Connors
©1967 CROWN VETCH MUSIC
(SOCAN) All rights reserved.

1.

C.
T - I - M - M - I - N - S .

That's gonna be my new address;
       G7.
'Cause I just got a new job workin'
    C.
In the mine, Hollinger Mine.

I'll work like a son-of-gun,

But as soon as that paycheck comes
       G7.   C.
I'm gonna buy me a diamond ring for Carolyne.

Chorus
   C.
Carolyne, sweet Carolyne.
                              G7.
I'm gonna make your pretty blue eyes shine,

Carolyne,

'Cause you're gonna wear that diamond ring
    C.
of mine;
 G7   C.
You're gonna wear that diamond ring of mine.

2.

T - I - M - M - I - N - S .
That's the town I love the best,
And we're gonna paint this Timmins town
Up fine, really fine.
All the people that we meet,
When we're strollin' down the street,
They're gonna stop and say,
"Oh, Look There's Carolyne".

Repeat Chorus

3.

T - I - M - M - I - N - S .
I'll advertize it in the Press,
'Cause I just got a new job workin'
In the mine, Hollinger Mine.
I'll work like I never before.
I don't care if my back gets sore,
I'm gonna buy that diamond ring for Carolyne.

Repeat Chorus Then Second Verse and
Chorus again

C.D. 19, SNG. 03

CASE CLOSED
(For The Holidays)

By T.C.Connors & G.Lepine
©1994 CROWN VETCH MUSIC
(SOCAN) All rights reserved.

1.

  A.
Case Closed and away she goes,
       E7.
Leaving me behind

I don't suppose she cares or knows
              A.
About this heart of mine

It's over now, the verdict's in,
       A7.   D.
We go our separate ways
 E7.
Case Closed and away she goes,
           A.
She's on her Holidays.

2.

Skirt's high and a smile 'goodbye',
She's heading for the plane
Another man will take her hand
While I just take the blame
The jury smiled all through the trial,
She's got those winning ways
Case Closed and away she goes,
She's on her Holidays.

3.

Case Closed and away she goes,
So happy to be free
The judge has ruled that I'm the fool
Just like she said I'd be
And how she grins each time she wins
Every game she plays
When the Case is Closed, away she goes,
she's on her Holidays.

4.

Case Closed and away she goes
With a twinkle in her eye
And I'll go home to be alone
And laugh until I cry
And then collect my Lotto cheque
And the million that it pays
Case Closed and what do you know?
She's gone away to stay. yay, ay, ay
Case Closed and Yippee I oh!
She's on her Holidays.

C.D. 04, SNG. 03

CHRISTMAS ANGEL.

By T.C.Connors

Chorus:

    D.   Gb
I get you on my mind
        G.   D.
Every year at Christmas time

                              A7.
As I trim every bough, branch and limb.
    D.   Gb.
But I don't want to see
    G.   D.
An angel on the tree
            G.   A7.   D.
'Til you're back in my arms once again.

1.

 D.   A7.
Christmas Angel, I have named you;

Since the day we first trimmed a
                D.
Christmas tree.

And the token of my love,
    A7.
I placed up above
            D.
A little angel,
            A7.   D.
For that's what you were to me.

Chorus:

2.

Christmas Angel, I have named you
For the Christmas tree I'm holding in my heart.
And I'm leaving a spot for your love on the top
Christmas Angel, even though we're far apart.

Repeat Chorus Twice:

C.D. 05, SNG. 07   **COAL BOAT SONG, The**

1.

D.
I left Cape Breton on the Coal Boat

A7.
For St. John's, Newfoundland;

And I met a little girl named Sally

D.
And I took her by the little white hand.

She shook her little head and said,

D7.   G.
No Way Fred, I won't go along with your plan.

D.
You've been workin' on a Coal Boat b'y,

A7.   D.
And you're nothin' but a dirty old man.

(Repeat last two lines)

(Spoken) Well, I had to think of somethin'
real fast, you know ....

2.

Yeah, well I'm gonna quit the dirty Coal Boat;
I wanna live in Newfoundland.
I'll buy a suit and get married;
Put a ring upon your little white hand.
She nodded her head and said, O.K. Fred,
Sally went along with the plan.
But I'm still workin' on the Coal Boat b'y,
And I'm nothin' but a dirty old man.

(Repeat last two lines)

3.

Well, it was some time later on the Coal Boat.
I got a little letter from home.
Sally said "Freddy was a good boy,
But the little beggar wanted to roam".
She said, it's too bad that he's got you for a dad
And I hope that you feel real grand;
He's gone workin' on the Coal Boat, b'y,
To be just like his dirty old man.

(Repeat last two lines)

4.

Well, I left Cape Breton on the Coal Boat
For St. John's, Newfoundland;
And good old Sally was a-waitin',
And I took her by the little white hand.
She shook her little head and said,
No way Fred, I won't go along with your plan.
You ain't gonna quit the Coal Boat, b'y,
'Cause I loves you ya dirty old man.

(Repeat last two lines)

5.

So, come all young fellers on the Coal Boat,
I hope you're gonna understand;
If you've got a pretty little girlfriend
And you take her by the little white hand.
If she turns her back and says, No way, Jack!
I won't go along with your plan,
Just keep workin' on the Coal Boat, b'y,
If you wants to be a dirty old man.
Just keep workin' on the Coal Boat, b'y,
And you'll be nothin' but a dirty old man.

C.D. 20, SNG. 07   **CONFEDERATION BRIDGE TO P.E.I.**

1.

G.
While Confederation bridges our nation

D7.
To an island so rich and so rare.

I'll be driving Northumberland

Strait, to that wonderland

G.
Garden that's cradled out there.

And I'll bet there's no bridges

Through high mountain ridges

C.
On land or on sea to compare

D7.
With the Confederation that bridges our nation

G.
To Prince Edward Island so fair.

Chorus.

C.
And it's calling, calling me over

The blue waters rolling

G.
And soon I'll be strolling out there.

D7.
Down by the ocean

Where the Island devotion

G.
To friendship is found everywhere.

Repeat Chorus ....

C.D. 08, SNG. 01   **CONSUMER, The**

By T.C.Connors
©1972 CROWN VETCH MUSIC
(SOCAN) All rights reserved.

Chorus:
(To be sung after each Verse or as required.)

   A.
Oh yes, we are the people,

Running in the race;
                B7.   E7.
Buying up the bargains in the old Market Place.
  A.   A7.
Another sale on something,
    D.
We'll buy it while it's hot;
          A.
And save a lot of money
    E7.   A.
Spending money we don't got.
   D.   A.
We save a lot of money
    E7.   A.
Spending money we don't got.

(All Verses Spoken)

1.
  A.
The Consumer, they call us.

We're the people that buy,

While everyone else is out to sell
B7.   E7.
Some kind of merchandise.
   A.   A7.
We run to the boss and tell him,
  D.
"We need a bit more gold".
            A.
Some tax deductions later
     E7.   A.
And we still wind up in the hole.

2.
The Consumer, they call us.
We always get a fair shake?
We buy a fridge that doesn't freeze
And a stove that doesn't bake.
We can't buy anything lasting
'Less we get that raise in pay;
Then they'd only charge us more
For the things that cost us less today.

3.
The Consumer, they call us.
We're fussy what we eat.
We look at the price of a T-Bone steak
And buy hamburg meat.
And all those fancy packages
We take down from the shelf,
They're always full of good fresh air
When they're not full of nothing else.

4.
The Consumer, they call us,
When the man comes in the door
To give us a 'deal' on a vacuum
If we buy a rug for the floor.
And how do we pay the finance
When the monthly bills arrive?
They just send down the bailiff
To re-possess the car we drive.

5.
The Consumer, they call us.
We're always deep in debt,
From buying drawers in discount stores
To fixin' the T.V. set.
We go to the bank for the money
And sign for another loan,
And pray the Lord doesn't see us stop
In the tavern half way home.

Note:
(This song was the Theme for the CBC TV
Series "Marketplace" from the year 1972 'til
about 1980.)

C.D. 10, SNG. 13

CORNFLAKES.

Chorus:
D.
Cornflakes,
               A.
That's what my baby makes
            E7.
Me feel like Cornflakes
         A.
With milk on top.
A7.   D.
And when I take
           A.
My "Little Sugar" she makes
        E7.
Me feel like Cornflakes,
            A.
When they crackle and pop.

1.

  A.
Before I found my "Sugar"
            E7.
My heart was an empty bowl.

Then she dropped a spoonful
         A.
Of sweetness in my soul.
  A7.   D.
Chorus (And I feel like Cornflakes .... etc.)

2.

Cornflakes in the night time,
Cornflakes in the day;
And as long as I get "Sugar"
Everything's okay ....
          A7.   D.
Chorus (On my Cornflakes .... etc.)

3.

I can't eat my supper,
And I don't want no cake.
All I want is sweet, sweet
Love, for heaven's sake.
         A7.   D.
Chorus (And my Cornflakes .... etc.)

C.D. 19, SNG. 05

COUNTRY JACK.
aka (Wino of Skid Row.)

1.
A.   A7. D.
If you're ever in our city,
     A.   E7.
On the back streets of our town
     A.   A7. D.
And you see an old man totin'
     A.   E7.
A small guitar around
     A.   A7. D.
That's Country Jack, the pickin' man,
 A.   E7.
A star of long ago
   A.   A7. D. E7.
An old tin cup on his guitar,
           A.
Now the Wino of Skid Row.

2.
He used to play on Main Street
'Till someone closed the door
Someone stole his big hit song
And he don't play there no more
But Country Jack's still singin'
The only song he knows
The one big song that broke his heart,
The Wino of Skid Row.

3.
So won't you give old Country Jack a nickel or a dime?
And don't you think his big hit song
Is worth a drink of wine?
And please don't judge old Country Jack
Or tell him where to go
'Cause he knows why you pass him by,
The Wino of Skid Row.

4.
So if you're ever in our city,
On the back streets of our town
And you see an old man totin'
A small guitar around
You may recall his melody, a song from long ago
Before old Country Jack became
The Wino of Skid Row.

5.
So, won't you give old Country Jack
A nickel or a dime?
And don't you think his big hit song
Is worth a drink of wine?
And please don't try to criticize the only song I know,
And this old man will play again,
The Wino of Skid Row.

C.D. 13, SNG. 08   **COWBOY, JOHNNY WARE.**   By T.C.Connors
©1976 CROWN VETCH MUSIC
(SOCAN) All rights reserved.

Chorus:

C.   G7.   F.   C.
Friendly, Courageous, Resourceful and Fair.

F.   C.
These are the pseudonyms

G7.   C.
Of a Cowboy, Johnny Ware.

1.

C.   C7.   F. C.
Johnny Ware was born in slavery around 1851,

To 'freedom' from the cotton fields,

D7.   G7.
He made his final run.

C.   C7.
The first part of his younger life

F.   C.
Is covered in travail.

F.   C.
Just a cow-poke on some cattle-drive

G7.   C.
Along the Chisholm Trail.

2.

My story starts in Idaho, in 1882,
When a Highwood River cattle-man
Came lookin' for a crew,
The day the big herd hit the trail
And dust was in the air,
Among the drovers on the drive
Was a Cowboy, Johnny Ware........Chorus.

3.

The mighty herd consisted of
3000 head or more,
Bound for old Alberta
To the Highwood River Shore,
While the big Bar-U- was waitin'
For the cattle to arrive,
The boss, Tom Lynch, had troubles
Keeping rustlers from the drive.

4.

The day they finally did arrive,
The stories that were told,
They said the deeds of Johnny Ware
Were something to behold,
He rode the meanest outlaw horse
And made him quite the pet,
Then he brought the cattle rustlers in
With just his lariet........Chorus.

5.

Now Johnny said he'd like to stay
To work the big Bar-U-,
And pretty soon there was no job
That Johnny couldn't do,
He could out-run any 3-year-old
And bull-dog any steer,
He could ride a bronco through a roll
Or stand him on his ear.

6.

He always took the hardest jobs
And made them look like fun,
He'd share his food and blankets
And his smile with any-one,
The old Fort McLeod Gazette
Said nothing could compare,
With the "Greatest Cowboy, All Around",
The Cowboy Johnny Ware........Chorus.

7.

He worked upon the Quorm Ranch;
They said he was the best,
His name was now a by-word
In the old Canadian West,
But Johnny said I've got to go
To the Town of Calgary,
Where I've got a little negro gal
And I hope she'll marry me.

8.

On a little ranch near Millarville
The couple settled down,
They soon became a family
With neighbours all around,
Honoured and respected by
The old folks and the young,
If only History could record
The praises that were sung........Chorus.

9.

By the year 1905, Alberta signed her name,
A Province now, of Canada, so proudly she became,
But while her jubilation
Was upon the whole Frontier,
Alberta lost her number-one cowboy pioneer.

10.

His smile and example
Are the "Spirit Of The Plains",
Never to be forgotten by the men who ride the range,
Some are born with character
And some have skill to spare.
But the "Greatest Cowboy of Them All"
Was the Cowboy, Johnny Ware........Chorus.

C.D. 07, SNG. 05 **CROSS CANADA.**
(aka C-A-N-A-D-A.)

By T.C.Connors
©1971 CROWN VETCH MUSIC
(SOCAN) All rights reserved.

1.

D.
C-A-N-A-D-A, Tell me, what's a Douglas Fir?
                    E7.   A7.
C-A-N-A-D-A, Bet you never heard a bobcat purr.
D.   G.
C-A-N-A-D-A, Have you ever seen a lobster crawl?
    D.   A7.   D.
In Canada, we get to see them all.

Chorus #1
    G.
We get to see the maple trees,

Maple sugar and the maple leaves,
E7.   A7.
We've got the biggest wheat fields growin' Tall.
    D.   G.
In C-A-N-A-D-A, where we see the Reversing Falls,
    D.   A7.   D.
In Canada we get to see them all.

2.

C-A-N-A-D-A, Tell me, what's a Tidal Bore?
C-A-N-A-D-A, Have you ever heard the ocean roar?
C-A-N-A-D-A, Just listen to that wild goose call.
In Canada, we get to see them all.

Chorus #2
We get to see the maple trees,
Maple sugar and the maple leaves,
We've got the biggest timber-woods, so tall.

In C-A-N-A-D-A, where adventure ever calls,
In Canada, we get to see them all.

3.

C-A-N-A-D-A, Have you ever hearda
Maple Creek?
C-A-N-A-D-A, Bet you never seen a mountain peak.
C-A-N-A-D-A, In the land of the big snow-ball,
In Canada, we get to see them all.

Chorus #3
We get to see the maple trees,
Maple sugar and the maple leaves,
We've got the biggest wheat fields growin' tall.
In C-A-N-A-D-A, in Niagara, the Horse Shoe Falls,
In Canada, we get to see them all.

4.

C-A-N-A-D-A, Have you ever seen a Magnetic Hill?
C-A-N-A-D-A, Or a Lady on a dollar bill?
C-A-N-A-D-A, Bet you never seen the Autumn fall?
In Canada, we get to see them all.

Repeat Chorus #2.

Final Tag Line:
I say, in Canada, we get to see them all

C.D. 08, SNG. 03 **CURSE OF THE MARC GUYLAINE, The**

By T.C.Connors
©1972 CROWN VETCH MUSIC
(SOCAN) All rights reserved.

Chorus:
    C.   G7.
Marc Guylaine, Marc Guylaine,
    F.   G7.
There's a curse upon your name,
        F.   G7.   Am.
And you must bear the shame, Marc Guylaine,
    C.   G7.   C.
You must bear the shame, Marc Guylaine.

1.

    C.   G7.
Three sister ships, in old Saint John,
        F.   G7.   Am.
Were built one day to sail upon the sea.
        C.   G7.
Lady Dorianne, the Marc Guylaine,
            F.   G7.
And the Lady O'Dette became their names,
            F.   G7.   Am.
And nobody knew what curses they would be.
    C.   G7.   C.
Three 'floating coffins' on the sea.

2.

In Nineteen-Seventy, a six-man crew
On the Lady Dorianne, off Isle Miscou,
went down.
Her sister ship, the Lady O'Dette,
With three more men, she ain't back yet;
And we don't know the reason they were
drowned.
We're not sure the reason can be found
Repeat Chorus:

3.

Captain Hashey tried in vain
To find a crew for the Marc Guylaine, but failed.
You can't get a man to make that trip
Aboard your 'floating coffin' ship,
When all the children whine and women wail;
They know the Marc Guylaine will never sail.

4.

Fishermen come, fishermen go,
And all the experts claim to know what's wrong.
The Marc Guylaine, they say, can sail,
So they built her down to a smaller scale;
And there in a tank of water the experts found,
The Marc Guylaine went sailing upside-down
Repeat Chorus:

5.

Two ships lost, nine men drowned
For some mistake that wasn't found before.
So, until our ships are safely made
The herring fish can die of old age
And wash against the north New Brunswick
shore;
And the name of the Marc Guylaine shall be
no more ... Repeat Chorus:

C.D. 13, SNG. 07 **DAMN GOOD SONG FOR A MINER** **By T.C.Connors**
(Muckin' Slushers)

1.

A.   A7.
Come on, you Muckin' Slushers,
D.   A.
You jack-leg drillers and blasters;

The price of uranium is up
     E7.
And there's money to make.
A.   A7.
Come on, you big rock-bolters,
D.   A.
who answer to the name of 'miner',
D.   A.
This old boom-town is still around
E7.   A.
On the shores of Elliot Lake.

Chorus:
D.
Time cards in and out, up and down cages,

Gonna make a heaven out of hell-earned wages;
E7.
Come on, Quirke, pay me now,

I got eighteen holes a-goin' Pow, Pow, Pow;
D.   A.
And there ain't no music finer.

E7.   A.
She's a Damn Good Song For A Miner.
E7.   A.
A Damn Good Song For A Miner.

2.

When it's daylight on the townsite
It's midnight away down under;
And I can hear the shift boss say,
"She's a muckin' out well".
With hard-hats, boots and oilers
We're off to scale the stope, boys;
Goodbye town, we're a-goin' down
To the belly of a man-made Hell.

Chorus:

3.

When it's afternoon, we'll cage up
To the surface and home to supper,
But we'll all meet at "The Algodin" later tonight.
Where the wine and the beer and the singin'
Kinda gets a good miner swingin';
And we'll dance around this whole damn town
'Til the sun comes shinin' bright.

Repeat Chorus, First Verse, and Chorus Again.

C.D., SNG.
Not In Discography

DIAL AN ISLAND
(The Eight-Double-Zero Jingle)

By T.C.Connors
©1972 CROWN VETCH MUSIC
(SOCAN) All rights reserved.

60 Seconds:

1.

A.
If you'd like to feel just right,
E7.
Laugh and have some fun;

Meet some friendly people
A.
And get some fishing done.

You can dial Prince Edward Island,
D.
It won't cost you none.
A.
For information on vacation,
E7.   A.
phone the Land of Fun.

2.

A.
Eight, double zero, five, six, five;
E7.
Seven, four, two, one.

A.
That's the Magic Number, free for everyone.

Just phone and say, "We're on our way"
D.
To the Island in the Sun.
A.
Eight, double zero, five, six, five;
E7.   A.
Seven, four, two, one.

3.

A.
Golf the courses, play the horses,
E7.
Nothing's out of reach;
A.
Fishing for the Tuna or bathing at the beach.

We welcome all to make this call
D.
For Prince Edward Island fun.
A.
Eight, double zero, five, six, five;
E7.   A.
Seven, four, two, one.
A.
Eight, double zero, five, six, five;
E7.   A.
Seven, four, two, one.

C.D. 10, SNG. 09

DON MESSER STORY, The

By T.C.Connors
©1973 CROWN VETCH MUSIC
(SOCAN) All rights reserved.

Chorus:
A7.   D.   A.
Don Messer played rings around the mountains;
E7.
He played reels all across the plains.
A7 .   D.
He played all that kind of music
A.   E7.   A.
That has made this country proud to say his name.

1.

A.   E7.
He was born in old New Brunswick
A.
In the early part of May, Nineteen-O-Nine.
A7.   D.
Six years old, he played the fiddle
A.   E7.   A.
At the barn dance on the old York County Line.

2.

Every year, Don got better;
He dreamed about that fortune down the track.
Then he came down to Saint John City
Where he formed
The old New Brunswick Lumberjacks
Chorus:

3.

Soon his band would have a singer;
Charley Chamberlain would join the
Messer fleet.
And travel to Prince Edward Island
To play on radio for twelve bucks every week.

4.
On the air, right after supper,
Commencing in the year of Thirty-Nine;
The man would say, "It's old Don Messer,
And His Islanders from down the Maritimes"
Chorus:

5.
Coast to coast with Don and Charley,
Duke Neilson and Ray Simmons played it up;
Warren McRae, with Cec McEachen;
Now the Islanders went touring to the top.

6.
How Charley sang with Margaret Osborne,
And Waldo made the old piano twang;
For the Queen, they played in concert,
And it was magic how Don Messer's fiddle rang.
Chorus:

7.
Seventeen years on Television,
From Nineteen-Fifty-Six to Seventy-Three;
Don Messer made his mark forever,
The fiddling King of Country Music History.

8.
Throughout the world, it's undisputed;
Don Messer and the Islanders were tops.
And away down east, beside the ocean,
The kind of music they began will never stop
Chorus:

C.D. 05, SNG. 03   **DON'T OVERLOVE YOUR BABY.**   **By T.C.Connors**

Chorus:
  D.
Don't Overlove Your Baby,
        A7.
She may prove untrue;
  D.
Don't Overlove Your baby,
  A7.   D.
She may walk on you.
  A7.   D.
She may walk on you.

1.
  D.
I've been feelin' lonely,
  A7.   D.
I've been feelin' blue;
  G.   D.
Since my baby left me,
  A7.   D.
Well, I'm tellin' you.

Repeat Chorus

2.
Keep the love light burnin'
When you fall in love:
Keep her always yearnin',
To be your turtle dove.

Repeat Chorus: But, Don't Overlove......etc.

DON'T WRITE ME NO LETTERS.

1.

A.
Well, I'm out of a job and just roaming around,
 A7.   D.
 E7.
And that's only half
         A.
Of what's wrong with this town.
            A7.   D.
The bar that I drink in, they gave me a note;
  E7.
It was signed by my wife
           D.
And here's what she wrote.

Chorus...
A.
Don't Write Me No Letters,
  A7.   D.
Don't call on the phone.
  E7.   A.
Don't knock on my door, there's nobody home.
              A7.   D.
I'm tired of hearing you won't take the blame
  E7.   A.
So go find another and I'll do the same.

2.

You're drinkin', you're smokin',
You're swearin' too much,
And when it comes to good lovin',
You're away out of touch.
You spend all your time in that dirty saloon,
And by the time you get home,
You're a perfect baboon. - Chorus.

3.

So, here in my new place, I'm watchin' T.V.
Beside my new woman who cherishes me.
I've cut out my drinkin', I'm workin' each day;
And when it comes to good lovin',
I'm doing Okay.

4.

And as I go walkin' down by the saloon
I can see at the bar, there's another baboon.
He's out of a job and he's wasting his life,
Receiving those notes
I once got from my wife. - Chorus.

DON VALLEY JAIL.

1.

C.   G7.   C.
I left my love to seek my fortune,
             G7.   C.
Though she told me not to go;
             G7.   C.
I said goodbye to Nova Scotia,
        G7.   C.
Travelled to Ontario.
                G7.   C.
There I chose the wrong companions
        G7.   C.
And we tried to rob the mail;
            G7. C.
Now I'm in Toronto city,
           G7.   C.
In the old Don Valley Jail.

Chorus:
  C7.   F.
Little darlin' do a favour for me,
  C.
Don't tell mom and dad.

It would break their hearts to know
                              G7.
Their only son has turned out bad.
          C.
And if you should see my sisters,
  C7.   F.   C.
Please don't tell them I'm in jail;
C7   F.   C.
I still love you, little darlin',
              G7.   C.
I'll be waiting for your mail.

2.

Here among my few belongings
I have pictures of the sea,
But the picture that I cherish
Is that one of you and me.
I'll be tryin' for probation,
There's a man that comes around;
Keep your fingers crossed and pray
That I'll be Nova Scotia bound... Chorus:

3.

As I write, I think of someone
Who once said, it always seems
When they take your freedom from you
Then you'll know what 'freedom' means.
Now, I hope you get my letter
In the Nova Scotia mail;
But don't forget me in Toronto
In the old Don Valley Jail... Chorus:

Tag Line after Last Chorus:
I'll be waiting for your mail
In the old Don Valley Jail.

C.D. 22, SNG. 07

DOWN NOVA SCOTIA WAY.

By T.C.Connors

1.

E.
One night in June beneath the moon
B7.
I heard those fiddles play

E.
Down Nova Scotia Way, Down Nova Scotia Way.

And as my boat began to float
B7.
Across that moonlit bay
E.
I found a cabaret Down Nova Scotia Way.

2.

E.
And as I walked upon the dock
B7.
Where friendly people say,

You're welcome here to stay,
E.
They stole my heart away.

And when the dance led to romance
B7.
I fell in love that day
E.
Down Nova Scotia Way, Down Nova Scotia Way.

Chorus:
B7.
And the moon was shining bright
E.
As heaven whispered
B7.   E.
Tell her that your heart will never stray.

B7.   E.
Take her in your arms and when you kiss her,
Gb7.   B7.
Tell her that you'll never sail away.

3.

E.
But the dawn was coming on
B7.
And I just couldn't stay

Down Nova Scotia Way.
E.
But I'll go back some day.

And my boat again will float
B7.
Across that moonlit bay

To where those fiddles play
E.
Down Nova Scotia Way.

Repeat Chorus & 3rd Verse.

4. (Tag Verse)
And my boat again will float
Across that moonlit bay,
To a little cabaret, Down Nova Scotia Way.
And that is where I'll stay.
Down Nova Scotia Way.

DOWN ON CHRISTMAS.

1.

A.
Well, here I am Down on Christmas,
E7.
After bein' up all year;

Broke my hip, caught the grippe
A.
And my good wife disappeared.

I hit the floor like an apple core
A7.   D.
when Doc took me off the beer;
E7.
It's hard to be Down on Christmas,
A.
After bein' up all year.

Chorus
A.   E7.   A.   A7.   D.
After bein' up all year; I can't find any cheer.
E7.
It's hard to be Down on Christmas,
A.
After bein' up all year.

2.

Yeah, here I am Down on Christmas,
And I can't eat nothin' fried;
Had a slice of meat that was cut so thin,
It only had one side.
I feel a lot like a dirty sock
That Santa Claus won't come near;
It's hard to be Down on Christmas,
After bein' up all year...... Chorus

3.

Here I am Down on Christmas,
And to add to my concern;
I got some coal in the kitchen stove,
Gauranteed not to burn.
And I'd like to tell that guy with the bell
He can go shove it into his ear.
It's hard to be Down on Christmas,
After being up all year...... Chorus

4.

Here I am, Down on Christmas,
And my credit's off at the store;
Some religious group sent a box of soup,
But it came to the guy next door.
I thumped the wall, but he never called,
And I'd like to say right here,
It's hard to be Down on Christmas,
After bein' up all year...... Chorus

EMILY, THE MAPLE LEAF.

1.

C.
Emily, the Maple Leaf lived with her family
G7.
High upon the maple tree;

Her sisters and her brother leaves

And all of the other leaves
C.
Used to laugh at Emily.

2.

C.
Everything that they said

Used to turn her face red;
G7.
Just as red as red can be.

But even when she felt bad,

She would never look sad,
C.
She took it all so cheerfully.

Chorus: 1.

   F.   C.
Then one day, the leaves all say,
   G7.   C.
Emily was taken far away.
   F.   C.
She was picked while playing tag,
    G7.   C.
And she was placed on Canada's Flag.

3.

Emily, the Maple Leaf, on the flag of Unity
Waving o'er the Nation wide;
Just to see her when she flips
On the masts of mighty ships,
Emily will stir your pride.

4.

All of us, we love her. There is none above her;
Blowing in the breeze, so free.
Her sisters and her brother leaves
And all of the other leaves,
We shout, "Forever Emily".

Chorus: 2.
She's our way to live each day,
In city style or country way;
From the valleys green to the mountain's crag,
Here's to Emily, Canada's Flag.

5.

Emily, the Maple Leaf, stands for the harmony
We share alike from sea to sea;
For this, our fathers sighed for,
Lived and loved and died for,
And we'll preserve it constantly.

6.

Where leaves are bound together,
We're Emily's forever;
We're all for one with each for all.
Our sisters and our brother leaves,
And all of the other leaves,
We'll never let the Red Leaf fall.

Chorus: 3.
Here we stand, all hand in hand;
O CANADA!, we're at your command.
And let not one be found to lag,
Where Emily waves on Canada's Flag.

C.D. 15, SNG. 13 **ENTRY ISLAND HOME.** By T.C.Connors

1.

  A.   A7.
Another day in Ontario,
  D.
Workin' to pay the debts I owe,
  A.   E7.
Living in a world I've never known;
  A.   A7.
And when I go to sleep at night
 D.   A.
I hold my pillow tight, while dreaming.
  E7.   A.
I dream about my Entry Island Home.

2.

And there again before my eyes,
A little boat from Paradise
Will carry me o'er the deep blue foam.
And then I'll be alive again;
My heart will anchor in the harbour.
In the harbour of my Entry Island Home.

3.

And to those hills and little farms,
Blue skies and open arms,
I'll renew my promise not to roam;
Where little children laugh with glee,
People of sincerity surround me,
And take me to my Entry Island Home.

4.

And when the fishing boats return,
Fiddles play, my heart will yearn,
And once again, my dreams,
They will have flown;
For I hear the bells on buoys warn,
There's gonna be a storm, and I waken,
Far away from my Entry Island Home.

Repeat First Verse with:
(Far away in Ontario... etc.)

Now Repeat Second Verse and Finish.

C.D. 21, SNG. 06

ERIKA NORDBY.
(Canada's Miracle Child)

By T.C.Connors
©2001 CROWN VETCH MUSIC
(SOCAN) All rights reserved.

1.

A.
One day in cold February
        E7.
In the year of two thousand and one,

From Edmonton City, Alberta
        A.
This remarkable story had come.

While sleeping one night with her mother,
  A7.   D.
Just a baby of thirteen months old;
        A.
Little Erika Nordby awakened,
 E7.   A.
Then crawled out of bed in the cold.

2.

A.
Out through a door that was open
        E7.
To a night that was thirty below;

By the time her poor mother came looking,
        A.
Her baby was froze in the snow.

In panic, she called paramedics
  A7.   D.
But much to her sorrow they said,
        A.
Little Erika's heart wasn't beating,
 E7.   A.
And they told her.... her baby was dead.

Chorus...
D.   A.
Erika Nordby, Erika Nordby
        E7.
Captured the world with her smile.
     D.   A.
Oh come hear the story of Erika Nordby,
   E7.   A.
Canada's Miracle Child.

3.

Then soon at the medical centre,
From her head to the tips of her toes,
There was no way to give intravenous;
All the veins of her body were froze.
But after some gradual heating
And much to their learned surprise;
Her faint little heart starting beating
While doctors had tears in their eyes.

4.

Then up in the arms of her mother,
When they saw little Erika smile,
All the media published her picture
And they called her "The Miracle Child".
But they couldn't believe how it happened,
This baby who froze in the snow;
And how she completely recovered
Was a mystery no mortal could know.

Repeat Chorus... end.

C.D. 20, SNG. 03

EXCUSE ME.

1.

E.   B7.   A.   B7.
Excuse Me for using our love, Babe,
                 E.
As a memory when I am blue, oo oo.
             B7.   A.   B7.
Excuse Me for needing your love, Babe,
               E.
That's the only love I ever knew.

2.

E.   B7.   A.   B7.
Excuse Me for acting like a fool, Babe,
              E.
I can't seem to realize we're through, oo oo.
        B7.   A.   B7.
Excuse Me for not playing cool, Babe,
            E.
That's because I love you like I do.

CHORUS.

B7.   E.
I will need your love to go on, Dear,
B7.   E.
As a memory when I'm blue, oo oo.
             B7.   A.   B7.
Excuse Me for using our love, Babe,
              E.
That's the only love I ever knew.

3.

Excuse Me for losing my mind, Babe,
I can think of nothing only you, oo oo.
Excuse Me for losing my heart, Babe,
That's because my heart belongs to you.

REPEAT 2ND VERSE AND CHORUS.......

C.D. 14, SNG. 05

FAREWELL TO NOVA SCOTIA.

Chorus:
  G.
Farewell to Nova Scotia, the sea bound coast;
        Em.
Let your mountains dark and dreary be.
     G.   D7.
For while I'm far away on the briney ocean tossed,
     Em.
Will you ever heave a sigh or a wish for me?

1.

  G.
The sun, it was setting in the west,
    Em.
The birds were singing on every tree.
     G.   D7.
All nature seemed inclined to rest,
    Em.
But still there was no rest for me. Chorus:

2.

The drums, they do beat and the wars do alarm,
The captain calls and I must obey.
So farewell, farewell to my Nova Scotia's charms,
For 'tis early in the mornin' I'll be far, far away.
Chorus:

3.

I grieve to leave my native land;
I grieve to leave my comrades, all.
And my parents, whom I love so dear,
And the bonny, bonny lassie that I do adore.
Chorus:

4.

I had three brothers but they are at rest;
Their hands are folded on their chests.
While a poor simple sailor-boy, just like me,
Must be tossed by the high winds
Of the deep blue sea.
Chorus:

C.D. 15, SNG. 02

FIDDLER'S FOLLY.

1.

A.
When I was a little lad of two or three
E7.
I learned to play the fiddle on my old dad's knee
A.
And the first little diddle that he hung on me
E7.   A.
Was a tune called Fiddler's Folly.

2.

I played it on the fiddle every time that I could
Till the old man said,
"Now, he's gettin' pretty good"
Then it didn't take long
'Til the whole neighbourhood
Was dancin' to the Fiddler's Folly.

3.

My school days came and I fiddled them away
Cause I didn't want to work, all I did was play
And my chest puffed up a little more each day
By the Devil and the "FIDDLER'S FOLLY".

4.

Now when my head got bigger
Than my little home town
I thought my fortune could be found
Playin' in a big band, tourin' all around
With a heart full of "FIDDLER'S FOLLY".

5.

And my girl in the country, I left her blue
Got another in the city and I left her too
And the only kind of love this fiddler knew
Was a love called "FIDDLERS FOLLY".

6.

I played my fiddle till I fiddled everywhere
And I tried to get a break
But there wasn't any there
And I found myself in a deep despair
A victim of "FIDDLER'S FOLLY".

7.

Now I took my fiddle and I took my bow
And I went back home and I put on a show
But I lost my shirt when they all said 'No',
Get away with your "FIDDLER'S FOLLY".

8.

And now there's a fiddler not so grand
He's livin' all alone like a broken man
A worn out fiddle in the Devil's hand
And fooled by the "FIDDLER'S FOLLY".

9.

So come all you fiddlers, old and young
When you let your fiddle get a little high strung
Remember the little fiddle-diddle I've sung
And the tune called "FIDDLER'S FOLLY".

C.D. 02, SNG. 04
C.D. 09, SNG. 03

FIRE IN THE MINE.

1.

D.
There was grief among the people

Of that northern Timmins town
A7.
When someone hollered, "Fire,
G.   D.
The mine is burnin' down".

Then rushing to the surface

Came those McIntyre men
A7.   G.   D.
To make ready and prepare to let the fire-fighters in.
G.   A7.   D.
There's a Fire way down in the mine.

2.

It was February second, in the year of Sixty-five;
A miner's life was taken in the carbon-monoxide.
The gas had been created way down a mile or so,
In the McIntyre hell-fire, six thousand feet below.
There's a Fire way down in the mine.

3.

The call went through the northland
For men to fight the flame,
From Sudbury to Noranda
And from everywhere they came.
With oxygen and gas masks
They worked for a month of days
In a hundred and fifty degrees of heat
They fought that gassy blaze.
There's a Fire way down in the mine.

4.

The deadly gas kept rising in the McIntyre, high,
'Till it seeped through the walls and fire-doors
To the Hollinger mine nearby.
For nearly a thousand miners, now,
There was no work below,
The word came from the office, "Boys,
We'll have to let you go".
There's a Fire way down in the mine.

5.

With their smiles of hope now faded,
Many faces wore a frown;
"Must we see our children hungry,
Must we have to leave the town"?
"Will they have to close the mines up,
Bringing trouble, strife and woe,
Or will they beat that gassy hell-fire,
Six thousand feet below?"
There's a Fire way down in the mine.

6.

Then at last it was all over,
They had sealed the fire in;
As it died they called the miners
Slowly back to work again.
Some may say that it was nothing
And the world may pass it by,
But the people up in Timmins
Will always hear that awful cry:
There's a Fire way down in the mine.

C.D. 12, SNG. 08

FLEUR DE LIS.

By T.C.Connors
©1975 CROWN VETCH MUSIC
(SOCAN) All rights reserved.

Chorus:
```
    G.        G7.          C.
Fleur De Lis, Fleur De Lis,
          D7.                G.
Je vous aime beaucoup, cherie.
             G7.          C.
Till the moon falls in the sea,
          D7.              G.
You will be my Fleur De Lis.
```

1.

```
  G.                        D7.
I met her by the Riviere De Loup,
                              G.
Where we shared a moonlight rendezvous.
             G7.      C.          A7.
I told her I'd return as we let the candle burn
  D7.                      G.
Out across the sea of endless blue,
  D7.                      G.
Out across the sea of endless blue.
```

2.

Now, every night alone, as I reflect,
I journey through that town in old Quebec.
And though I can't return, I see the candle burn
For me, across the sea of endless blue,
For me, across the sea of endless blue.

C.D. 01, SNG. 16
C.D. 16, SNG. 02

FLYIN' C.P.R.

1.

E.   E7.
I've been from old Vancouver,
    A.   E.
Right down to Newfoundland,
    B7.
I've travelled through old Canada
                            E.
And I'll travel through again.
    A.
My heart is like the three wise men,
                        E.
Once guided by a star;
B7.   E.
I left my blues to wander on the Flyin' C.P.R.

2.

Can ya hear that big eight wheeler
Go clickin' down the rail,
We're on the Flyin' C.P.R.
And believe me she can sail;
Oh take me flyin', whizzin' on
Away from a triflin' girl,
'Cause I know by the way that whistle whines
We're gonna span the world.

3.

Go rumble through the mountains,
Go flashin' by the sea,
Go flyin' through the countryside
To keep the blues from me;
Now tell me Mr. Porter can I play my old guitar,
I'll sing a song to the passengers
'Bout the Flyin' C.P.R.

4.

You've heard of the mighty rocket train
And the old time Cannonball,
Well it looked like they were goin' backwards
Man, when the flyer passed them all
The Canadian Pacific boys is hard to beat by far,
You'll get your life time thrill I know
On the Flyin' C.P.R.

5.

I told my two-time girlie,
When I heard that whistle moan,
That means your daddy is a gonna scram
And I'm leavin' town alone;
I've got another little mama friend
That'll mend my heart "by gar",
I'm gonna go roll my blues away
On the Flyin' C,P,R.

C.D. 18, SNG. 01

FOOTBALL SONG
(aka Wakin' Up The Grey Cup Team)

1.

A.
We'll see you down at the Football Game
                E7.
See you in the crowd
    A.
And we're gonna cheer our team this year
    B7.   E.
Till there aint no cheerin' as loud
    A.
And if someone down at the Football Game
        A7.   D.
Says, "Hey! Why do you scream"?

They're gonna realize
                A.
When we get the (big) "Prize"
    E7   A.
We were Wakin' Up The Grey Cup Team.

Chorus... (After Each Verse)
A7.   D.
With a 'First Down', 'Second Down',
        A.
a 'First Down' again
    B7.
'Snap' it to the Quarter-back
                            E7.
And flip it to the wind
    A.
Catch it on the '40 yard' and never turn around

(Then you) Run it to the 'End Zone'
        E7.   A.
And get a 'Touch Down'.

(Optional Last Line Of Chorus)
    A.   E7.   A.
Rush it to the 'End' and get another 'Touch Down'.

(Repeating Last Line of Each Verse is Also
Optional).

2.

Now, when it's 'Scrimmage' time,
At the '2 yard line'
We 'Bulldoze' in to score
Then the 'Kicker' kicks, and it's 'over the sticks'
And that's 'Six and one point more'
Then a '2 point sack' on their Quarter-back
And a 'Field Goal' just to be mean
And our screams and shouts
Don't leave any doubt
We've been Wakin' Up The Grey Cup Team.

3.

Now, when the Football shoots
From the Punter's boot
Their 'Receiver' can be sure
If he don't duck, he's gonna get struck
By a 'Tank' from the 'Second World War'
Then watch him fall down and 'fumble' the ball
And make a big 'Turn-Over' scene
And the cheering fans will make him understand
We've been Wakin' Up The Grey Cup Team.

C.D. 08, SNG. 08   **GASPE BELLE FAYE.**

1.

E.
I love the St. Lawrence River,
      B7.
I love the Bay Chaleur.

But the sweetest girl in all the world
      E.
Lives on the Gaspé shore.

From Mont Joli to Bon Ami,
      B7.
I love you through and through,

But paradise is in the eyes
         E.
Of the one I'm wanting to... always...

Chorus:
 E.
Be my Gaspé Belle Faye,
B7.   E.
My Belle Faye of the Gaspé;

Be my Gaspé Belle Faye,
B7.   A.   B7.
And I'll just hang around Gaspé Town;
      E.
Bound to the love I've found.
B7.   E.
Bound to the love I've found.

2.

From Campbellton Town, New Brunswick,
I drove to New Carlisle;
It's five o'clock around Percy Rock,
And it's forty-six more miles.
I'll soon be there with loving care
To do the things we do;
Kiss and hug my Gaspé love,
The one I'm wanting to... always...
Chorus: Be my Gaspé... etc.

Repeat First Verse and Finish with Chorus:

C.D. 04, SNG. 11

GLORIA.
(Angels We Have Heard.)

1.

C.
Angels we have heard on high;

Sweetly singing o'er the plains.

And the mountains, in reply,

Echo back their joyous strains.

Chorus:
C.   G7.   C.   G7.
Glo, o-o-o-o-o, o-o-o-o-o, o-o-o-o-oria,
C.   G7.
In excelsis Deo;
C.   G7.   C.   G7.
Glo, o-o-o-o-o, o-o-o-o-o, o-o-o-o-oria,
C.   G7. C.
In excelsis Deo.

2.

C.
Shepherds, why this jubilee,

Why your joyous strains prolong?

Say what may the tidings be,

Which inspire your heavenly song?

Chorus:

3.

C.
Come to Bethlehem and see

Him whose birth the angels sing.

Come, adore on bended knee,

Christ, the Lord, the new born king.

Chorus:

C.D. 01, SNG. 08

GOIN' BACK UP NORTH.

1.

C.   G7.
I'm Goin' Back Up North
                        C.
When the weather gets warm;
        G7.   C.
I'm gonna see my Mabel and I'm gonna reform.
        F.
I've been blue the winter through,
        C.
There's only one thing left to do,
        G7.
I'm Goin' Back Up North
                        C.
When the weather gets warm.

First Chorus:
C7.   F.   C.
When Mabel hears me say. I'm sorry I went away,
    D7.   G7.
I know shell take me back into her arms.
            F.
When the robins on the wing,
    C.
Sing their song of Spring,
        G7.
I'm Goin' Back Up North
                        C.
When the weather gets warm.

2.

I'm goin' back up north when the weather gets warm
I'm gonna be with Mabel when the maple buds form
When the ground turns to brown
And the grass grows all around
I'm goin' back up north when the weather gets warm.

SECOND CHORUS:
When Mable takes my hand, I know she'll understand
How I've been yearning for her tender charms
When the sun begins to gain
And the rose blooms in the lane
I'm goin' back up north when the weather gets warm.

3.

I'm goin' back up north when the better day's dawn
I'm gonna treat my Mable like I've been never gone
I can still see the hill and the stream run by the mill
I'm goin' back up north when the weather gets warm.

THIRD CHORUS:
When Mabel hear's me say, I'm sorry I went away
I know she'll take me back into her arms
When the summer's on the climb
And there's no more winter time
I'm goin' back up north when the weather gets warm,
I'm goin' back up north when the weather gets warm.

C.D. 10, SNG. 12

GOLDEN GONE BY.

1.

C.   D7.
Do you ever sit and think a bit
 G7.   C.   G7.
Of me, in the days gone by;
          C.   D7.
When our love was new, and oh how I loved you,
 G7.   C.
In the beautiful Golden Gone By.

Chorus
 D7.   G.   D7.
Visions of your memory
                     G7.
Haunt me as the day slowly dies;
 C.   D7.
I wonder if you ever think of me, too,
 G7.   C.
In the beautiful Golden Gone By.

2.

Do you ever weep instead of sleep
As the night time steals on by?
Are you happy at last
Or are you living in the past,
With me, in the Golden Gone By.

Repeat Chorus:

C.D. 03, SNG. 14
C.D. 16, SNG. 14

GONE WITH THE WIND. (I'll Be)

1.

A.   E7.   A.
Today is the day that I'm gonna say goodbye;
  E7.
I'm gonna close the cover
        A.
On the book of you and I.
 A7.   D.
You should hang your head
       A.
For the way you trifled on,
    E7.
But I know you'll never do it,
            A.
You'll be happy when I'm gone.

1st Chorus:
D.   A.
Gone With The Wind, like the leaves in the fall;
 B7.
Like time and tide I'm gonna wait
      E7.
For no one at all.
     D.   A.
And you won't even find me at the rainbow's end;

Gone with the breeze,
   E7.   A.
I'll be Gone With The Wind.

2.

Oh, two-timin' woman, I hope you'll never be,
Trickin', foolin', triflin' on no one like you did me.
Every dog has his day,
That's the way it's always been,
So far you've been lucky
But you'll pay for every sin.

2nd Chorus:
Gone with the wind like the drifting winter snow,
And if you're ever lonely
Don't you look for me no, no,
'Cause you won't even find me
At the rainbow's end,
Gone with the breeze, I'll be gone with the wind.

3.

I see now that somehow you had me on a string,
I'll give you credit there
'Cause you took care of everything,
But I hope you see the day
That you'll cry for me again,
You'll be here alone
And I'll be gone with the wind.

3rd Chorus:
Gone with the wind like the clouds in the sky
Gone with my sailboat, gone with the tide,
And you won't even find me at the rainbow's end,
Gone with the breeze, I'll be gone with the wind.

GOOD MORNING MR. SUNSHINE.

1.

D.
Drivin' down the Four-O-One,

Another day has just begun;
A7.   D.
Good Morning, Mr. Sunshine, how do you do?

Won't you ride with me a while,

I could use your winning smile,
A7.   D.
It sure could help my style to shine like you.

Chorus:
A7.
If you could do my smiling for me,
D.
How the people will adore me,
E7.   A7.
I'll bet they'd say good morning to me, too.
D.
If your smile could be mine

I could feel so devine,
A7.   D.
And shine, Mr. Sunshine, just like you.

2.

I could whistle on my way
When I hear the people say,
"Good morning Mr. Sunshine, how do you do?"
It's so nice when you arrive
All the world comes alive,
When you're with me
I feel like shining too.

Chorus:

3.

Everyday from now on
I will sing my favorite song;
Good morning, Mr. Sunshine, how do you do?
When you smile upon my chores
You'll be mine and I'll be yours
And we'll shine together me and you.

Chorus:
I want to shine Mr. Sunshine just like you

GUM-BOOT CLOGGEROO.
(GUMBOOT CLOGGIN'.)

1.

A.
Oh! We sailed away at the break of day
E7.
To pull traps, in oil-skin trousers;

On the "Suzie Jack", but tonight we're back,
A.
With a thousand pounds of lobsters.

Oh! Shanty Town, we're gonna tear you down;
E7.
I got money comin' out of me stockin's.

Tonight I'm do to 'bushwack' Sue,
D.   A
And take her to the Gum-Boot Cloggeroo,
E7.   A.
And we'll do a little Gum-Boot Cloggin'.

2.

Gimme fish and brewis and a Qua-Hog stew
And a bowl of clam chowder;
Just see me reach for that Newfie Screech,
When they diddle up the fiddle-jig louder.
Hear the French girls sing and the guitars ring
And the squeeze-box squeek-a-dee squawkin',
Me and my Sue gonna whoop-dee-doo,
Take her to the Gum-Boot Cloggeroo
And we'll do a little Gum-Boot Cloggin'.

3.

There's 'Boots" Bernard and the rough Richards
And the girls from 'way down Tracadie;
How many Blue-Nosers and Herrin'-Chokers
We just don't know exactly.
Pack 'em all in tight and we'll dance all night,
Get the old barn floor just a-rockin';
Buy a ring-dang-doo for P.E.I. Sue,
And take her to the Gum-Boot Cloggeroo
And we'll do a little Gum-Boot Cloggin'.

C.D. 12, SNG. 12   GYPSY CHANT.

Chorus

  Am.   Dm.
Where the Gypsies wander, wander,
Am.   E7.   Am.
I would like to know;
                  E7.
When the Gypsies wander,
  Am.   E7.   Am.
I wonder where they go.

Refrain:

  Am.   E7.   Am.
Hey ho she bah bah bah,
            E7.   Am.
Hey ho she bah bah bah,
    Dm.   Am.
Hey ho, hey ay ay ay ay ho,
            E7.   Am.
Hey ho she bah bah bah.

1.

A.   E7.
I fell in love with a Gypsy
                    A.
Where a strange pale moon does shine;
            E7.
I fell in love with a Gypsy,
                    Am.
But I never, never, never made her mine.

Repeat Refrain:

2.

Down where the stars are shining,
She told me she'd always stay;
But I heard the whip-poor-will pining,
So lonesome when she wandered away.

Repeat Refrain: Then Repeat Chorus and
Refrain and... End.

C.D. 14, SNG. 03   HANDY-MAN BLUES.

1.

 D.
I got the "I don't know
                    Bm.
How to fix the damn thing, blues";
       A7.
I'm just a "Handy-Man" to have around
                D.
When you're drinkin' booze.

I can't mend my broken heart
                G.
With a hammer, nails and screws;
    A7.
I'm a "Handy-Man" with the "I don't know
                D.
how to fix the damn thing, blues."

1st Chorus:

 A7.
You're just gonna have to come back
  G.   D.
To mend my broken heart;
    E7.
'Cause every castle I ever built
             A7.
Was a dream that fell apart.

2.

I got the "I don't know
How to fix the damn thing, blues";
I'm a "Handy-Man"
To make dreams that don't come true.
All I have is a broken heart
And a tool-set I can't use;
I'm a "Handy-Man" with the "I don't know
How to fix the damn thing, blues."

2nd Chorus:

I used to be the ambitious kind,
To keep things in repair;
But ever since you said, good-bye,
I guess I've lost my 'flair'.

Repeat 1st Verse and.... End.

HAPPY HOOKER, The

By T.C.Connors
©1977 CROWN VETCH MUSIC
(SOCAN) All rights reserved.

1.

A.
Oh! The land of liberation,
             E7.
It's a funny, funny world;

In every occupation
              A.
You'll always find "That Girl".

And I met her this morning
A7.   D.
On my doorstep, dressed in red;
E7.
Pointing to her bundles,
          A.
She winked at me and said:

Chorus:
 A.
I'll lay them in the bedroom, sir,
                    E7.
I can lay them in the hall;

If I hook them in the kitchen,
               A.
I can hang them from the wall.
                         A7.
I'm an expert on your carpet, sir,
           D.
I'm the best in all the world,
 E7.   A.
I'm "The Happy Hooker", your Rug-Sales-Girl.

2.

My mats and rugs and carpets.
I can hook them plain or shag,
And if you're patriotic,
I'll weave one like the flag.
Here inside my bundles
I've got everything you need;
I got rugs for all occasions
And my hookin's guaranteed.

Repeat Chorus:

3.

Well, of all the sales jargon
You get from door to door,
This had to be the best pitch
That I ever heard before.
She untied her bundles,
Took her money with a shrug;
Before I knew what happened,
She was layin' down the rug.

Repeat Chorus:

C.D. 19, SNG. 15

HEY, HEY, LORETTA

By T.C.Connors & G.Lepine
©1994 CROWN VETCH MUSIC
(SOCAN) All rights reserved.

Chorus:
E.
Hey, Hey, Loretta,
E7.   A.
Why don't you write a little letter?
E.   B7.
Hey, Hey, Loretta, why don't you phone?
E.
I could feel a little better
E7.   A.
If you write a little letter,
E.   B7.   E.
Hey, Hey, Loretta, please telephone home.

1.
A.
I've been drivin' up and down
E.
Every street in this old town
B7.
Asking all our friends, but they don't know
E.   E7.
All they do is shake their heads
A.
And say it's something that I said
E.   B7.   E.
Well, I'm sorry baby, now, where did you go?

To Chorus.

2.
Whatever happened to our song?
They're playin' all the music wrong
I can hear my heart beat on the stereo
The movie goers at the Mall
Say you don't come around at all
And as my curtain falls, where did you go?

To Chorus.

3.
I can't eat and I can't sleep,
And I can't make up if we can't meet
How can I ever say, "I love you so?"
I know you're somewhere in this town,
And before I turn it upside down
Won't you tell me now, where did you go?

To Chorus.

C.D. 12, SNG. 03

HIGH, DRY AND BLUE.

By T.C.Connors
©1975 CROWN VETCH MUSIC
(SOCAN) All rights reserved.

1.
D.   D7.
With a long, lonesome cry,
G.   D.
Right where you left me, high and dry;

And "Old Dreamboat"
A7.
Can't stay afloat with out you.
D.   D7.
All alone, I'm lost at sea;
G.   D.
All my dreams abandon me;
A7.   D.
And I'm HIGH, DRY AND BLUE.

Chorus:
D.   G.   D.
High. Dry and Blue tonight
A7.   D.
On this ocean of emotion where I lie.
G.   D.
Blue for you, my lonely heart cries,
A7.   D.
On this ocean of emotion I could die.

Repeat 1st Verse, Then Chorus and First
Verse again... End.

C.D. 22, SNG. 01

HOCKEY MOM TRIBUTE.
(aka My Hockey Mom.)

By T.C.Connors
©2004 CROWN VETCH MUSIC
(SOCAN) All rights reserved.

1.

G.   D7.
When I was young, I do recall

                              G.
We would go to school in the early Fall;

                              D7.
But on the days when there was no school,

                              G.
We'd learn to play by a different rule.
G7.   C.
Get out of that bed, you sleepy head,

My Hockey Mom would say;
 G.
Grab your skates and don't be late,

                      D7.
There's a hockey game today.
    C.
And poor old Dad was feelin' bad

Because he couldn't come;
      G.
He'd have to go to work and so
              D7.   G.
I took my orders from, My Hockey Mom.
                    C.   D7.
Tag: My Hockey Mom: She was my Chum;
              G.
My Hockey Mom.

2.

And then we drove to the rink in town,
And I'd hit that ice by fallin' down;
Then I'd score for the other team,
And you could hear my mom stand up and scream.
"Get off o' that ice, I told you twice

To skate the other way."
And every year she bent my ear
Until I learned to play.
And when my stick got pretty quick
And the puck to me would come,
Each time I scored I knew for sure
Where the loudest cheer was from.
My Hockey Mom.

Tag: My Hockey Mom: My day will come;
My Hockey Mom.

3.

And then one day, a stranger came
From far away, and he took my name.
And very soon, for the N.H.L.
I came to play and Mom came to yell.
Get on that puck and stir things up;
Show some 'winning pride'.
And every time she said that line
I'd bang that puck inside.
And here's my Dad, all Mister Glad,
He knew this night would come.
We're all lined up for the Stanley Cup
And the tears are rolling from, My Hockey
Mom.

Tag: My Hockey Mom: Aint she the 'plum';
My Hockey Mom.

Last Tag: My Hockey Mom: Forever young;
My Hockey Mom.

C.D. 08, SNG. 06

HOCKEY SONG, The

By T.C.Connors
©1971 CROWN VETCH MUSIC
(SOCAN) All rights reserved.

1.

C.
Hello, Out There! We're on the air,
              G7.
It's Hockey Night tonight;

Tension grows, the whistle blows,
                          C.
And the puck goes down the ice.

The goalie jumps, the players bump
          C7.   F.
And the fans all go insane;

                              C.
Someone roars, "Bobby Scores",
      G7.   C.
At the good old Hockey Game.

Chorus:
C.
Oh, the good old Hockey Game
                              G7.
Is the best game you can name;

And the best game you can name,
                              C.
Is the good old Hockey Game.

2.

Speak: "Second Period"!

Where players dash with skates a-flash
The 'home team' trails behind;
But they grab the puck and go bursting up,
And they're down across the line.
They storm the 'crease' like bumble bees,
They travel like a burning flame;
We see them slide the puck inside,
It's a one-one Hockey Game.

Repeat Chorus:

Speak: "Third Period! Last game in the
Playoffs, too."

3.

Oh, take me where the hockey players
Face off down the rink;
And the Stanley Cup is all filled up
For the Champs who win the drink.
Now, the final flick of a hockey stick
And the one gigantic scream;
"The puck is in", the 'home team' wins
The good old Hockey Game.

Repeat Chorus as Often As Required

C.D. 14, SNG. 14   **HOME ON THE ISLAND.**   By T.C.Connors

1.

A.   E7.
Just arriving Home on the Island,
                A.
The people on the ferry were smilin';
                E7.
Dad was on the telephone, dialin',
              A.
Tellin' everybody, I'm home.
              E7.
The old folks gather in the parlor
                  A.
To tell me what they're doin' at the harbour,
              E7.
And how many fishin' boats are there?
              A.
Gee, Mom, it's good to be Home again,
E7.   A.
Gee, Mom, it's good to be Home.

2.

I missed all your cookin' and your pan-cakes,
But don't start fussin' now for 'land Sakes'
Tell me what they're doin' up at Frank's place
And how is old Josey Jerome?
I see Dad's been workin' up the back land,
The cream-truck's droppin' off the milk-can,
And here comes Alfie, the mail-man.
Gee! Mom, it's good to be home again,
Gee! Mom, it's good to be home,

3.

I see the price of potatoes in the paper,
It just don't pay to grow an acre,
The dog's out barkin' at the grader,
And the hay smells great when it's mown.
We only get a holiday together,
But someday it's gonna be forever,
You can't beat the Island though, for weather.
Gee! Mom, it's good to be home again,
Gee! Mom, it's good to be home,

4.

The wind died down and the moss came,
And Joe's old truck went out the Knox Lane,
Here comes Roy, we'll have a card-game,
And maybe Aunt Maggie will phone.
We'll all get to talkin' 'bout the old days,
I guess I'll remember them always,
My heart must he made out of Red Clay,
Gee! Mom, it's good to be home again,
Gee! Mom, it's good to be home.

C.D. 18, SNG. 07
HONEYMOON IS OVER, The
(aka Poochi Pie)

1.

F.
Oh, The Honeymoon Is Over,

Poochi Pie, Poochi Pie,

C7.
And I wonder if the marriage is gonna fly

Hmm Hmm Hmm

I know were still together

And no one said Goodbye,

F.
But The Honeymoon Is Over, Poochi Pie.

2.

Oh, The Honeymoon Is Over,
Poochi Pie, Poochi Pie,
And I wonder why the nights are draggin' by.
Hmm Hmm Hmm

And if we don't find the answer,
Someone's gonna cry,
Cause The Honeymoon Is Over, Poochi Pie.

3.

Oh, The Honeymoon Is Over,
Poochi Pie, Poochi Pie,
And we're losing our direction, You and I.
Hmm Hmm Hmm
We've gotta stoke the fire, before the embers die,
Cause The Honeymoon Is Over, Poochi Pie.

4.

Oh, The Honeymoon Is Over,
Poochi Pie, Poochi Pie,
And I think we'd better give 'Old Love' a try.
Hmm Hmm Hmm
We can always hang our troubles
On the New Moon in the sky,
But The Honeymoon Is Over, Poochi Pie.

REPEAT VERSES NECESSARY.

C.D. 18, SNG. 02
HORSE CALLED FARMER.

1.

C.
On the shores of Entry Island,
C7.   F.
In the far off Magdalenes,
   G7.   C.
It was morning on the old Atlantic Sea;

When the early sun came rising,
   C7.   F.
Grandpa woke the sleeping kids,
          G7.
For there was something in the barn
             C.
They would have to see.

2.

As they clamoured to the stable
And they climbed upon the gate
The old brown mare was looking quite serene
And there beside his mother,
As the children jumped for joy,
Was the sweetest little colt they had ever seen.

3.

In the fur upon his forehead
Was the shape of the letter "F'"
And Grandpa said that Farmer was his name
All the children came to love him
More and more and every day
Their little 'Horse Called Farmer" did the same.

4.

He would love them every summer
When he hauled them through the fields
On his wagon load of Entry Island hay
And he would love them in the winter
When the channel filled with ice
And he could haul them to those islands
Far away.

5.

Now there came a winter's evening,
When the kids were all in bed
His master hitched him up to take a ride
And with many men and horses
He would cross the 'bridge of ice'
And bring his master safely to the other side.

6.

There was music at the party,
While the men were playing cards;
The bets were high and someone had to 'fold'
When the night was finally over,
No one seemed to understand
But the little "Horse Called Farmer"
Had been sold.

7.

He was forced upon a journey
Over many, many miles
With a man who lived on far away Grosse Ile
Where the barn was cold and drafty
And the cuttings from the whip
Only magnified the hungers he could feel.

8.

He was lonely in the Winter,
And even more so in the Spring
Till they put him in the field
Where he could graze
But the gate was rather shabby,
Just a kick might knock it down,
And our little "Horse Called Farmer" ran away.

9.

After many weeks of roaming
Many miles along the shore
There was something he was sniffing in the air
It was coming off the ocean
From an island far away,
And when he looked across the waters,
It was there.

10.

As he dove into the channel
Of the ocean deep and wide
In the same place where the 'ice bridge' was before
He was overcome with panic,
'Till he thought he heard the kids,
They were calling from his Entry Island Shore.

11.

It was hard to keep on breathing
When the waves went o'er his head
But he finally touched the bottom, just in time
He was now across the channel
Where he ran toward his barn
With the shouts of happy children right behind.

12.

Just a little "Horse Called Farmer"
In the far off Magdalenes,
You may not find him in the books of history
But the day our little "Farmer"
Swam back home to all us kids
Shall remain forever in my memory.

C.D. 06, SNG. 07

HORSESHOE HOTEL SONG.

By T.C.Connors
©1971 CROWN VETCH MUSIC
(SOCAN) All rights reserved.

1.

D.
Come all you big drinkers

And sit yourself down,
  A7.
The Horseshoe Tavern waiters
    D.
Will bring on the round;
    G.   D.
There's songs to be sung and stories to tell
  A7.
*Here at the hustlin', down at the bustlin',
          D.
*Here at the Horseshoe Hotel. Hotel!
    A7.   D.
*Right here at the Horseshoe Hotel.

*Last 3 Lines to be Sung at the End of Each
Verse:

2.

Now, there's Harvey, the hunter,
Just back from the kill,
Stanley, the storeman and bulldozer Bill;
And Marvin, the moocher,
We know them all well,
They drink at the hustlin',
Down at the bustlin',.....etc.*

3.

Oh, we've got the best waiters,
They do their job fast;
Before you're done drinkin'
They pick up your glass.
And Big Ted, the trucker, and needless to tell,
He drinks at the hustlin',
Down at the bustlin',.....etc.*

4.

Now, here's Stompin' Tom,
Who thinks he can sing;
But like an old rusty bell,
He's got no ding-a-ling.
But still he's okay, 'cause we all know well,
He drinks at the hustlin',
Down at the bustlin',.....etc.*

5.

Now, all you good people,
When morning is come,
You're back on your jobs
And your head's really numb;
I hope you recall when it's achin' like hell,
*You drank at the hustlin', down at the guzzlin',
*Here at the Horseshoe Hotel. Hotel!
*Right here at the Horseshoe Hotel.

Tag: You got sloshed at the Horseshoe Hotel.

C.D. 19, SNG. 04

HOW DO YOU LIKE IT NOW?

By T.C.Connors & G.Lepine
©1994 CROWN VETCH MUSIC
(SOCAN) All rights reserved.

1.

E.
Well, now, how do you like that G.S.T.?
B7.
The Loonie and Free Trade?

What do you think of Mulroney now,
E.
And the promises he made?

How do you like those fishing laws
E7.   A.
'Way down in Newfoundland?
E.
And how will the folks in the fishing boats
B7.   E.
ever understand?
E.
From the packing plants in the Maritimes
B7.
To the growers of our grain

They're fading away into yesterday
E.
Like the disappearing trains

And I wonder how the rancher feels
E7.   A.
And the farmer with his plow
E.
That great big chin had a beautiful grin,
B7.   E.
But HOW DO YOU LIKE IT NOW?

CHORUS:

HOW DO YOU LIKE IT NOW?
E7.   A.
To live with a broken vow?
E.
There's a lock on the door of the corner store,
B7.   E.
And HOW DO YOU LIKE IT NOW?

2.
How do you like them apple trees
They pulled up from the ground?
And how do you like those companies
That moved away from town?
And how do you like those million jobs,
The one's we could never find?
And the way we fret now to pay our debts,
well, it boggles up the mind.

They're breaking the social safety net
From New Brunswick to B.C.
And they're breaking the backs
Of the lumberjacks in the logging industry.
The young men roam from the broken homes
While the old men wipe their brow;
From the workin' girl to the mother's world,
Hey, HOW DO YOU LIKE IT NOW?

HOW DO YOU LIKE IT NOW?
Can we survive somehow?
They're on a roll; we're gettin' rid of the dole;
So HOW DO YOU LIKE IT NOW?

3.
They cooked our moose
And the Canada goose
While the eagle flies above,
And some can't wait now to separate
From the land they used to love.
From the Northern mines to the Maritimes,
the cheques are gettin' small,
And they'll tax away all your pension pay,
If it ever comes at all.

The only good things in the 90's
Are the things that used to be
Before Mulroneys Loonie,
Free Trade and the G.S.T.
And don't forget our war-time vets
Who saved our flag somehow;
You might have been sore about life before,
But HOW DO YOU LIKE IT NOW?

HOW DO YOU LIKE IT NOW?
Remember the gasoline row?
The price was high in days gone by,
But HOW DO YOU LIKE IT NOW?

HOW DO YOU LIKE IT NOW?
There's no milk in the Golden Cow,
When you kneel to thank your Piggy Bank,
HOW DO YOU LIKE IT NOW?

HOW DO YOU LIKE IT NOW?
Will you break the law somehow?
The crooks have guns, but you can't have one,
And HOW DO YOU LIKE IT NOW?

REPEAT LAST LINE AND FINISH

C.D. 02, SNG. 02

HOW THE MOUNTAIN CAME DOWN.
(Story of the Frank Slide)

By T.C.Connors & L.West
©1968 CROWN VETCH MUSIC
(SOCAN) All rights reserved.

Recite Verses: 1.

  D.   D7.   G.
On April, Twenty-second, of Nineteen-O-three,
          A7.
From the Indian reservation
         D.
Came a withered old Cree;
           D7.   G.
He came to the Pass of the old Crow's Nest,
    A7.
In the rugged Rocky Mountains
        D.
Of the Great North-West.
                D7.
He came to warn the white men
  G.
To leave their mining town,
     A7.
For the top of the Turtle Mountain, he said,
    D.
Was soon to come crashing down.
                D7.
He said, that before another sun
  G.
Would ever come to show,
    A7.
That a million tons of rock would slide
           D.
To the valley, far below.

Chorus:

  A7.
And O My God!
       G.   D.
How The Mountain Came Down;
  A7.
Oh, How The Mountain
      G.   D.
Came Down, Down, Down.
            D7.
The whole town of Frank
  G.
Was buried in the ground;
A7.   G.   D.
O My God! How that Mountain Came Down!

Sing A Chorus After Each Verse OR
As Necessary:

2

They laughed at the warning
And they paid him no heed
For who could trust the ravings, they said,
Of a crazy old Cree?
That rock had been surveyed
And the mining engineers
Said the mountain would be standing there
For another thousand years.
So nobody listened and the old man left
And the miners were now descending
For the mid-night shift.
The whole town was quiet now
Like nothing was a-foul
But a dog was heard to whimper
With the strangest kind of howl.

3.

All the men were workin' in the coal down below
And the monster rock was moving
Ever slow, slow, slow,
The stealthy mountain creeping
Sealed the mine like a tomb
On the twenty-third of April,
On that dark day, of doom.
The sun had almost risen,
With the miners in despair
When the top of the Turtle Mountain,
It went rising up in the air
With a mighty beastly grumble,
Like all Hell was at the door,
The giant rock had tumbled
All across the valley floor.

4.

Now everything was silent
Where life once used to be
No mine, no town, no people,
Not a shingle could he seen
When someone found a wee baby;
From out of the rock she cried
She became the sole survivor
And they called her "Frankie Slide"
No amount of excavation
Could save another soul
The day that Turtle Mountain
Took its deadly human toll;
And throughout the Rocky Mountains,
Friends, even to this very day,
Many people still whisper about it
And they shudder when they say

REPEAT CHORUS

C.D. 15, SNG. 14

I AM THE WIND.

1.

A.   E7.   A.
I Am The Wind, I Am The Wind:
       E7.   A.
Without foe, without friend.
         A7.   D.
I have no home, no cares to tend;
      E7.   A.
All alone, I Am The Wind.

1st Chorus:
A.   A7.   D.
I Am The Wind, I Am The Wind:
      E7.   A.
Where I go is where I've been.
        A7.   D.
I'm here today, and gone again,
      E7.   A.
On my way; I Am The Wind.

2.

I AM THE WIND; lazy wind;
Gentle breeze in Lover's Glen;
In the awesome tales of fishermen,
Testing sails; I AM THE WIND.

2nd Chorus:
I AM THE WIND; contrary wind;
Here to serve my Maker's end;
I don't believe I've ever sinned;
I only know I AM THE WIND.

3.

I AM THE WIND; swirling wind;
Stripping trees at Summer's end;
But I'm the song of Spring again;
Right or wrong, I AM THE WIND.

3rd Chorus:
I AM THE WIND; eternal wind;
Around the Door between gods and men;
And if you see how I go in,
You'll have the Key, and know the wind.
You'll have the Key, my friend,
To know the wind.

C.D. 22, SNG. 12

I BELONG TO GLASGOW.

Chorus:
E.   E7.   A.   E.
I Belong to Glasgow, dear old Glasgow town,

Hey! What's the matter wi' Glasgow, boys,
    Gb7.   B7.
She's goin' around and 'round.
     E.   E7.   A.
I'm only a common old workin' chap
         E.   B7.
As any one here can see.
       A.   E.
But when I get a couple of drinks on a Saturday
Gb7.   B7.   E.
Glasgow Belongs To Me.

Verse No. 1.
    E.   B7.   E.   E7.
I'd been out wi' a few of me cronies,
  A.   E,
Just a few lads of the clan.
    Gb7.
Went in the hotel, we did very well,
              B7.
And then we came back out again.
   E.   B7.   E.   E7.
But then we went in tay another;
       A.   E.
And that's why I'm broke and I'm blue.
    Gb7.
Had a wee Dock in Doris,

And you know the chorus,
           B7.
I wound up in jail wi' the crew.
     E.
Singing.... I Belong to Glasgow... etc.

Repeating Chorus.

C.D. 09, SNG. 04   **I CAN STILL FACE THE MOON.**

1.

C.   E7.   F.
I Can Still Face The Moon, any time;
     G7.   C.   G7.
I can honestly say I was true.
     C.   E7.   F.
I Can Still Face The Moon, any time;
     G7.   C.
But I can't say the same about you.

Chorus:
     C7.   F.   C.   G7.   C.
You forgot that night that you and I
                              G7.   C.
Walked alone except for stars up in the sky;
                                   C7.   F.
And you left the yellow moon wondering why,
                         D7.   G. G7
We pledged our love, but then you said goodbye.

(Repeat Verse One Then Chorus Then Verse
One again... End.)

C.D. 20, SNG. 04   **IF A MEMORY WAS A MELODY.**
aka (Memories & Melodies)

1.

D.
If a Memory was a Melody
     G.   D.
And a Heartache was a song

Love would always rule the world
     E7.   A7.
And be forever strong
     D.
And I'll just bet we'd all forget
     G.   D.
Just who went right or wrong

If a Memory was a Melody
     A7.   D.
And a Heartache was a song.

2.

If a Memory was a Melody
And a Heartache was a song
Each lonely day would pass away
And the nights wouldn't be so long
And you'd be back within my arms
Like you were never gone
If a Memory was a Melody
And a Heartache was a song.

3.

If a Memory was a Melody
And a Heartache was a song
And a little boy and a baby girl
Were back where they belong
I'd sing and play my heart away
And nothing could be wrong
If a Memory was a Melody
And a Heartache was a song.

REPEAT VERSES No.1 & 2.... and Finish.

C.D. 22, SNG. 09 ## IF I HURT ANY MORE.

By T.C.Connors
©2004 CROWN VETCH MUSIC
(SOCAN) All rights reserved.

1.

A.   E7.
If I hurt any more, I won't have to cry
                                    A.
If I hurt any more, I'll be willing to die
                          A7.   D.
You've been running around, I told you before
                        A.   E7.   A.
They'll be putting me down If I Hurt Any More.

2.

A.   E7.
If I hurt any more, I won't have a heart
                                    A.
If I hurt any more, I'll be falling apart
                        A7.   D.
Get this into your head, you better open the door
                      A.   E7.   A.
'Cause I'm gonna be dead, If I Hurt Any More.

Chorus:
A7.   D.   A.
If I hurt any more, I'll be leavin' you girl
              D.   E7.
If I hurt any more, I'll be leavin' the world
            A.   A7.   D.
So you better behave, while I'm up on the floor
                  A.   E7.   A.
'Cause I'll be in the grave. If I Hurt Any More.

3.

If I hurt any more, there won't be a sound
If I hurt any more, 'cause I won't be around
If you're gonna be cold, I can tell you for sure
There'll be nothing to hold, If I Hurt Any More.

4.

If I hurt any more, you'll be singin' the blues
You'll be walkin' the floor,
When you're hearin' the news
And if you try to pretend,
You were true to the core
You'll cry in the end, If I Hurt Any More.

Chorus:
If I Hurt Any More, I'll be leavin' you girl
If I Hurt Any More, I'll be leavin' the world
So you better behave, while I'm up on the floor
'Cause I'll be in the grave, If I Hurt Any More.

C.D. 19, SNG. 16 ## I'LL DO IT FOR YOU.

By T.C.Connors & G.Lepine
©1994 CROWN VETCH MUSIC
(SOCAN) All rights reserved.

1.

A.   E7.
I'll Do It For You, love, I'll Do It For You

I'll take an old dream, love,
                    A.
And I'll make it come true
                        A7.   D.
I'll give you my promise, everything that I do
              A.   E7.   A.
I'll Do It For You, love, I'll Do It For You.

2.

I'll give you my heart, love,
Every moment of time
It's only a start, love, if you can be mine
I'll give you my word, love, everything that I do
I'll Do It For You, love, I'll Do It For You.

3.

I'll build you a dream world,
I'll build you a dream
With rivers and rainbows on ribbons of green
In a garden of roses where the heavens are blue
I'll Do It For You, love, I'll Do It For You.

REPEAT 1st and 2nd Verses.

C.D. 21, SNG. 08

I'LL DREAM ALONE.

By T.C.Connors
©2002 CROWN VETCH MUSIC
(SOCAN) All rights reserved.

1.

A.
Deep down inside of me
      D.
The only dream I see
      A.
Is when you came to me
      E7.
To be my own.
        A.
And though you said to me
      D.
This dream can never be
      A.
With all those memories
  E7.   A.
I'll Dream Alone.

1st Chorus.
A.   D.
And in my picture book
     A.
I'11 often take a look
     E7.
To see the one I love
     A.
The one I'm dreaming of.

And though you can't be mine
     D.
All through the years of time
     A.
I'll take this dream of mine
  E7.   A.
And I'll Dream Alone.

2.

Deep down inside of me
The only dream I see
Is when you came to me
To be my own.
And though you said to me
This dream can never be
With all my memories
I'll Dream Alone.

2nd Chorus.

And in my picture book
I'll often take a look
To see our baby laugh
And kiss your photograph.
And though you can't be mine
All through the years of time
I'll take this dream of mine
And I'll Dream Alone.

REPEAT 1st Chorus and Finish.

C.D. 19, SNG. 10

I'LL DREAM YOU BACK.

By T.C.Connors
©1995 CROWN VETCH MUSIC
(SOCAN) All rights reserved.

1.

A.   B7.
Every dream always seems
  E7.   A.
To bring you back, and then
     B7.
When I awake my heart breaks
  E7.   A.
From losing you again.

2.

A.   B7.
How can I even try
  E7.   A.
To make a brand ncw start
      B7.
With memories of a 'used to be'
  E7.   A.
Still burning in my heart.

CHORUS...
 D.
To give myself to someone else
  A.
Is not the thing to do;
 D.
I could meet you on the street
  B7.   E7
And fall all over you.

3.

A.   B7.
And that's the way it is today
  E7.   A.
My heart won't set me free
          B7.
But that's all right, 'cause every night
  E7.   A.
I'll dream you back to me.

C.D. 12, SNG. 09

I'LL LOVE YOU ALL OVER AGAIN.

Chorus:
A7. D.   E7.
I want to love you forever;
                                 A.
Forever means never to end.
       D.   A.
And after I love you forever,
      E7.   A.
I'll Love You All Over Again.

1.

     D.   E7.   D.   A.
Please take my old way of dreaming
     E7.   A.
And give me a new life to start;
     D.   A.
Please take what I thought was freedom
     B7.   E7.
And make me a slave to your heart.

Chorus:
          D.   E7.
'Cause I want to love you forever .... etc.

2.
I have no mountains of silver
And I have no mansion of gold.
All I have for you is sunshine,
And something that never grows old.

Repeat Chorus

C.D. 15, SNG. 05

I NEVER WANT TO SEE THE WORLD AGAIN.

1.

 E.
It's a quarter after three,

There's nothing on T.V.,
                         B7.
And I've got every pocket novel read;

It's time again to take the glass

Filled with memories of the past
                            E.
And drink to all the lonely hours ahead.

Your note did not explain

Why you could not remain,
           E7.   A.
Or why there was a teardrop on the end;
  B7.
So I'll wait up for you 'til dawn,

And if, by then, you're really gone,
                         E.
I Never Want To See The World Again.

2.
It's a quarter after four,
You're still not at the door,
And down upon the carpet there's a fool;
An empty glass beside my knees,
I'm all out of memories,
I guess I've gone and broke the 'drinking rule'.

If you're not here by five,
My heart will not survive
To see another dawn come rolling in;
If all the love we shared so long
Is not enough to bring you home,
I Never Want To See The World Again.

C.D. 11, SNG. 10

I SAW THE TEARDROP.

By T.C.Connors & G.Lepine
©1969 CROWN VETCH MUSIC
(SOCAN) All rights reserved.

Chorus:

E.   E7.   A.   E.
I Saw the Teardrop in the corner of your eye;
                                 B7.
And the time had finally come to say goodbye.
            E.   E7.   A.   E.
You didn't have to say a word to tell me why;
                     B7.   E.
I Saw the Teardrop in the corner of your eye.

Recite:

                   1.
E.   E7.   A.
Oh, sweetheart, we had learned
              E.
To love each other so,

And then on the night you said
              B7.
I'd have to let you go;
       E.   E7.   A.
My broken heart had finally learned
         E.
The reason why.

I Saw the Teardrop, Darling,
   B7.   E.
In the corner of your eye.

Repeat Chorus:

Recite:

                 2.
It reminded me of the happiness
That we had shared:
It reminded me of your sweet love
And how much you cared.
But it also told me that someone else
Really owned your heart;
Though we're in love, the Teardrop said,
We'd have to part.

Repeat Chorus

C.D. 09, SNG. 02

ISLES OF MAGDALENE.

By T.C.Connors
©1971 CROWN VETCH MUSIC
(SOCAN) All rights reserved.

                   1.
D.   D7.
In the Gulf of St. Lawrence,
    G.
Off the coast of P.E.I.
    A7.   D.
There are treasures this world has seldom seen;
                   D7.
When I dream, I dream of them,
    G.
Shining there like little gems,
      A7.   D.
They're the beautiful ISLES OF MAGDALENE.
      A7.
Where the high cliffs of red
      D.
And the blue sky over head
      E7.   A7.
Lend the ocean its deep romantic sheen;
    D.   D7.
While the long warm lagoons
        G.
Lap the shining crystal dunes,
    A7.   D.
Heaven smiles on the ISLES OF MAGDALENE.

                 2.
Where the boats all come and go,
Slowly rocking to and fro,
On the breeze of the sea so fresh and clean;
And the hardy fisherman
Are away from home again,
Fishing lobsters
Off the ISLES OF MAGDALENE.

From Grosse Ile to Entry Isle
You may drive along and smile,
Through that little town of Grindstone
In between;
Where the children love to play
Round the barracks on the hay,
While the sun shines
On the ISLES OF MAGDALENE.

3.

To this haven of the Gulf
Many feathers from the south,
Build their nest among those hills
Of grassy green;
They sing je vous aime beaucoups
Like the friendly people do,
For they love those
Little ISLES OF MAGDALENE.

When the blue of the skies
Bring the tears to my eyes,
I go back to those islands of my dreams;
Where the little fishing towns
Dot the coast line all around,
I return to THE ISLES OF MAGDALENE.

C.D. 15, SNG. 03   # IT'S ALL OVER NOW, ANYHOW.   **By T.C.Connors**

I.

A.   D.   A.
Well, chuck my worries, what's my hurry?
                              E7.
I might as well unhitch the plow.
     A.   D.   A.
The wife went giddy with a guy from the city
               E7.   A.
And It's All Over Now, Anyhow.

2.

     A.   D.   A.
There's no harm in pigs and farmin',
                    E7.
Just enough to start a row.
          A.   D.   A.
She ran to her honey with a farm boy's money,
               E7.   A.
And It's All Over Now, Anyhow.

Chorus One:
E7.
No, No, Father; Don't you bother,
D.   A.
It's too late to call her now,
               D.   A.
Call the Auctioneer, John Watson;
            E7.   A.
It's All Over Now, Anyhow.

3.

I'll pay my neighbours for all their favours
Trade my tractor, sell my cow;
My life went wrong but I'll get along.
Cause It's All Over Now, Anyhow.

4.

Oh, I can't deny that I felt like dyin'
On that day she broke her vow;
But all her schemes were just a bad dream
And It's All Over Now, Anyhow.

Chorus Two:
No, No, Father; Don't you bother,
It's too late to call her now;
Call me a lawyer and I'll divorce her,
It's All Over Now, Anyhow.

5.

Well, I may be broke but I'm not croakin
I'm just pausin' to wipe my brow;
Then I'll drive them roads till my truck explodes
Cause It's All Over Now, Anyhow.

6.

So Chuck my worries, what's my hurry?
I might as well unhitch the plow;
The wife went giddy with a guy from the city
And It's All Over Now, Anyhow.

Chorus Three:
No, No. Father; Dont you bother,
I won't need that mortgage now;
Call the bank and just say Thank You,
It's All Over Now, Anyhow.

(Repeat Chorus One and finish)

C.D. 12, SNG. 06   **JACK OF MANY TRADES.**   **By T.C.Connors**

Recite:
  D.
Down in the manpower office

I was lookin' for work
                        A7.
When along comes a feller in a big white shirt;
  D.
He said, "You'll have to state

Your occupation, son";
      A7.
He broke the lead of his pencil
          D.
When I said, "Which one?"

Chorus: (To be sung after each verse).
  A7.   D.
I'm the Jack Of Many Trades;
                  A7.
I took a hundred school grades;

I wore out more axe blades;
      D.
Hammers, picks and dulled spades;
  A7.
I'm the Jack Of Many Trades
                      D.
And the Master of them all.

Recite Verses:
              1
      A7.
I'm a fisherman, a fireman,
  D.
Repairman, a cowboy,
  A7.
Roof-thatcher, dog-catcher,
  D.
Pay-master, bell-boy,
  A7.
Giant killer, diamond-driller,

Pig-swiller, milk-man
  D.
Gas-pumper, coal-dumper,

Bounty-hunter, baker-man,
  A7.
Surveyor, brick-layer, hockey-player, Dee-Jay,
  D.
High-rigger, grave-digger,

Cotton-picker, chess-player;... To Chorus.

2.
I'm a farmer, snake charmer, doctor, a lawyer,
Muleskinner, cat-skinner, poker player, sawyer,
Floor sweeper, meter reader,
Miner, bum and roamer,
Moss raker, ticket taker, lumber jack, astonomer,
Blood donor, matador, stevedor, a gun slinger,
Pub singer, bell ringer,
Book maker, dry cleaner;... To Chorus.

3.
I'm a blacksmith, junkman,
Factory worker lawman,
Busdriver, cabdriver, truckdriver, weatherman,
Squid jigger, babysitter, carpenter, psychiatrist,
Bodyman, serviceman, tailor, archaeologist,
Home maker, lawbreaker, leaf raker, paperboy,
A busboy, waterboy,
Batboy, loverboy;... To Chorus.

4.
I'm an oil man, trainman, a garbage collector,
Mechanic, professor, teacher, movie director,
Shoemaker, cook, painter, bartender, veterinary,
Plumber, tobaccoman, barber and typesetter,
Reporter, salesman, postman, jailorman,
Storeman, butcherman,
Hydroman, potatoman;... To Chorus.

TAG: (At the end of Last Chorus.)
      A7.
And if you have a job around, sir,
  D.   A7.   D.
I'd be the man to call, sir, I'd be the man to call.

C.D. 14, SNG. 02

JACQUELINE.

By T.C.Connors
©1977 CROWN VETCH MUSIC
(SOCAN) All rights reserved.

1.

A.   D.   A.
From the Bay Chaleur, o' Nouveau Brunswicka
          E7.   A.
Comes a mademoiselle of Canada.
                                    D.   A.
On a fine guitar like you never saw
          E7.   A.
She plays her hilly-billy musica.
     D.   E7.   Am.   A.
Jacqueline, Jacquelin;
          E7.   A.
She win de hearts of de fishermen; Yeah,
          E7.   A.
She win de hearts of de fishermen.

2.

Well I see her once by de water moon
And she play one herrin' choker tune
And de fishermen, dey go agin de law
When she plays her hilly billy musica.
- Jacqueline, Jacquelin. -
She meets a man from de television, Yeah,
She meets a man from de television.

3.

He say, from Nouveau Brunswicka
She's a mademoiselle of a Canada
On a fine guitar a-what she love to play
And to be for "Star" he come for take her away.
- Jacqueline, Jacquelin. -
Should play De guitar for de cameramen, Yeah,
Should play De guitar for de cameramen,

4.

Now all de people in de fish home town
Dey keep de eye a-lookin' on de ground
Cause de "Big Buck Man"
He come from Ottawa
And takes away all de musica.
- Jacqueline, Jacquelin. -
Come back to de North Shore fishermen, Yeah,
Come back to de North Shore fishermen.

5.

Well de summer time, she soon pass away
And de snow, she comes on de winter's day
When a picture known as "Jacqueline"
She come to show on de T.V. screen.
- Jacqueline, Jacquelin. -
We so surprise a-when we listenin', Yeah,
We so surprise a-when we listenin'.

6.

From de Bay Chaleur, Nouveau Brunswicka
She's a mademoiselle of a Canada
On a fine guitar like you never saw
She plays her hilly hilly musica.
- Jacqueline, Jacquelin. -
You make us so proud, all de fishermen, Yeah,
You make us so proud, all de fishermen.

JENNY DONNELLY.

1.

E.   E7. A.
On a bright moonlit night over Lucan,
    B7.   E.
Strolled the "Belle of Biddulph" and her beau;
       E7.   A.
He would soon have to leave for St. Thomas,
  B7.   E.
And he quietly begged her to go.

1st Chorus:
       E7.   A.
Come away, come away. Jenny Donnelly;
  B7.   E.
From Lucan I beg you to flee.
       E7. A.
Come away, come away, Jenny Donnelly;
   B7.   E.
Come and live in St. Thomas with me.

2.

There's a great cloud of hate over Lucan
And a black shadow strangles this land
So tonight let us go to your father
And there I will ask for your hand.
SECOND CHORUS:

Come away, come away, Jenny Donnelly
For the love in my heart you can see
Say goodbye, say goodbye, Jenny Donnelly
To this land with its dark destiny.

3.

They were married and lived in Saint Thomas
Where their children did happily grow
They were gay 'til that day came the message
Proclaiming its tidings of woe.

4.

As it read your family's dead
They've been murdered
Can you come they'll be buried today
Deep inside Jenny cried at the funeral
Till beside her she heard someone say.

REPEAT FIRST CHORUS:

JINGLE JANGLED AEROPLANE.
(aka Jingle Jangle.)

Chorus:
C.
Jump when the band plays Jingle Jangle,
F.
Swing with a single tingle tangle,
D7.   G7.
Dance in the Christmas Jingle Jangle way;
C.
Jump with a Jingle, Jingle Jangle,
F.
Swing with a single tingle tangle,
C.   G7.   C.
Dance the Jingle Jangle, Christmas Day.

1.

C.   G7.
I was wondering if the fans
         C.
Rock 'n roll in foreign lands;
      G7.
So my aeroplane and me
         C.
Flew around the world to see.
       G7.
I found out they rock 'n roll
         C.
In every place but the old North Pole;
      G7.
There I saw them swing and sway,
        C.
And I could hear old Santa say:

Repeat Chorus:

2.
So I flew down and landed there,
By Mrs. Claus' rockin' chair,
The reindeer jingle jangled by
And Rudolph held his red nose high,
Hear the Christmas fairies sing,
Watch the brownies sway and swing,
Then they taught me how to prance
The Christmas jingle jangle dance.

REPEAT CHORUS:

3.
Before I left the old North Pole,
I forgot how to rock 'n roll,
The jingle jangle in my brain,
Began to affect my aeroplane;
It must have heard old Santa say,
To jingle jangle all the way
'Cause now its in the Hall of Fame,
My jingle jangled aeroplane.

REPEAT CHORUS:

TAG:
Hey, Dance the jingle jangle Christmas day.

C.D. 17, SNG. 01

JOHNNY MAPLE.

By T.C.Connors
©1991 CROWN VETCH MUSIC
(SOCAN) All rights reserved.

1.
D.
Have you heard in Quebec City,

There's a law they would decree;

To separate John Maple
      E7.   A7.
From his lovely Fleur De Lis?
       G.
Well, my name is Johnny Maple,
       D.
And they'll never make no laws
     E7.   A7.   D.
That'll keep me from my little "Quebecois".

2.
Yeah, my name is Johnny Maple
And I'm from the Beaufort Sea,
And those high Laurentian Mountains,
They won't keep her love from me.
It's gonna take an army
Led by Big Joe Mufferaw
To keep me from my little Quebecois.

3.
They will have to move the mountains;
They'll have to stop the tides;
They'll have to burn the bridges
On a thousand rivers wide.
They'll have to move their province
Down to Nicaraug-oo-ahh
To keep me from my little Quebecois.

4.
So won't you come and join our wedding
Underneath the maple tree?
The wedding of John Maple
To the lovely Fleur De Lis.
And upon our waving banner
Of the Maple Leaf, I'll draw
One Fleur De Lis for my little Quebecois.

5.
There will he no 'separation';
Let the whole world come and see.
My name is Johnny Maple
And I love my Fleur De Lis.
We're gonna start a family
In my Northern Shangrila;
My provinces and my little Quebecois

REPEAT 2ND VERSE and finish.

C.D. 15, SNG. 10

JOLLY JOE MacFARLAND.

By T.C.Connors
©1988 CROWN VETCH MUSIC
(SOCAN) All rights reserved.

1.

G.
Hey, Hey. What do you say?
D7.　　　　　　　　　G.
I lost my job and I got no pay;
　　　　　　　　　　　　D7.　　　　　G.
My gal, she ran away, and now I got no darlin'

Ho, Ho, What do you know,
　　D7.　　　　　　　G.
I got no gal and I got no dough;

These are the troubles, Oh!
　　D7.　　　　　G.
Of Jolly Joe MacFarland.

Chorus No. 1.
　　D7.　　　　　　G.
Sold my car to get some dough;
　　D7.　　　　　　　　G.
Bought me a pocket radio;
　　D7.　　　　　　　G.
Now the battery's gettin' low;
　　A7.　　　　　　　　　　D7.
Here I come Ontaree-Yodel-ayee-o,wo,wo,wo,
　　G.
Hee, hi, and away we go,
　　D7.　　　　　　　G.
Down the road like an old hobo;

These are the troubles, Oh!
　　D7.　　　　　G.
Of Jolly Joe MacFarland.

2.

Hey, Hey, What do you say,
I got a new job yesterday,
My new gal, she said O.K.,
She's gonna be my darling.
Ho, Ho, What do you know,
The boss took off with the girlee oh,
These are the troubles Oh!
Of JOLLY JOE MacFARLAND.

Chorus Two:
Can't collect no pogey oh;
Will you buy my radio?
Give me a ride, Westward Ho?
Here I come Vancouver,
Yodel ayee oh wo wo wo
Hee Hi and away we go,
Down the road like an old hobo
These are the troubles Oh!
Of JOLLY JOE MacFARLAND.

3.

Hey, Hey, What do you say,
I fell in to the English Bay
I got pneumonee ay
And a mermaid is my darling.
Ho, Ho, What do you know,
Her father drives a UFO,
These are the troubles Oh!
Of JOLLY JOE MacFARLAND.

Chorus Three:
I got no job, I got no dough,
I might as well go home-ee-oh
When the spuds begin to grow,
Here I come P.E.I. Yodel ayee oh wo wo wo
Hee Hi and away we go,
Down the road like an old hobo
These are the troubles Oh!
Of JOLLY JOE MacFARLAND.

J.R.'s BAR.

C.D. 16, SNG. 05

1.

C.
Just two more jars down at old J.R.'s
        C7.   F.
Will drown my lonesome blues;
   G7.
I'm the only guy in P.E.I.
         C.
With nothin' more to lose.

She used to be right here with me
        C7.   F.
But she's nowhere now in sight;
   G7.
There's an empty stool beside a fool
        C.
In J.R. 's Bar tonight.

2.

There's an empty stool beside a fool
In J.R.'s BAR tonight;
There's a great big clown in Charlottetown
Who thinks he's always right.
And for awhile he tries to smile,
Then he cries with all his might;
There's an empty stool beside a fool
In J.R.'s BAR tonight.

3.

I didn't know when I let her go
How quickly I could fall;
I thought my friends would prove again
We're good friends after all.
But now today she's gone her way
And I know it serves me right;
There's an empty stool beside a fool
In J.R.'s BAR tonight.

JUST A BLUE MOON AWAY.

C.D. 18, SNG. 05

1.

G.   D7.
I'm Just A Blue Moon Away from your

world today,
                    G.
A Blue Moon Away from your world;
               D7.
No dreams of my own, I'm just here alone,
            G.
A Blue Moon Away from your world.

2.

G.   D7.
I'm A Blue Moon Away from your

love today,
                    G.
A Blue Moon Away from your world;
               D7.
Like the stars up above, I'll fade from

your love,
                G.
Just A Blue Moon Away from your world.

Chorus....

C.   D7.   G.
For you, there's a new moon rising,
     D7.   G.
He shines in your eyes like a pearl;
                     D7.
And though I appear, to be gone, I'll be here,
                      G.
Just A Blue Moon Away from your world.

C.D. 22, SNG. 04

JUST AN OLD TRAIN.

By T.C.Connors

1.

A.   A7.   D.
I'm just an Old Train, baby, Goin' Nowhere
E7.   A.
Cryin' over what you put me through
                 A7.
You're not a bad dream, baby,
      D.
You're a Nightmare
          E7.
And I'm the wreck that's always
              A.
Rollin' back to you.

2.

A.   A7.   D.
I'm just an Old Train, baby, Goin' Nowhere
E7.   A.
And you're the one that's breaking me in two
               A7.
You're not a bad dream, baby,
      D.
You're a Nightmare
         E7.
And I'm the wreck that's always
           A.
Rollin' back to you.

Chorus....
   E7.   A.
Every time I feel like going somewhere
   E7.   A.
You're kissing me and telling me to stay
   E7.   A.
But every time I feel like moving closer
   B7.   E7.
You make me think I'm only in your way.

3.

E7.   A.   A7.   D.
Just like an Old Train, baby, Goin' Nowhere
E7.   A.
Never knowing what to say or do
               A7.
You're not a bad dream, baby,
      D.
You're a Nightmare
         E7.
And I'm the wreck that's always
          A.
Rollin' back to you.

REPEAT 1st Verse & Chorus....

4.

Just like an Old Train, baby. Goin' Nowhere
I'll never find a way to say we're through
You're not a bad dream, baby,
You're a Nightmare
And I'm the wreck that's always
Rollin' back to you.

C.D. 10, SNG. 03

KEEPIN' NORA WAITIN'

By T.C.Connors & K.Brockwell

1.

C.
I got no money but I gotta see my hon,
          G7.
She lives in old Kenora;

If I don't get work she'll think I'm a jerk,
              C.
So I gotta get a ring for Nora.

CHORUS:
   C7.   F.   C.
'Cause I love her, and I need her,
     G7.   C.
And I dont want to keep her waitin' any more.

2.

I'll work like a dog doin' any old job,
And like I told Manpower;
Before I'll quit I'll shovel... DIRT,
For nineteen cents an hour.

3.
They got me a job out drivin' cat,
And now I'm excavatin;
I've got the ring and everything
And me and Nora's datin'.

4.
Tomorrow at dawn we're movin' on,
To work upon the highway;
The pay is big for drivin' this rig,
And things are goin' my way.

REPEAT CHORUS:

5.
Oh Nora dear, "Come here, come here",
No longer shall we linger;
I took her hand and I put the band
Of gold around her finger

REPEAT CHORUS:

6.
Now we live in a trailor camp,
And married life is started;
The trailor home goes with the job,
Just so we don't get parted.

REPEAT CHORUS:

Tag line:
No I don't keep Nora waitin' any more.

C.D. 03, SNG. 02

KETCHUP SONG, The

1.
A.
There was a guy from P.E.I.
E7.
They used to call "Potato";

He met this young Leamington,
A.
Ontario, "Tomato".

But he had eyes for other girls
E7.
And she was a little mushy;

So they said, "Well, let's get wed,
A.
There's no sense being fussy".

CHORUS:
D.   A.   E7.
Big size French Fries; how they love tomatoes!

So dress 'em up with Heinz Ketchup;
A.   E7.   A.
Ketchup loves Potatoes: Ketchup loves Potatoes.

2.
Well, he went down to Windsor town
To buy a ring on Monday.
Saturday, they said "O.K.
We'll cut the cake on Sunday".
But Sunday came and what a shame,
They had no one to fetch it.
Without a cake they just sat and ate
Potato Chips and Ketchup.

REPEAT CHORUS:

3.
And so this guy from P.E.I.
They used to call Potato,
He's got two boys and a little girl
(Two Spuds and one Tomato).
They romp and run 'round Leamington
And boy when they get hungry,
The bottle drips all over the chips
Way down in the Ketchup Country.

REPEAT CHORUS:

C.D., SNG.
To Be Re-Recorded

KEVIN BARRY.

By T.C.Connors (Trad. Arr.)

1.

E.
In Mount Joy, one Monday morning,
    B7.
High upon the gallow tree;

Kevin Barry gave his young life
    E.
For the sake of Liberty.

2.

E.
Just a lad of eighteen summers,
    B7.
That nobody can deny;

Kevin Barry faced the hangmen,
    E.
And these words he did reply.

3.

Shoot me like an Irish soldier,
Do not hang me like a dog,
For I fought to save Old Ireland
In that cold November fog.

4.

And before he faced the gallows
In that lonely prison cell,
Foreign soldiers tortured Barry;
They said, Now we'll make you tell.

5.

You'll tell the names of your companions
And the others that you know.
Turn 'informer' or we'll kill you.
Kevin Barry answered, "No".

6.

Then his comrades, they stood attention
As he bid the last farewell
To his broken hearted mother,
In her grief, too sad to tell.

7.

Shoot me like an Irish soldier,
Was the last request he made.
But they hung young Kevin Barry
On that cold November day.

TAG: And they hung young Kevin Barry
On that cold November day.

C.D. 04, SNG. 06

KISS ME THE NEW YEAR IN.

By T.C.Connors

1.

C.   G7.   F.
I got no dough to buy you clothes,
C.   G7.   C.
I know your shoes are thin;
    F.   C.
But I dropped a pile at a poker game
D7.   G7.
And I spent the rest on gin.
C.   G7.   F.   C.
But this New Year is a-gonna be
        C7.   F.
What the old Year should have been;
            C.   D7.
So hug me the old Year out, love,
C.   G7.   C.
And Kiss Me The New Year In.

CHORUS:

C.   G7.   C.
Kiss Me The New Year In;
            C7.   F.
Kiss Me The New Year In.
                C.   D7.
Hug me the old Year out, love,
    C.   G7.   C.
And Kiss Me The New Year In.

2.

I'd like to quit those cigarettes
But that's so hard to do
But there's one thing sure,
I'll be home more to spend more time with you
'Cause I know you've been wishin'
I could change the way I've been.
So hug me the old year out, love
And kiss me the New Year in.

3.

When its time for Auld Lang Syne,
I'll drink my last one down
And you're gonna see when you look at me
That a new man you have found
And I shall be so resolute
I just can't wait to begin
So hug me the old year out, love
And kiss me the New Year in.

REPEAT CHORUS:

Kiss me the New Year in.

C.D. 19, SNG. 06

KITCHEN SHOW.

By T.C.Connors & G.Lepine

1.

G.
Well, the Kitchen Show is over
               D7.
And everyone's in bed

But I can't sleep for I still have
               G.
That old song in my head

The one I wrote so long ago,
               D7.
The one I like the best,

And the kitchen stove won't let me go
               G.
Without one last request.

2.

G.
Oh, the Kitchen Show is over,
               D7.
They clapped and they went to bed

But I'll stay up to chase the dreams
               G.
Running through my head

And I may be just a dreamer
               D7.
But my songs will be known
                   G.
Even if I have to do my Kitchen Show alone.

3.

Now, they say when you get older,
You'll never make the grade,
But I've got a song that's on the Top
Of the Kitchen Hit Parade;
And though I'll make no money,
I'm never feelin' low,
As long as friends and neighbours come
To hear my Kitchen Show.

REPEAT VERSE NO: 1..... Then to verse 4.

4.

Now, the kitchen stove is colder,
It's almost half-past four;
And the old dog tries to stay awake
Beside the bedroom door.
And with his one eye open
He wants to let me know
How much he likes the song I've written
For my Kitchen Show.

REPEAT VERSE NO: 2..... Then Repeat last
two lines of verse 2.

C.D. 15, SNG. 01

LADY, k.d. lang.

Chorus:

A7.   D.   A.
Little "k", little "d", little "l-a-n-g",
     E7.   A.
Her name was just plain "k.d. lang";
         D.
But her main claim to fame
              A.
Was how she sang with a 'twang',
     E7.
And jumped around like a 'rang-ee-tang:
         A.
Lady, k.d. lang.
A7.   D.   A.   E7.
k.d. lang, k.d. lang; She jumped around
                          A.
Like a 'rang-ee-tang; Lady, k.d. lang.

1.

   A.   E7.
Where the wild roses grow in Alberta,
                          A.
On the banks of the Gooseberry Lake;
                            E7.
There's a 'rose' I suppose that you've heard of,
                     A.
She's as mild as a wild Irish Wake.

2.

Like a thorn, she was born to be contrary;
Like a boy, it was her joy raising cane.
The wildest rose that ever drove on the prairie
Behind the wheel of a big truck-load of grain.

Repeat Chorus:

3.

From her home down in Consort Alberta
Near the tracks of that old railroad line
With her hair she could scare Old Medusa
While she sang like a young Patsy Cline.

4.

It wasn't long till her songs got her landed
On the stage with those outrageous clothes
There were skirts over shirts, boots and trousers
Hanging down from this wild Alberta rose.

Repeat Chorus:

5.

Now she toured north and south of the border
And recorded with many famous names
Though her style, it was wild and outrageous
Her star just kept rising to fame.

6.

With her voice that was new and exciting
She was called to those juno Awards
She made a leap on the stage and she got one
And took it home to Alberta, Boy George!

C.D. 16, SNG. 10

LAND OF THE MAPLE TREE.

1.

   A.
Where the Coureur de Bois met the Iroquois,
     A7.   D.
The Micmac and the Cree,
                    A.
The Trapper and the Woodsman came
         E7.
And left this legacy;
   A.
To roam the woods, to fish and hunt
     A7.   D.
And always to be free,

                                A.
And to stand up for our Culture
     E7.   A.
In the LAND OF THE MAPLE TREE.

2.

On our snow-shoe webs we often tread
Our True North Wonderland,
So far away from city life
Where folks don't understand,
The beauty and tranquility that's here on every hand;
And there's no better place on earth
Than living in this land.

3.
By swift canoe we paddle through
Those rivers, lakes and streams,
Then sit beside our campfires
And stare at the bright moonbeams;
Our way of life is not as tough
Or as harsh as it may seem,
This is the life that most men live,
But only in their dreams.

4.
In our mackinaws we stand in awe
Of the beautiful sights we see,
Those woods and lakes and rivers
From Newfoundland to B.C.
Where the beaver and the otter swim
And the moose and deer roam free
This is the Land of Manitou
And it's always calling me.

5.
Where softer men have never been,
We portage with our gear,
Where the distant call of a waterfall
Is an echo sounding clear.
Where the salmon hide by the riverside
We'll camp for another day,
And tonight we'll dream of 'That Other Stream"
In the distant Milky Way.

6.
Where the Coureur de Bois met the Iroquois,
The Blackfoot and the Cree
The Trapper and the Woodsman came
And left this Legacy;
To roam the woods, to trap and hunt
And always to be free,
And to stand up for our culture
In this LAND OF THE MAPLE TREE

C.D. 14, SNG. 01   **LEGEND OF MARTY AND JOE.**   By T.C.Connors

1.
```
A.              A7.     D.      A.
```
Of all the great stories of Maritime glories
```
                              E7.
```
I'll bet I've got one you don't know;
```
       A.          A7.
```
How the land was divided
```
       D.        A.
```
With an ocean beside it.
```
                    E7.         A.
```
In the Legend of Marty and Joe: Ho, Ho!
```
       E7.                    A.
```
The Legend of Marty and Joe.

2.
Now Newfoundland Marty
To a Mainlander's party
Is something that surely don't go;
And when they got drinkin'
That Newfie got winkin'
At the girl-friend of Mainlander Joe. Ho! Ho!
The girl-friend of Mainlander Joe.

3.
They showed their great muscles
And clenched for the tussle
And struck with such powerful blows;
The land disassembled and everyone trembled,
And if any survived we don't know. Ho! Ho!
How many survived we don't know,

4.
In turbulent fashion the ocean was crashin',
While foe threw great boulders at foe;
And Newfoundland drifted
While New Brunswick shifted,
In whatever direction they'd go. Ho! Ho!
This Legend Of Marty And Joe.

5.
Now the battle grew hotter till up in the water
The Isle of Prince Edward did show;
And Gaspe' was much closer to old Nova Scotia
Till Cape Breton Island let go. Ho! Ho!
And Cape Breton Island let go.

6.
Now when they were tired
And peace was desired
That's when they both came to know;
Some guy took that girly
That made them go squirrely,
And he hit for old Ontario. Ho! Ho!
He took her to Ontario.

7.
For many years after the story brought laughter
That rang to the rafters and so;
That's why when they're fightin'
These "Coasters" are likened,
To the Legend Of Marty And Joe. Ho! Ho!
This Legend Of Marty And Joe.

C.D. 17, SNG. 06

LENA KATHLEEN.

By T.C.Connors
©1991 CROWN VETCH MUSIC
(SOCAN) All rights reserved.

CHORUS:

A.   A7.   D.   A.
Lena Kathleen, Lena Kathleen;
              E7.   A.
Light of my love, Queen of my dreams.
              A7.   D.   A.
Lena Kathleen, no moon have I seen,
                    E7.   A.
That could hold a beam to my Lena Kathleen.

1.

A.   E7.   A.
I've travelled the ocean; the world I have seen;
                    E7.
With mountains and valleys
                    A.
And beautiful streams.

                                E7.
But there was no beauty
                          A.
Compared to my dreams
                    E7.   A.
Of old Entry Island and Lena Kathleen.

CHORUS:

2.

And now as I ramble, far over the sea,
To all the fair cities, I take her with me.
For there is no beauty compared to my dreams
Of old Entry Island and Lena Kathleen.

CHORUS:

C.D. 18, SNG. 10

LET'S SMILE AGAIN.

By T.C.Connors
©1993 CROWN VETCH MUSIC
(SOCAN) All rights reserved.

1.

      E.
(So)... Let's Smile Again, for a while again,

And for a while again
                          B7.
A smile could be in style again;

And when the style again, is to Smile Again,

We may learn to sing the song of life
              E.
And laugh again.

1st Bridge.....
        A.
Whatever happened to the friendly smile?
        E.
I haven't seen a good one for a while.
        A.
Lately, when I'm walking down the street,
    Gb7.
People look as if
                              B7.
They haven't got a friend to meet. (greet)
    E.
So Let's Smile Again... Repeat 1st Verse...

2nd Bridge.....

Whatever happened to the friendly smile?
I haven't seen a good one for a while.
Lately, when I hear a friendly joke,
Someone looks as if
They're just about to have a stroke.

So Let's Smile Again... Repeat 1st Verse...

C.D. 02, SNG. 11

LITTLE BOY'S PRAYER.

Chorus:
```
C.          C7.    F.
```
I thought that I had troubles,
```
      D7.             G7.
```
So I took them to the Lord.
```
            C.      C7.        F.
```
While I was praying in an old fashioned chapel,
```
      G7.           C.
```
This little boy I overheard.

Recitation:
(Spoken to the Above Chord Progression.)

Dear God, I'm sorry I'm cryin',
'Cause mom told me never to cry,
She told me that I was a big boy now,
But this morning, God, she died.
She was, always so sick, God,
And early this morning my dad,
He got drunk and he started to beat her,
The only mom that I ever had.
Oh God, tell me why did you take her,
Is it 'cause I must have been bad,
Well, I'll be a good boy now, God,
So please, don't take my dad.

They come and they took him to jail, God,
And they said he was guilty, too,
What does guilty mean God,
And what are they gonna do.
Please, don't make him die, God,
I'll try not to be bad,
You took my mom away, God,
But please, don't take my dad.
I love you God, and I love my mom
But I love my daddy, too.
He's sorry, God, don't make him die,
Oh God, tell me, what will I do.

I watched the boy then leave the church,
And the tears were just streaming from his eyes.
I turned around then to say him a little prayer,
But then I heard that screeching cry.
I rushed out the door but it was just to late,
A car was speedin' by.
But God, and you, and I know folks,
It's better I guess, that he died.

I thought that I had troubles,
But I'm sorry for saying so, lord.

C.D. 14, SNG. 10

LITTLE OLD FORGETFUL ME.

1.
```
A.                 E7.    A.
```
Here comes Old Forgetful Me,
```
A7.       D.         A.
```
Down the Road of Tragedy.
```
A7.       D.         A.
```
I can't recall or bring to mind,
```
            E7.              A.
```
Why you should leave such love behind.

2.
```
A.                    E7.    A.
```
And when you break another heart,
```
A7.       D.         A.
```
And you take his world apart;
```
A7.       D.                A.
```
Won't you please come back and see
```
        E7.        A.
```
Little Old Forgetful Me.

Chorus:
```
A.            E7.                    A.
```
There's been times my heart would say,
```
            E7.                   A.
```
You're no good, why don't you stay away?
```
A7.        D.              A.
```
But when you're home, who's all a-glee?
```
        E7.        A.
```
It's Little Old Forgetful Me.

REPEAT FIRST VERSE
THEN GO TO VERSE NO: 3.

3.
When you've chained another fool
To that dream that don't come true;
Won't you please come back and see
Little Old Forgetful Me.

REPEAT CHORUS

NOW REPEAT FIRST VERSE and Finish.

C.D. 01, SNG. 14
C.D. 09, SNG. 11

LITTLE WAWA.

By T.C.Connors
©1967 CROWN VETCH MUSIC
(SOCAN) All rights reserved.

Chorus:

  D.
Honk, Honk, said Little Wawa;

Honk, Honk, my Gander Goo;
  G.   D.
In goose-talk, that means "I love you,
  G.   D.
And I always will be true."
  G.   A7.   D.
"I always will be true".
                      G. D.
REFRAIN: Little Wawa, Little Wawa.

1.

  D.
Little Wawa was a wild goose,
  G.   D.
Who from the southland flew,
  G.   D.
In a V-shaped flock of wild geese
    G.   D.
With her lover, Gander Goo;
  G.   A7.   D.
Her lover Gander Goo.

They flew across North Michigan
    G.   D.
To see the sights below,
      G.   D.
'Cause they were on their honeymoon
    G.   D.
To North Ontario;
    G.   A7. D.
To North Ontario.

Chorus:

2.

The night was fast approaching,
A dreadful hissing sound,
'Twas an arrow from an Indian bow
And Gander Goo shot down,
Gander Goo fell down.
The wild geese kept on flying
But Wawa would not go,
She stayed to find her lover
In the bushland far below,
In the bushland far below.

REPEAT CHORUS:

3.

A goose that died of heartbreak,
A legend she became,
But now she'll live forever
In a town that bears her name,
A town that bears her name.
If you should see her statue
On Highway Seventeen,
You'll know that you're in Wawa
And her love-song you will sing,
Her love-song you will sing.

REPEAT CHORUS:

LAST REFRAIN:
                  G. D.   A7. D.
Little Wawa, Little Wawa, Little Wawa.

C.D. 19, SNG. 01
C.D. 20, SNG. 13

LONG GONE TO THE YUKON.

By T.C.Connors & G.Lepine
©1994 CROWN VETCH MUSIC
(SOCAN) All rights reserved.

CHORUS:

E7. A.   B7.   E.
I'm Long Gone to the Yukon.
     A.   B7.   E.
Those northern lights I want to see
   A.   B7.   E.   E7. A.
I'm Long, Long Gone to the Yukon, boys,
     E.   B7.   E.
'Cause the Yukon is callin' for me.
         B7.   E.
Yeah, the Yukon is callin' for me.

1.

E.
Well, brother, I just got your note this morning,
                                     B7.
And you tell me that you've found a little gold,
             E.   E7.   A.
And before another day is dawnin'
   B7.   E.
On that long northern train I'm gonna roll.

2.

E.
I can see a little cabin by the mountains;
                                        B7.
I'll soon be there to share the gold with you;
        E.   E7.   A.
'Cause I want to live a life like Robert Service,
B7.   E.
Old Sam McGee and Dangerous Dan McGrew.
(To Chorus.)

3.

Where the wind along the river will be music
And the midnight sun is always riding low
I'll paddle my canoe along the Klondike
And I'll pan the gold and be a sourdough.

4.

And when I pull into Dawson City, Yukon,
I'll be headin' for old Diamond Gert's Saloon.
I'll gamble to a honky-tonk piano,
And I'll chase the dancin' girls around the room.
(To Chorus:)

5.

Well, they say that once you've heard
Those mystic voices,
From the 'Silence of the North' you can't return.
Now, I hear that lonesome timber wolf a-callin'
By the fire where I watch the 'bannock' burn.

6.

And it won't be long before I'm pickin' nuggets;
My brother says they're lyin' everywhere.
And my boss is gonna want to be my butler,
'Cause when I get back I'll be a millionaire.
(To Chorus:)

C.D. 17, SNG. 11   **LOOKIN' FOR SOMEONE TO HOLD.**   By T.C.Connors

Chorus:
    G.   D7.   G.   G7.
I'm Lookin For Someone To Hold again,
    C.   G.
Lookin' For Someone To Hold;
        G7.   C.
And if it's alright can we make it tonight
        G.   D7.   G.
'Cause I'm Lookin For Someone To Hold.

1.

    G.   G7.   C.
Come join in the crowd where the music is loud
        G.   D7.
And I'll sing of the brash and the bold;
    G.   G7.
With lessons I've learned
        C.
About bridges I've burned
        G.   D7.   G.
And the roads of regret that I've strolled.

2.

So long I have roamed
Without friends or a home
And I still haven't found any gold;
And here at the end of my rainbow again,
I'm Lookin' For Someone To Hold.

Chorus:

3.

There once was a day
That my love walked away
From the lies I shouldn't have told;
And there in the storm, my world, it was torn
And I found myself out in the cold.

4.

My love was all gone but my heart carried on
With dreams I could never unfold;
It's a long time ago but I want you to know
I'm still Looking For Someone To Hold.

Repeat Chorus... Then Verses 1 & 2 and
Finish with Chorus.

C.D. 16, SNG. 06

LOSER'S ISLAND.

By T.C.Connors
©1990 CROWN VETCH MUSIC
(SOCAN) All rights reserved.

1.

G.   G7.   C.   G.
I've been marooned all alone on Loser's Island;
          D7.   G.
On Loser's Island, in Heartbreak Sea.
          G7.   C.   G.
I count the waves that break on Loser's Island,
          D7.
For all those days and ways
                              G.
You've made a fool of me.

2.

I walk the shores forever more on Loser's Island,
On Loser's Island, with the memory.
Those sands of time, they're mine
On Loser's Island,
But all those plans we carved in sand
Can never be.

3.

I watch the moon shine blue on Loser's Island,
On Loser's Island, in Heartbreak Sea.
I count the years through my tears
On Loser's Island,
While dreaming dreams that used to seem
So true to me.

4.

I've listened well to the shells on Loser's Island,
On Loser's Island, where can she be.
Sad breezes sigh, I want to die
On Loser's Island,
While my burning ship of love
Goes down at sea.

Repeat first verse...

C.D. 17, SNG. 05

LOVER'S LAKE.

By T.C.Connors
©1969 CROWN VETCH MUSIC
(SOCAN) All rights reserved.

1.

D.   E7.
Kiss me while the moon is smiling
  A7.
Dreams on Lover's Lake.

My love is yours to take,
                  D.
My heart is yours to break.
              E7.
Oblivious, in your caress,
      A7.
I'm captured by your charm;
                                          D.
Smothered in your arms, I'm deep in love.

Chorus:
        G.
Since ecstasy's come over me
          D.
I feel desire's flame;
      E7.
And if this night of dreams should end
          A7. E7.   A7.
I'll never be the same.
      D.   E7.
So kiss me while the moon is smiling
  A7.
Dreams on Lover's Lake,

And hold me through the breaking
        D.
Dawn of love.

2.

Kiss me while the moon is smiling
Dreams on Lover's Lake;
Dreams that only make
My love live for your sake.
And as I hold you in this golden
Mirror of the moon,
Starlight breezes croon my song of love.

Repeat Chorus:

C.D. 16, SNG. 09

LOVE'S NOT THE ONLY THING.

By T.C.Connors

1.

G.   D7.
You could love me today and just walk away;
                                 G.
That's not the only thing I fear.
D7.   G.   D7.
You could just take my heart and tear it apart;
                                 G.
But that's not the only thing I fear.

Chorus:
        D7.   G.
The word's goin' round all over town;
A7.   D7.
It maybe just a smear, but nothing's really clear.
                G.
And though love may be strong
        D7.
And may not be wrong,
                                G.
Love's Not The Only Thing I fear.

2.

You could bring me to shame;
Dishonor my name;
That's not the only thing I fear.
I could live with disgrace
And the laugh on your face,
But that's not the only thing I fear.

Chorus:
The word's goin' round all over town;
It may be just a smear,
But nothing's really clear;
And though Love may be strong
And may not be wrong,
LOVE'S NOT THE ONLY THING I FEAR.

C.D. 03, SNG. 05
C.D. 06, SNG. 11

LUKE'S GUITAR.
(Twang, Twang.)

By T.C.Connors
©1989 CROWN VETCH MUSIC
(SOCAN) All rights reserved.

Chorus:

  F.   C.
Twang Twang a diddle dang,
  F.   C.
A diddle dang a twang a twang a

Twang twang a diddle dang,
  G7.   C.
Another dang twang,
    G7.   C.
And another dang twang,
    G7.   C.
And another dang twang.

1.
 C.
I've been married now, for a year or more,
    G7.
And my old guitar hangs by the door;
   F.   C.
That women of mine says, "Hock that, Luke",
    G7.   C.
'Cause your mama, dear, needs a brand new suit".
  C.
Well, I hocked my watch and I sold my dog
                  G7.
And I pawned the gasoline stove;

I hocked my ring and everything
                 C.
Just to keep that woman in clothes.

I even pawned the cat and I hocked my boots
             G7.
And I sold the family car;
     F.
But that woman of mine
    C.
Will be a hundred and nine
    G7.   C.
Before I hock my old guitar. (Repeat Chorus:)

2.
She went out one day last week, I guess,
And she won't come back until I say "yes".
In answer to her 'HOCK THAT LUKE"
My old guitar for a swimmin' suit.
That'll be the day, when I pawn my heart,
Like I pawned the gasoline stove;
I hocked my ring and everything,
Just to keep that woman in clothes;
I even pawned the cat and I hocked my boots
And I sold the family car;
But that woman of mine
Will be old and blind,
Before I'll hock my old guitar.

3.
If she don't come back, I won't be sore,
'Cause I don't give a hoot about her no more;
A man gets tired of, "HOCK THAT LUKE"
That woman of mine's too bad to shoot.
Well, I hocked my watch and I sold my dog
And I pawned the gasoline stove;
I hocked my ring and everything,
Just to keep that woman in clothes;
I even pawned the cat and I hocked my boots
And I sold the family car
But that woman of mine'll
Be in a box of pine,
Before I hock my old guitar.

REPEAT CHORUS:
(After last chorus, talk) This song ain't over yet;
(sing refrain) Still another dang twang, and
another dang twang
And another dang twang, and another dang
twang, (fade)

C.D. 16, SNG. 08   MADE IN THE SHADE.   **By T.C.Connors & A.Hawes**

1.

A.   A7.
Yeah! When I was goin' to high school,
   D.
In my late twenties,
   E7.
Cigarettes and booze
                          A.
Was takin' most of my money.
                     A7.   D.
So I got a factory job, away from them grades;
   E7.
'Cause that's the only way, man,
                          A.
You'll ever have it made.
   E7.   A.
Yeah! MADE IN THE SHADE.

2.

So I bought me a car, just a beat up old crate,
To cruise around town till I found me a date;
She said she was a country gal
And she wasn't afraid
To ride beside her "Sweety Pie'
So I could have it made.
Yeah! MADE IN THE SHADE.

3.

Well, I wined her and I dined her
And I took her to the shows,
We talked about her school days
And talked about her clothes;
In her school of thought
There was no panty raid,
It's after the wedding
That you really have it made.
Yeah! MADE IN THE SHADE.

4.

Well, after we got married,
I was waitin' to be happy,
Till she marched out her kids
And told them all to call me "Pappy";
And when she went to dances,
It was home I stayed,
And I began to realize,
"Some one" had it made.
Yeah! MADE IN THE SHADE.

5.

Well, it wasn't me that made it,
So I found another "Honey"
But the wife took the car
And took the house and all the money,
And then the "Honey" left me
For another guy she played,
And I began to wonder if I'd ever have it made.
Yeah! MADE IN THE SHADE.

6.

Well, I finally bought a book
On "How To Play The Guitar",
And I was on the road, Man, soon to be a Star;
The song I wrote was called,
"MADE IN THE, SHADE"
And when she hit the top, boys,
I knew I had it made.
Yeah! MADE IN THE SHADE.

7.

Well, the day finally came,
And I ran to get my cheque,
Fell down the stairs and I...... broke my neck,
And the Undertaker chap
That put me in the grave
Said, "here's another Sucker gettin' laid,
instead of Made."
Yeah! LAID IN THE SHADE.

C.D. 22, SNG. 06

MAGGIE.
(When You And I Were Young)

By G.Johnson & J.Butterfield 1864
Updated & Arranged By T.C.Connors

1.

A.   A7.   D.
I wandered today to the hill, Maggie
A.   E7.
In search of the scenes down below
A.   A7.   D.
By the creek and the rusty old mill, Maggie
A.   E7.   A.
Where we strolled in the long, long ago.

1st CHORUS...
D.   A.
And though we are aged and we're gray, Maggie
                     E7.
And few are the treasures we've won
A.   A7.   D.
Let us sing of the days that are gone, Maggie
A.   E7.   A.
When you and I were young.

2.

The green grove is gone from the hill, Maggie
Where all the red roses did grow
But I still see you there just as fair, Maggie
As you were in the days long ago.

2nd CHORUS...
And though we are aged and we're gray, Maggie
Trials of our life nearly done
Let us sing of the days that are gone, Maggie
When you and I were young.

3.
Now in place of the mill, there's a field, Maggie
Where all of our friends lay at rest
So far from the soil where they toiled, Maggie
They have gone like the sun in the west.

REPEAT 1st CHORUS...

4.
And I'll roam never more to the hill, Maggie
With steps that are feeble and slow
For the creek and the rusty old mill, Maggie
They have gone like the long, long ago.

REPEAT 2nd CHORUS...

END...

C.D. 14, SNG. 04

MAN FROM THE LAND, The

By T.C.Connors

1.

C.
I keep my left arm around my baby girl,
                        C7.
I keep the right one braced against the world,
F.
And if you try to harm one little curl,
G7.
You'll find your mind go blindly in a swirl,
C.
And you'll come to understand
G7.
That you don't force the hand
                 C.
Of the Man, From The Land.

2.

I keep my left arm around my baby boy,
I've got the right one ready to destroy
Anyone who tries to break a toy,
Will have the world's worst head-ache to enjoy,
And he'll come to understand,
That you don't force the hand
Of THE MAN FROM THE LAND.

3.
I keep my left arm around my little wife,
I've got the right one to conquer any strife,
And if you should bring danger to her life,
You could be lookin' down the wrong end
of the knife,
And you'll come to understand,
That you don't force the hand,
Of THE MAN FROM THE LAND.

4.
I keep my left arm around my family,
I've got the right to guard their Liberty,
And if you try to take this right from me,
You might just wind up hangin' from a tree,
And you'll come to understand,
That you don't force the hand
Of THE MAN FROM THE LAND.

MANITOBA.

By T.C.Connors

1.

A.   A7.
When you mention Manitoba,
  D.
I'll be mindful of the prairie
  A.   E7.
In the province where the old Red River flows;
  A.   A7.
It's a land of shining water
    D.
Where the beaver and the otter
  A.   E7.   A.
Play together where the Prairie Crocus grows.

Chorus:
A7. D.   A.
Manitoba, you're my sunshine,
  D.   A.
My twilight and repose;
A7. D.   A.
Manitoba, you're my heaven,

Because it's heaven
    E7.   A.
Where the Prairie Crocus grows.

2.

When you mention Manitoba
I'll be mindful of her beauty,
In the evening when the sunset fades away;
And the moon of golden glimmer
On the wheat field seems to shimmer,
And the night bird sings the closing of the day.

REPEAT CHORUS:

3.

When you mention Manitoba
I'll be mindful of her valleys,
And the old brown hills calling me away;
Where the favors of Our Giver
Dwell among the lakes and rivers,
From the U.S. line
To the shores of the Hudson Bay.

REPEAT CHORUS:

It's my heaven where the Prairie Crocus grows.

MAPLE LEAF WALTZ.

By T.C.Connors & G.Lepine

1.

D.   D7.   G.   D.
The Band, it was playing the Maple Leaf Waltz
A7.   D.
A soldier was saying goodbye
      D7.
He whispered, "My Snowbird,
 G.   D.
I'll come back to you,"
  A7.   D.
As he brushed a sad tear from her eye.

Chorus:
  G.
He held her so tight
    D.
As they danced 'round the hall
    G.   E7.   A7.
And you'd wonder, tonight, if it happened at all
  D.   D7.   G.   D.
For here they are dancing down memory lane
  A7.   D.
To the beautiful Maple Leaf Waltz.

C.D. 16, SNG. 01   **MARGO'S CARGO.**   **By T.C.Connors**

REFRAIN:

   D.   D7.   G.
Reggie's got the rig; Reggie's got the rig;
              D.
Margo's Got The Cargo, B'ye,
   A7.   D.
And Reggie's got the rig.

1.

   D.   D7.
Have you heard the news in Newfoundland,
   G.   D.
Rollin' around the "Rock"

How Reggie brought for Margie home,
   E7.   A7.
A "Cowsy Dungsy Clock?"
   D.   D7.
With Margo bein' a farm girl,
   G.   D.
She almost took a fit,
   G.   D.
To find the "Cowsy Dungsy Clock"
   A7.   D.
Was really made of.... "IT".

2.

   D.   D7.
The Clock was from Toronto
       G.   D.
And her mind was soon made up;

She said to Reggie, "Get the cow
   E7.   A7.
And load 'er on the truck",
   D.   D7.
"We're headin' for Ontario
      G.   D.
And we're off to make 'er big;
   G.   D.
'Cause MARGO'S GOT THE CARGO, B'ye,
   A7.   D.
And Reggie's got the rig. -- Sing REFRAIN.

3.

Now, they're rollin' through the Maritimes,
The truck was nearly full;
The cow began to bawl,
She was lonesome for the bull.
The Mountie pulled them over,
"Is there something I can do"?
"Go right ahead, Sir", Margie said,
"Climb in the back and moo."

4.

Now, when they got to Montreal,
They missed the 'Auto Route'
But they found that everyone in town
Was glad to 'help them out';
"The sooner you hit Toronto", they said,
"The sooner you'll make'er BIG";
'Cause MARGO'S GOT THE CARGO, B'ye,
And Reggie's got the Rig. -- Sing REFRAIN.

5.

The truck was over flowin'
When Toronto hit their eyes;
The 401 was full of dung
And the cab was full of flies.
"We're losin' lots of money, Reg,
We can't afford to stop;
We gotta find the place that makes
The Cowsy Dungsy Clock".

6.

Well, I wish you could have been there,
On the corner of Queen & Yonge
When Margo found the 'Company'
And she dumped her load of dung;
And when she found the 'office'
She was singin' and doin' a jig;
MARGO'S GOT THE CARGO, B'yse,
And Reggie's got the Rig. -- Sing REFRAIN.

7.

It was later in the evenin'
When they heard from 'Mr. Judge',
"I don't know what to give ya,
But I'll never hold a grudge;
I think a thousand dollars
Would be fair to hand you down,
And 30 days of 'lodging'
Will be free upon the town".

8.

Well Margo says to Reggie,
"What a hell of a deal we struck;
We might have lost the cow, B'ye,
But still we got the truck".
And now they're back in Newfoundland,
They're loadin' up the pig;
'Cause MARGO'S GOT THE CARGO, B'ye,
And Reggie's got the Rig. -- Sing REFRAIN.

C.D. 01, SNG. 02
C.D. 08, SNG. 07

MARITIME WALTZ.

By T.C.Connors
©1967 CROWN VETCH MUSIC
(SOCAN) All rights reserved.

1.

C.   C7.
When the moon gives her light
  F.
On the harbour tonight,
  G7.   C. G7.
We'll dance the Maritime Waltz;
    C.   C7.
When the boats are tied in
     F.
And we're together again,
  G7.   C.
We'll dance to the Maritime Waltz.

Chorus:

C7. F.
The fiddles will play
    C.
And our hearts shall be gay,
  G7.   C. G7.
For tomorrow, the sea again calls.
  C.   C7.   F.
So kiss me once more while I am ashore,

    G7.   C.
And we'll dance to the Maritime Waltz.

C.D. 10, SNG. 04   **MARTEN HARTWELL STORY.**   **By T.C.Connors**

Chorus:

  F.   C.
Lost, up in no man's land,
         G7.   C.
Of the Northwest Territories;

They were Lost, up in no man's land,
         G7.   C.
The Marten Hartwell Story.

1.

  C.
On November the 8th of Seventy-two,
 G7.   C.
North of the Arctic Circle,

A plane took off from Cambridge Bay
        G7.   C.
And the pilot's name was Hartwell.
  F.   C.
He had to make it to Yellowknife
 G7.   C.
Although the night was stormin',
  F.   C.
To save the lives of an Eskimo boy
    G7.   C.
And a pregnant Eskimo woman.

2.

Oh Mr. Hartwell, said the nurse,
I pray that you will guide us,
To save this woman with her child
And the boy with appendicitis;
But the wind it blew and the storm it grew
And the signal of Contwoyta,
They missed by miles and flying wild
They crashed beside Lake Hotta.

REPEAT CHORUS:

3.

Now Judy Hill the federal nurse,
She never lived to waken,
And the life of the mother and her child
Were both soon after taken;
But the pilot woke to find himself
And the Eskimo boy were livin',
Left in pain beside the plane
To search the skies of heaven.

4.

Day by day the pilot lay
With both his ankles broken,
And it took the lad everything he had
To keep the fire stoken;
While in the sky, too far away,
The rescue teams were seekin',
A signal wave that might be traced
To Hartwell's radio beacon.

REPEAT CHORUS:

5.

After nineteen days the aerial search
Was said to be completed,
But someone cried "They're still alive",
And the search must be repeated;
And the day the "BEEP" was finally heard
Is a day we'll all remember,
The man was found safe and sound
On the ninth day of December.

6.

Hartwell said he should have died
At thirty-five below zero,
And the reason Hartwell did survive,
The boy had died a hero;
He brought me food when I couldn't move,
While he himself grew feeble,
Yes, Davie Kootook died a saint
And a credit to his people.
Davie Kootook died a saint
And a credit to his people.

REPEAT CHORUS: Then fade....
The Marten Hartwell Story, The Marten
Hartwell Story,
The Marten Hartwell Story.

C.D., SNG.
To Be Re-Recorded

MARY OF THE WILD MOOR.

By T.C.Connors (Trd. Arr.)
©CROWN VETCH MUSIC
(SOCAN) All rights reserved.

1.

G.   D7.   G.
It was on one cold winter's night

                             D7.
And the wind blew across the wild moor;
   G.   C.   G.   C.
As Mary came wandering home with her child,
       G.   D7.   G.
And she came to her own father's door.

2.

   G.   D7.   G.
Oh, father, dear father, she cried,

                        D7.
Won't you come down and open the door;
    G.   C.   G.   C.
For the child in my arms, it will perish and die
      C.   D7.   G.
From the wind that blows across the wild moor.

3.

Oh, why did I leave this fair spot
Where I was once happy and free?
For I'm now doomed to roam
Without friends or a home
And no one to take pity on me.

4.

But her father was deaf to her cries;
Not a sound of her voice could he hear;
Though the watch-dog did howl
And the village bell tolled
And the wind blew across the wild moor.

5.

Oh, how the old man must of felt,
When he came to the door the next morn;
And he found Mary dead,
But the child still alive,
Closely wrapped in his dead mother's arms.

6.

In anguish he tore his grey hair,
And the tears down his cheeks they did pour;
When he saw how, that night,
She had perished and died
From the wind that blew across the wild moor.

TAG LINE:
And the wind blew across the wild moor.

C.D. 01, SNG. 05

MAY, THE MILLWRIGHT'S DAUGHTER.

By T.C.Connors
©1967 CROWN VETCH MUSIC
(SOCAN) All rights reserved.

1.

D.   A7.
In a little town called Ansonville,
                       D.
Not very far from the paper mill;
                     G.
There lives the girl I'm thinking of,
                D.
May, the Millwright's Daughter,
 A7.   D.
The girl I really love.

Chorus:
 A7.   D.
Soon I'm gonna be leavin' Moosonee,
 E7.   A7.
The James Bay job will soon be through,

Then I'll shove
   D.
On back to Ansonville,
    E7.
And my old job at the mill,

 A7.   D.
And May, I'm a-comin' home to marry you.
 A7.   D.
May, I'm a-comin' home to marry you.

2.

Most every night, I sing a song,
For all the boys when they gather round,
They come to hear me tell them of
May the Millwright's daughter,
The girl I really love.

REPEAT CHORUS:

3.

You're gonna quit the restaurant
'Cause I'm gonna bring that ring you want,
I'm headin' down the Moosonee line,
And May the Millwright's daughter,
I'm a gonna make you mine.

REPEAT CHORUS:

C.D. 20, SNG. 10

MEADOWS OF MY MIND.

1.

E.
And the winds of November
     E7.
  A.
Blew cold I remember
    E.   B7.
On that little house of love I left behind
    E.   E7.
Where the light from her window
  A.
Casting her shadow
B7.   E.
Fell across the Meadows Of My Mind.

2.

I dreamed of the hours
Sweet wildwood flowers
In the springtime of the year that she was mine
Then the change of the season
Brought blame without reason
And a prison where the sun don't ever shine.

3.

I have an old love letter
I'll cherish it forever
From an old rose faded from the vine
And the day they release me
She'll be there to greet me
In those fields of eternal summer time.

4.

And the winds I remember
Blew cold in November
On that little house of love I left behind
Where the light from her window
Casting her shadow
Still falls across the Meadows Of My Mind.

REPEAT 2ND, 3RD, AND 4TH VERSES.

C.D. 04, SNG. 02

MERRY BELLS.

1..

D.   D7.
Oh give me the time
       G.
When the Merry Bells chime
      D.   A7.
And the mistletoe hangs in the hall;
      D.   D7.   G.
When gone is all care and life seems so fair,
      D.   A7.   D.
And happiness reigns over all.

CHORUS:
  A7.   D.
Ring Merry Bells ring;
             A7.
Oh, cheerily, cheerily chime;
      D.   D7.
With peace and good will
      G.
Our hearts we shall fill
      D.   A7.   D.
And welcome the glad Christmas Time.

2.

When the merry bells chime,
Hearts closer entwine
There's gladness and joy all around.
Though branches be bare, though frosty the air,
Yet warmth in our hearts shall be found.

3.

We'll banish each sigh,
Let the yule log burn high,
Let its brightness shine out to the world;
Give a greeting to all,
Pray that blessings may fall,
And the banners of peace be unfurled.

REPEAT CHORUS:

C.D. 04, SNG. 01

MERRY CHRISTMAS EVERYBODY.

By T.C.Connors

CHORUS:

A.
Merry Christmas, Everybody,

E7.
And a Happy New Year, too,

May your Holidays be merry

A.
And every wish come true;

May you always be remembered

A7.   D.
By those so dear to you,

A.
Merry Christmas, Everybody,

E7.   A.
And Happy New Year all year through.

D.   A.
Merry Christmas, Everybody,

E7.   A.
And Happy New Year all year through.

1.

A.
Well, there's old grand pappy,

And he sure looks happy,

E7.
With granny just a-slappin' her knees;

There's old aunt Mary with funny uncle Harry

A.
And they're tryin' to give the baby a squeeze.

There's long-lost cousins, kiddies by the dozens,

A7.   D.
And they're gonna stay the whole day long;

A.
Get together now, friends and neighbours,

E7.   A.
Sing a happy holiday song.

REPEAT CHORUS:

2.

The turkey's on the table now,
And when you're feelin' able,
You can take another helpin' if you will,
But soon as you eat it,
I'm afraid you got to beat it,
'Cause you got to give the chair to brother Bill.
And hey uncle Marty, it's an all night party,
And don't you pour the drinks to strong.
Get together now friends and neighbours,
Sing a happy holiday song.

REPEAT CHORUS:

C.D. 22, SNG. 14

MIRAZHA.
aka (Good Night Mirazha.)

By T.C.Connors

Chorus.

A.   E7.   A.
Good Night, Mirazha. Good Night to you.

E7.
Good Night, Mirazha.

A.
May all of your dreams come true.

1.

A.
I met her in April, we married in June

E7.   A.
We went to Niagara on our honeymoon;

Got broke and came home

And then what did she do?

E7.   A.
She went back to Niagara with sombody new.

2.

And now that it's over I guess I'll be fine
As long as I take it one day at a time.
But today in the paper, I was so appalled,
Some forsaken lover jumped over the Falls.
(Alt: Heartbroken lover).

3.

Oh, where is Mirazha, the girl of my dreams?
Just like a mirage, she's not what she seems.
Beware of her kisses, they will make you glow;
Then it's over the Falls of Niagara you go.

START WITH CHORUS
AND REPEAT AFTER EACH VERSE.

C.D. 09, SNG. 06

MOON-MAN NEWFIE.
(The Man in the Moon is a Newfie)

By T.C.Connors
©1971 CROWN VETCH MUSIC
(SOCAN) All rights reserved.

CHORUS:

D.   G.
You might think it's goofie,
          A7.   D.
But the Man in the Moon is a Newfie;
          D7.   G.
And he's sailin' on to glory,
     A7.   D.
Away in the 'golden dory'. (Repeat line.)

1.

  D.
Codfish Dan, from Newfoundland,
     A7.   D.
He dreamt that he had three wishes.

He took Mars and all the stars
          A7.   D.
And he turned them into big fishes.

He said the sky was much too dry
          A7.   D.
And he made a wavy motion;

And the moon, like a boat, began to float
     A7.   D.
Upon the 'starry ocean'.

REPEAT CHORUS:

2.
One night he strayed to the Milky Way
To cast his nets upon it,
When he spied the tail
Of what he thought was a whale,
He harpooned Haley's Comet.
He never had a pot for the fish that he caught,
So he had to use the big dipper;
And the sun, By Jove, was a very good stove
For cookin' up smelts and kippers.

REPEAT CHORUS:

3.
Now the northern lights that seem so bright
Like nothin' could be grander,
Well they're just waves of the moon-boat made
By the Newfoundland Commander.
And don't you sigh and say Oh My!
What gross exaggerations;
Cause he'll tell you the dream was true
When Codfish Dan awakens.

REPEAT CHORUS:
He's sailing on to glory, away in the
golden dory.

REPEAT CHORUS:
Sailing on to glory, away in the golden dory.

C.D. 10, SNG. 06

MOONLIGHT LADY.

By T.C.Connors
©1973 CROWN VETCH MUSIC
(SOCAN) All rights reserved.

1.

  D.   G.   A7.   D.
Moonlight Lady, dancing around;
          G.   A7.   D.
All night, up tight, all day lay down.
          G.   A7.   D.
Moonlight Lady, Queen of the show;
              G.   A7.   D.
Daybreak come Baby, Lady lay low.

Chorus:

  D.   D7.   G.   D.
Lady, lay low, Lady, lay low;
              G.   A7.   D.
Daybreak come Baby. Lady lay low.
G.   A7.   D.
My Moonlight Lady.

2.
Moonlight Lady, up on the town;
Come bright daylight, Lady lay down.
Moonlight Lady, Queen of the show;
Daybreak come Baby. Lady lay low.

Repeat Chorus:

3.
Moonlight Lady, wherever you roam,
Come back, Baby, stay Lady home.
Moonlight Lady, Queen of the show;
Daybreak come Baby, Lady lay low.

Repeat Chorus:

C.D. 21, SNG. 12

MOONSHINE DADDY.

By T.C.Connors
©2002 CROWN VETCH MUSIC
(SOCAN) All rights reserved.

1.

C.   C7.
We can make our own moonshine, Baby;
F.   C.
We can make our own moonshine.

Stop what you're doin',

Get your mind on to brewin'
   D7.   G7.
Come on down and see me sometime.
C.   C7.
We can make our own moonshine, Baby;
 F.   C.
And if you want to really unwind;

Come and see Big Daddy,

You can drive my caddy,
         G7.   C.
And we can make our own moonshine.

2.

We can make our own moonshine, Baby.
We can make our own moon shine.
When no one's lookin'
We can just start cookin'
And we can take our own sweet time.
We can make our own moonshine, Baby.
Moonshine, sweeter than wine,
We'll spend money
Like the bees make honey, Baby.
We Can Make Our Own Moon Shine.

3.

We can make our own moonshine, Baby.
We can make our own moon shine.
When the hops are a-hoppin'
And the corks are poppin'
We can have a high old time.
We can make our own moonshine, Baby.
We're gonna make it work so fine
When a cool cucumber
Meets a red-hot number, Baby.
We Can Make Our Own Moon Shine.

(Repeat any verses if needed.)

C.D. 15, SNG. 07

MORNING & EVENING & ALWAYS.

By T.C.Connors
©1988 CROWN VETCH MUSIC
(SOCAN) All rights reserved.

1.

A.   A7.   D.
MORNING & EVENING & ALWAYS,
E7.   A.
We live just one room apart;
      A7.   D.
Morning and Evening and Always,
 E7.   A.
I'm climbing those walls in my heart.

2.

MORNING & EVENING & ALWAYS,
I find myself pacing the floor,
And one of these days down the hallway,
I'll make myself knock on your door.

3.

I know you're thinking of someone,
Someone you're longing to see,
You always say "Hi" in the hallway,
So maybe that someone is me.

4.

Cause MORNING & EVENING & ALWAYS,
We live just one room apart;
And MORNING & EVENING & ALWAYS,
I'm climbing those walls in my heart.

5.

MORNING & EVENING & ALWAYS,
I find myself pacing the floor;
And one of these days down the hallway,
I'll make myself knock on your door.

6.

Cause I hear the music you're playing,
And we watch the same on T.V.
I wonder when you lay down dreaming,
If you dream the same thing as me.

Repeat 4th Verse and FINISH.

C.D. 20, SNG. 01

MOVE ALONG.
(My Truckin' Song)

By T.C.Connors
©1999 CROWN VETCH MUSIC
(SOCAN) All rights reserved.

1.

D.   D7.   G.
It's time to Move Along: Write another song.
                        D.
You made a shmuck of a damn good trucker
    E7.   A7.
And done your daddy wrong.
    D.   D7.   G.
And as I roll along, hear my truckin' song;
                    D.
You made your play, now clear the way;
    A7.   D.
It's time to Move Along.

2.

It's time to Move Along: Time to Move Along.
There's another load on down the road
And a new love just beyond.
And as I roll along, hear my truckin' song;
I warned you twice, now pay the price,
It's time to Move Along.

3.

It's time to Move Along:
You tried to steer me wrong.
Now open your eyes and realize
Your truckin' daddy's gone.
And as I roll along, hear my truckin' song;
I'm all through with lovin' you,
It's time to Move Along.

4.

It's time to Move Along: Time to Move Along.
You tried to send me around the bend,
But I'll keep drivin' on.
And as I roll along, hear my truckin' song;
You've had your ride, now step aside,
It's time to Move Along.

5.

It's time to Move Along: Let me say it strong.
There's a place to cheat on down the street
With another guy named John.
And as I roll along, hear my truckin' song;
You're 'way too late to play it straight,
It's time to Move Along.

6.

It's time to Move Along: Time to Move Along.
You made a shmuck of a damn good trucker
And done your daddy wrong.
And as I roll along, hear my truckin' song;
You made your play, now clear the way,
It's time to Move Along.

Tag Lines:
I warned you twice, now pay the price,
It's time to Move Along.
I'm all through with lovin' you,
It's time to Move Along.

C.D. 09, SNG. 08

MOVIN' IN FROM MONTREAL.

By T.C.Connors
©1971 CROWN VETCH MUSIC
(SOCAN) All rights reserved.

1.

E.   E7.   A.
In this old train depot, just ten minutes ago,
                    E.
I was waiting anxiously
    B7.   E.
For the No.9 whistle blow.
                            E7.
The guy walks up and says, man,
                        A.
There's a woman on your brain,
    E.   B7.   E.
Movin' In, from Montreal by train.

2.

Then I heard the rumble
And I watched the engine crawl,
Right on by the station door,
I thought he'd never stall,
I couldn't wait to throw my arms
Around my Joli Jane,
Movin' in from Montreal by train.

3.

Crowds began to gather round
To welcome kinfolk home,
Movin' in from Montreal by train and all alone,
Then I heard the people say
Here comes a Quebec dame,
Movin' in from Montreal by train.

4.

There she stood within the door,
And the wolves began to howl,
I knew I'd have to make it fast
To catch my baby doll,
I pushed by way right through the crowd
To kiss my Joli Jane,
Movin' in from Montreal by train.

5.

Someone whispered
They sure grow them fine in Montreal,
She talks a little Frenchy
And she's curvy, dark and tall,
Joli Jane I love you so,
Your trip was not in vain,
Movin' in from Montreal by train.

6.

Now we're off to meet the man
That makes two lovers into one,
And Number Nine just rolled away
With one more good turn done,
For someone someday there may be
Another Joli Jane,
Movin' in from Montreal by train,
She'll come movin' in from Montreal by train.

C.D. 01, SNG. 04   **MOVIN' ON TO ROUYN.**   By T.C.Connors

1.

C.
The day I left Kirkland

My girl's head was circlin',
                G7.
I left her with only one shoe on.
   C.
My baby in Larder, she may take it harder,
  G7.   C.
'Cause I've got a new one in Rouyn.
  G7.   C.
I've got a new one in Rouyn.

CHORUS:
C.   G7.   C.
I'm a honky tonk player just drifting along;
  G7.   C.
I move like a leaf the wind blew on.

I'll love you tonight and I'll hold you so tight;
  G7.   C.
Tomorrow, I'll Move On to Rouyn.
  G7.   C.
Tomorrow, I'll Move On to Rouyn.

2.

Tonight if I gamble
Tomorrow I'll ramble
I'm a captain that don't take no crew on
Goodbye to my Shirley
She's been a cute girly
But I've got a new one in Rouyn
I've got a new one in Rouyn.

REPEAT CHORUS:

3.

Now love is a stranger
To some it's a danger
To me, It ain't nothin' to stew on
I'll play with your curls
And I'll call you my girl
But I've got a new one in Rouyn
I've got a new one in Rouyn.

REPEAT CHORUS:

LAST CHORUS:
I'm a honky took player just drifting along
I move like a leaf the wind blew on,
From Kirkland to Larder
Through V-Town and farther
I've just got to move on to Rouyn
'Cause I've got a new one in Rouyn
So I'm gonna move on to Rouyn

C.D. 08, SNG. 13

MR. ENGINEER.

By T.C.Connors
©1972 CROWN VETCH MUSIC
(SOCAN) All rights reserved.

1.

C.
Mr. Engineer, make your engine moan,
        G7.   C.
There's a little mama waitin' for you alone;
        C7.   F.
Mr. Engineer, you better hurry home,
        C.
You better burn some rail
    G7.   C.
And make your engine moan,

Boy, make it moan. Yeah!

Chorus:
  C.
Make it moan and groan for home,
         C7.
Make it moan and groan for home,
  F.
Make it moan and groan for home,
  C.
Make it moan and groan for home,
    G7.   C.
'Cause your baby's all alone, Mr. Engineer.

2.

Mr. Engineer, on a record run,
You've just become a daddy of a baby son.
Mr. Engineer, you better hurry home,
You better burn some rail
And make your engine moan,
Boy, make it moan. Yeah!

Repeat Chorus:

Repeat Verses and Choruses as required
for length

Tag Line:
Don't you think it's time to get home,
Mr. Engineer.

C.D. 19, SNG. 17

MRS. BLUE GUITAR.

By T.C.Connors & G.Lepine
©1994 CROWN VETCH MUSIC
(SOCAN) All rights reserved.

1.

A.
In the foggy mountain rain,
  E7.
There goes the midnight train
            A.
And we can't buy a ticket for the ride
      E7.
This crumbled dollar bill, Oh God, I hope it will
        A.
Take us to a bar where we can hide.

2.

A.
A shelter from the storm,
  E7.
Somewhere to keep us warm
          A.
For one more night of singing to survive
    E7.
Oh Mrs. Blue Guitar, how beautiful you are
        A.
For the years you kept this old hobo alive.

Chorus:
A7.   D.   A.
Oh, Mrs. Blue Guitar, you're all I have to hold
  D.   A.   E7.
If I had been a star, you'd wear strings of gold
    A.
But though I can't be worthy
    E7.
Of the lady that you are
             A.
I'll always love you Mrs. Blue Guitar.

(Repeat if necessary)

C.D. 04, SNG. 07

MR. SNOWFLAKE.

By T.C.Connors
©1970 CROWN VETCH MUSIC
(SOCAN) All rights reserved.

1.

C.
I went strolling one bright morning
C7.   F.
In December;
          G7.   C.
'Twas the first time this year we saw the snow.
                              C7.
I stopped to watch a little boy
          F.
Catch snowflakes,
          G7.
And to one great big snowdrop
                  C.
He whispered low:

CHORUS:
C.   C7.
Please Mr. Snowflake,
              F.
tell your friends to stay for Christmas.
          C.   G7.
Because no one wants to see them melt away.
  C.   C7.
Please Mr. Snowflake,
              F.
Tell your friends to stay for Christmas,
              C.   G7.
They will brighten up the world
                      C.
On Christmas Day.

2.

On your soft white snowy blanket
We go sliding,
Me and all the kids on our street,
And even dear old Santa Claus is happy,
'Cause snow don't hurt his tiny reindeers' feet.

REPEAT CHORUS:

3.

I've been hearing all big people
Sing of Christmas,
And they hope that every Christmas
Will be white.
So all your friends are welcome
Mr. Snowflake,
And please don't let them melt away tonight.

REPEAT CHORUS:

MUK LUK SHOO.
By T.C.Connors

1.

A.
Way up up up up up in Tuktoyaktuk
   E7.   A.
The Eskimo make big igloo;

Way up up up up up in Tuktoyaktuk,
   E7.   A.
You marry me, and I marry you;
     D.   A.   E7.   A.
And go dancin' to the Muk Luk Shoo.
E7.   A.   E7.   B7.   E7.
Ooo Ooo Ooo, Ooo Ooo Ooo, Ooo Ooo Ooo;

the Muk Luk Shoo.
     D.   A.   E7.   A.
Go dancin' to the Muk Luk Shoo.
E7.   A.   E7.   A.   B7.   E7.
Ooo Ooo Ooo, Ooo Ooo Ooo, Ooo Ooo Ooo;

2.

A.
Way up up up up up in Tuktoyaktuk
Come and go, everyone do,
Way up up up up up in Tuktoyaktuk
Come white bear and walrus too,
They come to do the Muk Luk Shoo
Ooo Ooo Ooo, Ooo Ooo Ooo, Ooo Ooo Ooo;
the Muk Luk Shoo
Come to do the Muk Luk Shoo.
Ooo Ooo Ooo, Ooo Ooo Ooo, Ooo Ooo Ooo;

3.

Way up up up up up in Tuktoyaktuk
In my old kayak canoe,
Way up up up up up in Tuktoyaktuk
We sail away, me and you,
And go bobbin' to the Muk Luk Shoo
Ooo Ooo Ooo, Ooo Ooo Ooo, Ooo Ooo Ooo;
the Muk Luk Shoo
We go bobbin' to the Muk Luk Shoo.
Ooo Ooo Ooo, Ooo Ooo Ooo, Ooo Ooo Ooo;

4.

Way up up up up up in Tuktoyaktuk
When the snow is baby blue,
Way up up up up up in 'l'uktoyaktuk
You and me have wee Goo Goo,
And teach him to do the Muk luk Shoo
Ooo Ooo Ooo, Ooo Ooo Ooo, Ooo Ooo Ooo;
the Muk Luk Shoo
And Goo Goo too do the Muk Luk Shoo.
Ooo Ooo Ooo, Ooo Ooo Ooo, Ooo Ooo Ooo;

5.

Way up up up up up in Tuktoyaktuk
We all do the Muk Luk Shoo,
Ooo Ooo Ooo, Ooo Ooo Ooo, Ooo Ooo Ooo;
the Muk Luk Shoo
We all do the Muk Luk Shoo,
Ooo Ooo Ooo, Ooo Ooo Ooo, Ooo Ooo Ooo;
the Muk Luk Shoo
Way up up up up up in Tuktoyaktuk
We all do the Muk Luk Shoo
Ooo Ooo Ooo, Ooo Ooo Ooo, Ooo Ooo Ooo;

MY BROTHER PAUL.
By T.C.Connors

Recitation:
  E.   E7.
Well, I've been sittin' round the house here,
  A.
Day by day,
  E.
I ain't got much to do
         B7.
But there's always lots to say;
      E.   E7.
Well, the doctor dropped in
          A.
And he said my blood was low,
  E.
So I ain't worked since, heh,
  B7.   E.
That's about five year ago.

2.

Oh, it's a brand new house,
Got nice pictures on the wall,
'Course it belongs to my brother,
Now his name's Paul.
I'm wearin' his suit, heh, he bought it brand new,
I drive a nice car, but that's his, too.

3.

There really ain't much mine, 'cept my overalls,
And they were dirty when I found them
Hangin' out there in the hall,
But my brother Paul, he's makin' a pretty big pay,
So I'm eatin' pretty regular, heh,
About ten times a day.

4.

Oh, once in awhile you know,
I step out for a munch,
'Cause my credit's always good
Down at my brother's lunch.
You know, I think I'll get married
Towards the end of the fall,
'Cause my girlfriend's tired
Of runnin' around with Paul.

5.

Now seein' that my brother's
Pretty good to me, heh,
I don't think, this here house
Would be too small for three.
But if the house starts gettin'
A little too small for the four,
Well, I think my brother's gonna have to
Sleep with the guy next door.

6.

But he's understandin' that way, my brother Paul,
I only hope that my brother can support us all.
'Cause if'n he can't do it,
I'm gonna have to get a divorce,
Less'n my wife then would rather
Start workin', of course.

7.

Oh yeh, I had a dream last night
About my brother and me,
You know, he grabbed a big gun and, heh,
I climbed a big tree.
Of course it was only a dream,
He wouldn't hurt his brother Tim,
Cause he's so good to me and, of course,
I'm so good to him.

8.

Well, they say a rollin' stone
Never gathers any moss,
So when I'm away,
I always leave him be the boss.
Oh gosh, I just remembered,
I lost my glass eye ball,
Hey there dog, don't swally that, heh,
That belongs to my brother Paul.

C.D. 13, SNG. 04   **MY DOOR'S ALWAYS OPEN TO YOU.**   By T.C.Connors

1.

  G.   G7. C.   G.
My Door's Always Open To You;
    D7.   G.
So come back whenever you're blue.
       G7.   C.   G.
No matter how often you treat me untrue,
    D7.   G.
My Door's Always Open To You.

Chorus:
D7.   G.
I will understand how it's been;
    D7.   G.
Craving the love you could not win.
      G7.   C.   G.
Each time you feel the same way that I do,
    D7.   G.
My Door's Always Open To You.

2.

My Door's Always Open To You,
While my heart is breaking in two;
Always remember whenever you're blue,
My Door's Always Open to You.

Second Chorus:
You'll have my heart till the end;
You may not be there but I'll pretend.
Till somebody loves you the way that I do,
My Door's Always Open To You.

Repeat lst Verse... end.

C.D. 01, SNG. 10
C.D. 17, SNG. 02

MY HOME CRADLED OUT IN THE WAVES.

1.

A.
There's a crescent shaped island
   E7.   A.
In the Gulf of St. Lawrence;
   E7.   A.
My Home Cradled Out in the Waves.
            A7.
My Garden of the Gulf,
     D.
It's my Million Acre Farm,
A.   E7.   A.
MY HOME CRADLED OUT IN THE WAVES.

1st Chorus:
   E7.   A.
I just can't wait for that good old Abegweit,
   E7.   B7.   E7.
While standing in Cape Tormentine;
      A.   A7.
She's the only ferry, fair,
      D.
True and humble as a prayer,
      A.   E7.   A.
She's the beauty of the land for which I pine.

2.

There's an old mellow moon
That shines there in June
He can tell you of the good old country ways
He'll tell you with a smile
There's no place like P.E.Isle
MY HOME CRADLED OUT IN THE WAVES.

Second Chorus:
Through those old northern lights
Maritime stars are bright
Shining brighter no stars can be found
From Tignish on the end,
Down to Souri, back again
You'll love our famous city, Charlottetown.

3.

On Old Prince Edward Island
Where the Silver Fox was born
Anne of Green Gables trod the ways
You should see the sunny tide
Down in good old Summerside
MY HOME CRADLED OUT IN THE WAVES.

Third Chorus:
The soil is so red and the ocean is fed
By the little rivers running to and fro
In the winding brooks around
All the lazy trout are found
While the tourists in "Old Home Week"
Come and go.

4.

Where "Old Friends Meet" you're welcome
On the shores of old "Spud Isle"
MY HOME CRADLED OUT IN THE WAVES.
My garden of the Gulf,
It's my million acre farm
MY HOME CRADLED OUT IN THE WAVES.
My little home cradled way out in the waves.

C.D. 19, SNG. 11 **MY HOME'S IN NEWFOUNDLAND.** By T.C.Connors & G.Lepine

1.

G.
I tried to wait for you to shake Toronto town D7.

You couldn't so you let me go
G.
And turned me down

You tried to change my Newfie ways,
D7.
I understand

Wrong or right, I'm home tonight,
G.
I'm Back in Newfoundland

2.

Down by the sea where life is free
I'm home again
Where I sail the blue and think of you
And what might have been
And if some day you can find a way
To change your plans
You'll find me here where there's no tears
Back Home in Newfoundland.

3.

My life goes on without your warm
And smiling face
Though every care has been to share
One more embrace
And as I write from home tonight
Please understand
You can always know I loved you though
My Heart's in Newfoundland.

4.

Where folks are real and people feel
So deep inside
And the sea just rolls right through the soul
Of Newfie pride
And if memories fold some day I'll hold
Another's hand
But I'll roam no more from Heaven's shore
My Home's in Newfoundland.

C.D. 05, SNG. 11 **MY LAST FAREWELL.** By T.C.Connors

1.

E. E7.
Walking by the river at midnight,
A.
Strolling in the falling rain;
E.
I can hear a whippoorwill calling,
Gb7. B7.
I can hear a far off train.
E. E7.
Here's what it's like to be lonely,
A.
Here's what it's like to be blue;
E.
I can't help but remember
B7. E.
My Last Farewell to you.

2.

I see the riverboat sailin'
Underneath the misty moon,
Rain filled willows are weeping
Down where the roses bloom.
My heart cries out to the water
Will there be a new love true,
But I'll never cease to remember
My last farewell to you.

REPEAT FIRST VERSE:

C.D. 03, SNG. 08 **MY LITTLE ESKIMO.** **By T.C.Connors**
©1969 CROWN VETCH MUSIC
(SOCAN) All rights reserved.

1.

C.
I'll make my way this Saturday
        G7.
To my darlin' oh so true;

Up north so far, 'neath the daylight star,
                        C.
And she lives in an ig-a-loo.

From Edmonton I'll make my way
                    G7.
To pay for the wrong I've done,
        F.   C.
My Little Eskimo, where the moon shines low
    G7.   C.
In the land of the midnight sun.

2.

I left the north and travelled south,
Many months ago
But I did find that your love is blind,
Down here where there ain't no snow
Of all the girls, that's in the world,
For me there's only one
My little Eskimo, where the moon shines low,
In the land of the midnight sun.

3.

Now polar bear and walrus hair,
May cover up her form
But don't you know, eighty-eight below
It isn't very warm
So rain or snow, I'm a gonna go,
'Cause she's the only one,
My little Eskimo, where the moon shines low
In the land of the midnight sun.

4.

In the cool of the night, when the Northern
Lights, are flashing everywhere
We'll be nose to nose, and love soon grows
In the world of away up there
So goodbye Jack, and I won't be back,
I'm off to see someone
My little Eskimo where the moon shines low,
In the land of the midnight sun.

5.

I'll make my way this Saturday
To my darlin' oh so true
Up north so far, 'neath the daylight star,
And she lives in an igloo
From Edmonton, I'll make my way,
To pay for the wrong I've done
My little Eskimo, where the moon shines low,
In the land of the midnight sun.
My little Eskimo, where the moon shines low,
In the land of the midnight sun.

C.D. 22, SNG. 08 **MY SILVER BELL.** **By T.C.Connors (Trad. Arr.)**
©2004 CROWN VETCH MUSIC
(SOCAN) All rights reserved.

1.

C.
Beneath the light of a bright starry night

Sat a lonely little Indian maid
        G7.   C.
No lover's sweet serenade has ever won me

As in a dream it seemed down a stream

He came paddling a shiny canoe
            G7.   C.
This Chieftain longing to woo sang her this song.

Chorus...
    C.   C7.   F.   C.
Your voice is ringing, My Silver Bell
    G7.   C.
And under its spell here I come to tell you

        C7.   F.   C.
Of the love I'm bringing o'er hill and dell
        G7.   C.
And so happy we will dwell My Silver Bell.

2.

Many swoons and tunes by the moon
Broke the echo of the still summer night
As the dawn came through so bright,
They go to dreaming
In his canoe only two sat to woo
As they listened to the sound of the breeze
That seemed to sing in the trees this sweet refrain.

Repeat Chorus.

C.D. 17, SNG. 10   **MY SLEEPING CARMELLO.**   By T.C.Connors & G.Lepine

1.

G.   G7.
One mystical morning
          C.   G.
Through her window, bright,
                              D7.
The sun, it was shining and yellow;
G.   G7.   C.   G.
The robin was chirping in sweet harmony
          D7.   G.
To the lyrical winds from the willow.

1st Chorus:
G.   D7.   G.
The fragrance of flowers came wafting along,
D7.   G.
As I arose from her pillow;
                G7.   C.   G.
And crowning this beautiful morning, so bright,
          D7.   G.
The Smile of My Sleeping Carmello.

2.

I slipped from the bedroom
And out of her world,
A restless and foolish young fellow;
And all through the years,
How I've kept in my heart,
These lessons I've learned from the willow.

2nd Chorus .....
Recalling that morning when life was a song,
Often with tears on my pillow;
I long for that wonderful world that I've lost,
And the Smile Of "MY SLEEPING
CARMELLO".

REPEAT 2nd Verse, 2nd Chorus... End.

C.D. 07, SNG. 01   **MY STOMPIN' GROUNDS.**   By T.C.Connors & R.A.Payne

1.

C.
I've been all across this country,
                              G7.
From the east coast to the west;

And I've been asked about a thousand times
          C.
What places I like best.

Well, I've had to base my answers
                              G7.
On the friendly people I've found;
                  C.
And if you're inclined to take the time
          G7.   C.
This is where you'll find MY STOMPIN'

GROUNDS.

CHORUS:
  C.
Just take a little piece of P.E.I.
              G7.
And old Saskatchewan,

Nova Scotia and New Brunswick,
  C.
Quebec and Newfoundland;

                                                          G7.
Alberta and Manitoba, Ontario and B.C.,
          C.   G7.   C.
And you'll have found the Stompin' Grounds
          G7.   C.
Of all my friends and me.

2.

There was a time, with a buddy of mine
When a freight train was our abode;
And we found people in this here land
That would help a guy along the road;
Some of them lived in the country,
And others lived in town,
But these are the people that made me proud
To say this is MY STOMPIN' GROUNDS.

REPEAT CHORUS:

3.

And now you've heard my answer,
It's one I hope you'll understand,
It's just my way of saying "Thank you"
To the people of this land;
And it doesn't matter, really where you're from,
You can spread the word around;
Where ever you find a heart that's kind,
You're in a part of MY STOMPIN' GROUNDS.

REPEAT CHORUS TWICE:

C.D. 01, SNG. 15

MY SWISHA MISS.

By T.C.Connors & B.Roberts
©1967 CROWN VETCH MUSIC
(SOCAN) All rights reserved.

1.

C.
When there's a Swisha Miss to miss you
    G7.
back in Swisha,
                                C.
And your heart is aching for her all the time;
                         C7.
And you grab your clothes to pack,
    F.
Leave the city and go back,
      G7.   C.
To that little Swisha Miss you left behind.

CHORUS:
C7.   F.
Oh, my little Miss of Swisha,
        C.
If you knew how much I miss ya
        G7.
When thoughts of home come stealin'

C.
through my mind;
    F.
If I could just be with ya,
    C.
My little Miss of Swisha,
        G7.   C.
Oh, my Swisha Miss I'd kiss ya all the time.

2.
Oh my Swisha Miss will meet me back in
Swisha,
When soon I cross that Quebec border line,
So goodbye Ontario,
I hate to leave but I must go
To meet my Swisha Miss to make her mine.

REPEAT CHORUS:

C.D. 07, SNG. 11

NAME THE CAPITALS.

By T.C.Connors
©1971 CROWN VETCH MUSIC
(SOCAN) All rights reserved.

1.
C.   G7.
Ottawa is a mighty good town,
                        C.
They never turn a Maple Leaf upside-down.
    C7.   F.
Here's to Ottawa, in the land we love;
    D7.   G7.
Can anyone here name the Capital of.....

British Columbia?

(Crowd Response)... "Victoria"...

C.   **2.**
Victoria is a mighty good town,
They never turn a Maple Leaf upside-down.
Here's to Victoria, in the land we love;
Can anyone here name the Capital of.....
Alberta?

(Crowd Response)... "Edmonton"...

3.
Edmonton is a mighty good town,
They never turn a Maple Leaf upside-down.
Here's to Edmonton, in the land we love;

Can anyone here name the Capital of.....
Saskatchewan?

(Crowd Response)... "Regina"...

4.
Regina is a mighty good town,... etc.

(Continue in this manner until all the
Provinces and their Capitals are named. Then
ask for the Capital of Canada.)

(Crowd Response)... "Ottawa"...

Last Verse.
    C.   G7.
Ottawa is a mighty good town,
                              C.
They never turn a Maple Leaf upside-down.
    C7.   F.
Here's to Ottawa, in the land we love;
    G7.
And here's to the Maple Leaf Flag that flies
                                C.
Up in Canada's sky, high above....

(Crowd Response.... "YAY !!!".

C.D. 10, SNG. 05

NEW BRUNSWICK AND MARY.

By T.C.Connors
©1973 CROWN VETCH MUSIC
(SOCAN) All rights reserved.

CHORUS:

A.
I get heartsick and blue
    B7.
For New Brunswick and you
    E7.   A.
Since I left for the west and the prairie;

And the stars up above
    B7.
Know the two things I love
    E7.   A.
Are my Home in New Brunswick and Mary.

RECITE (With same Chord Changes)

1.

I'll bet the salmon are all running now,
Up along the old Miramichi,
And in Woodstock the potatoes
Will be doing fine;

While away out west in the wheat fields,
With Mary still in my heart,
I've got far away New Brunswick in my mind.
REPEAT CHORUS:

RECITED:

2.

I can see the cattle just coming home now,
'Round Sussex where Mary lives,
As I catch a glimpse of a moose
In the lonesome pines;
While away out west in the wheat fields,
With Mary's love in my heart
I've got far away New Brunswick in my mind.

REPEAT CHORUS TWICE:

C.D. 16, SNG. 13

NO CANADIAN DREAM.

By T.C.Connors
©1986 CROWN VETCH MUSIC
(SOCAN) All rights reserved.

1.
    A.
The music of strangers they play in our homes
    E7.   A.
And tell us that we don't have songs of our own;
                    A7.   D.   A.
They give us no choices and make it quite clear,
    E7.   A.
They'll play what they want us to hear.
    D.   A.
Canadian Radio, boy, is it grand,
        E7.   A.
When you want to hear music from some other land;
            A7.   D.   A.
They tell us to like it and flow with the stream;
    E7.
We have No Canadian Dream.

Chorus:
    D.   A.
There's No Canadian Dream, my friends,
                        E7.
We have No Canadian Dream.

The Radio blares and the music declares,
                    A.
We have No Canadian Dream.

2.
We hear the American telling his son,
Of the battles he fought and the Freedoms he won,
He sings about Home and the Pride that he has,
And his son wants to be like his dad.

Canadian Radio, boy, is it grand,
When you want to hear stories from some
other land,
They teach us to long for those far away scenes,
Where there's NO CANADIAN DREAM.

Repeat CHORUS:

3.
No, we've got no cotton, and no Uncle Sam,
We've got no Texas and no Alabam;
From all of our singers, we don't hear a sound,
From St. John's to Vancouver Town.

We don't write letters, we don't use the phone,
We have no petitions to make our Cause known;
Even our Children don't know what it means,
To Dream A CANADIAN DREAM.

Repeat CHORUS:... END.

C.D. 19, SNG. 14

NO, NO, NO.
I'LL NEVER LET YOU GO.

By T.C.Connors & G.Lepine
©1994 CROWN VETCH MUSIC
(SOCAN) All rights reserved.

Chorus:
```
   C.                  D7.
```
No, No, No. I'll never let you go, go, go.
```
        G7.
```
You can tell all your friends, over again
```
C.                         D7.
```
I'll keep lovin' you right through to the end
```
     G7.                     C.  F.  C.
```
No, No, No. I'll never let you go, go, go.

1.
```
C.                        D7.
```
Somebody said I was an old Tom Cat
```
  G7.                          C.
```
Sportin' a suit-case and a ramblin' hat
```
                           D7.
```
Somebody don't want me hangin' around,
```
 G7.              C.
```
They want to see me gone.   (Chorus:)

2.
Somebody told you I'd be a train
Leavin' the station, out in the rain
Somebody said the station was you
And I'd be leavin' you blue.   (Chorus:)

3.
I'm tellin' you, Babe, I'll never leave
I'm really the one that you should believe
I'll always be there when everyone's gone
I'll never leave you alone.   (Chorus:)

C.D. 12, SNG. 01

NORTH ATLANTIC SQUADRON.

By T.C.Connors
©1975 CROWN VETCH MUSIC
(SOCAN) All rights reserved.

Chorus:
```
   C.
```
Away, away, with fife and drum;
```
 G7.              C.
```
Full of the devil and navy rum;

R-r-r-umpa-tum, tum-pa-tum, here we come,
```
     G7.         C.
```
The North Atlantic Squadron.

1.
```
 C.
```
All the girls in Cherry town,
```
     G7.                 C.
```
The ship was in and they all came down;

We took 'em aboard and showed 'em around.
```
     G7.         C.
```
The North Atlantic Squadron.

2.
The cabin boy, the cabin boy;
The dirty little nipper;
He stole a pearl from every girl
And he planted them on the Skipper: Chorus:

3.
All the girls in Harbour John,
They line the street beside the pond;
They love to get their clutches on
The North Atlantic Squadron;

4.
The engineer, the engineer,
He loved to play the clarinet;
But after the fight the other night,
The second mate was wearin' it; Chorus:

5.
All the girls in Harbour Jacks,
They're waitin down beside the tracks;
Tonight, the 'Skirts' are gonna attack
The North Atlantic Squadron.

6.
The boatswain had a talkin bird,
He took him out to the party;
But all we heard from out of the bird
Was "Give us another one, Marty!" Chorus:

7.
All the girls around the Bay
They came to hear the music play;
We played to them all and we sailed away;
The North Atlantic Squadron.

8.
Now all the boys are gone to war
And all the girls are on the shore
And they wave goodbye forevermore
To the North Atlantic Squadron. Chorus:

NORTHERN GENTLEMAN.

By T.C.Connors

1.

C.   G7.   C.
Here's to the Northern Gentleman
   F.   C.
Who brought the Northland fame,
        F.
Through the boundless snow
     C.
Where none dare go,
      D7.   G7.
The Northern Gentleman came.
    C.   C7.
He trapped the beaver and the northern fox
     F.   C.
And the great white polar bear;
     F.   C.
And the 'yellow stone' he found alone,
     G7.   C.
Had a gleam beyond compare.
   G7.   C.
Here's to the Northern Gentleman
    G7.   C.
Who named the northern towns,
     F.   C.
Where a husky sleigh was the only way
     D7.   G7.
The North Gent made his rounds.
    C.   G7.   C.
He called the Yukon, "YUKON",
     F.   C.
And the great bay, "HUDSON BAY",
     F.   C.
From Dawson down to Timmins town,
     G7.   C.
The North Gent made his way.

CHORUS:

C.   F.   G7.   C.
The Northern Gentleman,
    G7.   C.
Who crossed the northern plains.
   F.   C.
He's the Gent whose life was spent
     G7.   C.
To bring the Northland fame.

2.

Here's to the Northern Gentleman
Who braves the winter through;
He's still a-trek in North Quebec
And Kapuskasing, too.
He's a miner and a lumberjack,
He's a driller on a diamond drill;
He drives a crane and he stakes a claim
And he works at the old pulp mill.

Here's to the Northern Gentleman
Who wears a big mackinaw;
He might say, "How"! with an Indian bow,
Or he might say. "Comment ca va?".
So here's to the Northern Gentleman,
No matter what be his name;
He's the Gent whose life was spent
To bring the Northland fame.

Repeat CHORUS and finish.

NORTH OF OLD LAKE ERIE.

1.

C.   G7.   F.   C.   G7.
North of Old Lake Erie, South of Moosonee,
    F.   C.
Ontario, I'll have you know
        D7.   G7.
You're all the world to me;
          C.   G7.   F.
From Cornwall. to Kenora
          C.   G7.
My heart will always be
    F.   C.   G7.   C.
North of Old Lake Erie, South of Moosonee.

2.

North of Old Lake Erie, South of Moosonee,
Ontario, where trilliums grow
Beneath the Maple Tree
In a land of lakes and rivers always calling me
North of Old Lake Erie, South of Moosonee.

3.

North of Old Lake Erie, South of Moosonee;
The world can go to Mexico,
To Rome or Tennessee.
But every time I travel the only road I see
Is North of Old Lake Erie, South of Moosonee.

4.

North of Old Lake Erie, South of Moosonee,
Ontario, where lovers know the blissful harmony
Of a cottage in the valley, nestled in the trees,
North of Old Lake Erie, South of Moosonee.

5.

North of Old Lake Erie, South of Moosonee;
If you're a stranger looking for
The chance of being free:
In every town or village
A welcome there will be
North of Old Lake Erie, South of Moosonee.

6.

North of Old Lake Erie, South of Moosonee,
Ontario, I'll have you know
You're all the world to me;
From Cornwall to Kenora
My heart will always be
North of Old Lake Erie, South of Moosonee.

ODE FOR THE ROAD.

Chorus:
D.   D7.   G.   D.
Many years ago, so many years ago;

Come hear the Ode that I wrote for the Road,
    A7.   D.
Many years ago.

1.

D.   D7.
I left my home in the Maritimes;
G.
Worked the mills and I worked the mines;
A7.   D.
All them gals, I left behind, many years ago.
                                  D7.
I wandered down by the railroad tracks;
G.
Joined up with some lumberjacks;
    A7.
I took the train that never came back;
              D.
Many years ago. (Chorus:)

2.

I worked an oil-rig away out west
Bronco ridin' with the best
Cowboy hats and all the rest. Many Years Ago.
Rode the rails and thumbed the cars
Learned to play this old guitar
Hangin' 'round those Country Bars,
Many Years Ago.
(Chorus:)

3.

Pickin' spuds on P.E.I.
Castle building in the sky
There wasn't much that I wouldn't try.
Many Years Ago.
Whenever love came snoopin' around,
It wasn't long till I was found
Far away in another town. Many Years Ago.
(Chorus:)

4.

Then one day it occurred to me
Although I've been from sea to sea
I'm not the man I used to be. Many years ago.
So I came back home to the Eastern Shore
But all them widows around my door
Were all lined up like they were before.
Many years ago.

SECOND LAST CHORUS:

Many Years Ago, So Many Years Ago;
There was even more than there was before,
Many Years Ago.

REPEAT 1st Chorus End.

C.D. 11, SNG. 08

OH CHIHUAHUA.

By T.C.Connors

CHORUS:
  D.
Oh, Chihuahua; Hey, Chihuahua;
  A7.   D.
Not much bigger than c o o - c a - r a - c h a,
  A7.   D.
Not much bigger than c o o - c a - r a - c h a.

1.

  D.   A7. D.
Way down south in Mexico,
                       A7.   D.
We went down to the doggie show.

Some were big and some were small;
                       A7.   D.
But who's the best bow-wow of all?

REPEAT CHORUS:

2.

She won ribbons at the fair,
Now she wears them in her hair,
Well ain't she just a proud female,
You can tell by the wiggle in her tail.

3.

She spends hours in her room,
Paints and powders and perfumes;
Mirror, mirror on the wall,
Now whose the best bow-wow of all.

REPEAT CHORUS:

4.

Where's her boyfriend doggy date,
Poor senor, he has to wait,
She's so busy with her hair,
By manana she'll be there.

REPEAT CHORUS TWICE:

C.D. 09, SNG. 01

OH LAURA.

By T.C.Connors
©1971 CROWN VETCH MUSIC
(SOCAN) All rights reserved.

CHORUS:
  A.   E7.   A.
Oh, Laura; Laura, Laura;
          E7.   A.
Oh, Oh, Laura; how I love you Laura.

1.
  A.
Who turns my world? It's a beautiful girl
       E7.
called Laura;

My heart's aflame at the sound of her name,
  A.
Laura.
    A7.   D.   A.
Together, hand in hand we stray,

Down by the moon-lit water-way;
    E7.
How I love to be walkin', I love to be talkin'
    A.
with Laura.

2.
I just can't wait to have another date with Laura.
She's so sweet, she can't be beat, it's my Laura.
Maybe we'll get some sugar dips,
Maybe I'll get to kiss her lips,
I don't mind statin', I feel so great when datin'
my Laura.

3.
I strum my guitar and sing how lovely you are
my Laura;
Heavens above, Oh how I love you my Laura.
Honey! It'll soon be June,
Come on I wanna talk about a honeymoon,
I'll be all a-glory, my life'll be the story
of Laura.

REPEAT CHORUS:

C.D. 16, SNG. 12

OKANAGAN OKEE.

By T.C.Connors
©1989 CROWN VETCH MUSIC
(SOCAN) All rights reserved.

Chorus:
  C7.   F.   C.
Little Blossom, forever true;
  D7.   G7.
Okanagan Okee, I love you.
     C.   C7.
And of all the pretty flowers,
    F.
I have loved you from the start;
  G7.   C.
Okanagan Okee, Blossom of my heart.

1.
  C.   C7.
When the birds are singing "Spring Time"
   F.
In the mountains,
    G7.
And my heart is singing
         C.
"Apple Blossom Time";
          C7.   F.
Love is blooming in the Okanagan Valley,
  G7.   C.
And little Okanagan Okee, you're all mine.

2.
I don't care if all the world
Might think I'm 'hokey'
When I'm strolling in the moonlight
On the trail,
With my sweetheart Okanagan Okee;
She's the fairest little blossom in this vale...
(To Chorus:)

Repeat 1st & 2nd Verses and Chorus:

(Variation of Last Line at End of Last Chorus),

Little Okee, you're the Blossom of my Heart.

End.

C.D. 03, SNG. 07

OLD ATLANTIC SHORE. The

1.

E.
When the big moon shines in the Maritimes
　　　　A.　　　　E.
On the Old Atlantic Shore;

I'll be glad to be back to old Halifax
　　　Gb7.　　　B7.
And the girl that I adore.
　　　　　　E.　　　　　　　　E7.
When the Big Sky's blue I'll be coming to you
　　　　A.　　　　E.
With a love forever more
　　　　　　A.　　　B7. A.　　E. B7.　Gb7.
Where the high tides roll on the rocky shoals
　　　　E.　　B7.　　E.
Of the Old Atlantic Shore.

2.

Where the fishin' nets hang
And the buoy bells clang
You marvel at the stevedore's might

And the big long ships
From the docks they slip
Away in the silence of night.
How I reminisce your goodbye kiss
Standing in the shanty door;
I'm comin' back home never more to roam
From the Old Atlantic Shore

3.

It's a long ways down to Halifax town
Where the great white seagull flies,
But the big blue sea it's a-callin' to me
"Come back to your big blue eyes".
I can feel sea breezes comin' through the trees,
I can hear the ocean's roar,
I'll be home tonight dear to hold you tight,
On The Old Atlantic Shore.

(Repeat Verses as Needed for Time
Requirements)

C.D. 18, SNG. 06

OLD FLAT TOP GUITAR.

1.

E.
Well, I work all week, the wife does too;
　　　　　　　　　E7.
She gets a 'perm', and I buy 'brew';
　A.
We stock the fridge and pay the bills;
　E.
We don't get too many frills.
　B7.
But we got a house, a dog and a mouse
　　　　　　　　E.
And an Old Flat Top Guitar.

2.

Well, it's all right to dance and dine
By candle light with fancy wine.
But when we can't afford to roam,
We'll have a shindig here at home;
And dance around to the Country sounds
Of Old Flat Top Guitar.

3.

On Saturday nights we get some beer.
We sit outside, the old dog near;
Bang the old veranda boards;
Get the wife to strum the chords;
Shake the moon with a new set of tunes
On Old Flat Top Guitar.

4.

How the neighbours look
When they hear the sound.
They jump the fence and they gather 'round;
Dance the heels right off their boots;
Even the owls begin to hoot;
When the higher strings begin to ring
On Old Flat Top Guitar.

5.

Well, at half-past-two we hit the roof,
The old hound dog, he gives a "Woof".
That's his way of tryin' to speak;
"See you all again next week".
Walk right in, we'll pick it up again
With Old Flat Top Guitar.

C.D. 13, SNG. 12

OLYMPIC SONG, The

1.

D.
All the way from Mount Olympus,

Here they come,
A7.   D.
The Athlete with the Torch and the Flame;

Bringing Sacred Fire,

Goodwill, Courage and Desire,
A7.   D.
To the Heart of the World Olympic Games.

Chorus:
A7.
Swifter, Higher, Longer;
D.
The Skillful and the Stronger;

E7.   A7.
Performing for the "Five Great Links of Chain".
D.
And in 'revel-tones', wearing medals,

Going home;
A7.   D.
Great Winners of the World Olympic Games.

2.
How to play the best,
And to out-play all the rest,
For the eyes of the world to behold.
National hearts reel,
Cheering heroes on the field,
Competing for the "Silver, Bronze and Gold".

C.D. 04, SNG. 10

ONE BLUE LIGHT.

1.

A.   E7.
As he stood by the pole on the corner
                                              A.
Of the street where decorations shine so bright;
                              A7.
He could see in between
      D.
The array of red and green,
E7.   A.
To the house with One Blue Light.

First Chorus:
A7.   D.   A.
There's a house with One Blue Light, tonight,
D.   A.
On a Christmas Eve, so white;
                              A7.   D.
And a man with regrets, on his way to the steps
      E7.   A.
Of the house with One Blue Light.

2.
As he thought of what he'd done,
He couldn't blame her,
And he knew that she might turn him
From her sight,
But he knew in his mind,
What he'd lost, he'd have to find
At the house with one blue light.

3.
As he coughed he could hear people singing,
Unaware that he was out there in the night;
In his heart there was pain,
And he knew he'd remain
At the house with one blue light.

SECOND CHORUS:
There's a house with one blue light tonight,
On a Christmas eve so white;
And he dropped his cigarette
Where he fell by the steps
Of the house with one blue light.

TAG Line:
There's a house with one blue light.

C.D. 04, SNG. 12

OUR FATHER.

Verse 1.
```
A.        A7.              D.
Our Father, which art in Heaven,
A.      E7.           A.
Hallowed be Thy Holy Name.
                    A7.
Thy Kingdom shall come,
          D.                    A.
And Thy Will shall be done, in the Earth,
          E7.        A.
As it is in Thy Heavenly Domain.
```

Bridge:
```
E7.                           A.
Give us this day, our daily bread,

We need no more;
   B7.
And forgive us our debts
       E7.        B7.      E7.
As we forgive our debtors, Lord.
```

```
A.         A7.
And we beg you to lead
      D.                          A.
Us away from evil deed and temptation,
                          E7.          A.
That our Savior, Jesus, never died in vain.
```

Verse 2.
```
A.         A7.              D.
Our Father, which art in Heaven,
A.      E7.           A.
Hallowed be Thy Holy Name.
                         A7.
For the Kingdom is Thine,
            D.                    A.
And the Power Divine and the Glory,
                    E7.            A.
Stand in praise and there forever will remain.
```

TAG:
```
D.        A.                      E7.
Ahh, ah-ah-ah-ah, ah-ah-ah, ah-ah-ah-ah,
      A.
ah-ah-men. (Amen)
```

C.D. 17, SNG. 12

PAPER SMILE.

1.
```
G.                              D7.
While you grin through your thin Paper Smile
                    G.
You tell me that love is your style.

                              D7.
But your eyes show the lies and your guile
                              G.
While you grin through your thin Paper Smile.
```

Chorus:
```
G7.      C.              G.
You think cheating repeatedly is cool;
   C.              A7.      D7.
Hoping I'm deceived, thinking I'm a fool.
          G.                    D7.
But while your eyes try to hide your secret file,
                    G.
I see in through your thin Paper Smile.
```

2.
```
I see in through your thin Paper Smile,
And I guess I'll be leaving for a while;
With loving thoughts you could not reconcile,
And still grin through your thin Paper Smile.
```

Repeat Chorus:

3.
```
I see in through your thin Paper Smile,
Without a friend at the end of your mile.
And your smart broken heart takes a while
To wipe that grin from your thin Paper Smile.
```

Repeat Chorus if necessary.

C.D. 01, SNG. 11
C.D. 21, SNG. 09

PETERBOROUGH POSTMAN.

1.

C.   G7.   C.
I see the programs on T.V. are gettin' better,
                          G7.   C.
And the music on the radio is fine;
                          C7.
I've got lots of records too,
        F.
That I play and think of you,
        D7.   G7.
But that don't keep the worry from my mind.

CHORUS:
G7.   C.   G7.
When the Peterborough Postman passes by, I cry,
                                        C.
And I wonder why we ever said goodbye.

                                        C7.
'Cause I'm always home alone,
            F.
But you don't even phone,
                    C.   G7.   C.
And the Peterborough Postman passes by.

2.
Sometimes I want to leave this town forever,
But my heart won't let me go till you return;
And when all the house is still
I sit beside my window sill
Waiting, watching, worried while I yearn.

C.D. 08, SNG. 11

PIGGY-BACK RACE. The

Recitation: 1.
    A.   A7.   D.
'Twas July 32nd, on Piggy-back Day,
        E7.
And the crowds were all standing
        A.
In each other's way;
                          A7.
They came there to watch him,
        D.
That awful disgrace,
        E7.   A.
The annual champ of the Piggy-Back Race.

Refrain -
    A.   E7.   A.
Singing Chuckle-dee-Chuckle-dee-dee, dee-dee,
            E7.   A.
Singing Chuckle-dee-Chuckle-dee-dee.

2.
Now, The cabbage roll kid, just an overgrown Uke,
He was last year's champ cause he won by a fluke,
For old griptight Glenny was too thin to be seen,
And he lost his first prize to that cabbage machine.

3.
Now Leprechaun Johnny
Would not have entered this deal,
But he had no way of knowin'
All the pigs would be real,
And the Skinners Pond hippie
Had a laugh on his face,

To see Leprechaun Johnny
In a piggy back race..... To Refrain:
Singing chuckle dee chuckle dee dee, dee dee,
Singing chuckle dee chuckle dee dee.

4.
Now the crowd started lookin'
At a sight that was weird,
Just an old pair of boots with a nose and a beard,
And it said I can win any prize in this show,
And he signed himself in Pinochio Joe.

5.
Now all the contestants, there must have been ten,
Were all ready to jump on their pigs in the pen,
But the whistle got stuck and so did the gun,
And there wasn't a soul there could count higher
than one.

6.
At last they were off, each man to a hog,
For the hundred yard dash
Through that dirty old bog,
Where the leprechaun vanished
And left not a trace,
No more to return to the piggy back race.....
To Refrain:
Singing chuckle dee chuckle dee dee, dee dee,
Singing chuckle dee chuckle dee dee.

7.

Now the man with the nose
He was makin' good time,
He arrived with his hog at the finishing line,
They were covered with mud
And their noses so big,
There was no one could tell which one was the pig,

8.

Now old Griptight Glenny
Was no fool or no kook,
He slipped off his pig but came in on the Uke,
And if you see a pig with a cowboy hat on,
It belongs to that hippie from old Skinners Pond.

9.

Now Pinochio Joe he could never play chess,
But at piggy back ridin' we know he's the best,
So we gave him first prize, a pie in his face,
And we found our new champ
For the piggyback race.....
To Refrain:
Singing chuckle dee chuckle dee dee, dee dee,
Singing chuckle dee chuckle dee dee.

C.D. 10, SNG. 11

PIZZA PIE LOVE.

By T.C.Connors

CHORUS:

  C.
Oh, She-sa my-a leetle piece-a pizza pie-a,

b'ye-a,
                      G7.
Oh, She-sa my-a big-a moon up above;
  C.
Oh, She-sa my-a leetle piece-a pizza pie-a,

b'ye-a,
             G7.   C.
Oh, She-sa my-a leetle Pizza Pie-a Love.
                    Am.
L a - l a - l a - l a - l a - l a - l a - l a - l a a a,
         G7.   C.
L a - l a - l a - l a - l a - l a - l a - l a - l a a a,

1.

C.   C7.   F.
Well, I meets a leetle gallee up in T.O. town,
  G7.   Am.
She's come to from Itallee, makes me folly

she's around.
  C.   C7.   F.
She tell me come to her house and she make

some pizza pie,
     G7.   Am.
Oh, me gallee from Itallee, she's dee 'apple

of me eye'.

REPEAT CHORUS:

2.

She's make me eats a pizza and me head she
spins around,
She's giff me leetle keeses and me heart goes
up and down,
She say to me she's love me and she kootchy,
kootchy, koo,
Oh! me gallee from Itallee make me don't
know what to do,

3.

She's giff me hat and coat and say goo'bye
come back again,
But when you back come Tony, don't forget
to bring da ring,
Me tinks if I go buy for her to shop
of jewellery,
Me gallee from Itallee she's got some ting
nice for me.

REPEAT CHORUS:

C.D. 13, SNG. 06

POLE AND THE HOLE. The
(Bottomless Hole.)

1.

E.
When you're in the hole,

You know the 'money pole'
B7.
Is the ladder of all success.

But the guy with the 'roll' controls the pole,
E.
And the hole's in a hell of a mess.

You can bust your butt

And give it all that you got,
E7.   A.
Till you feel it in the pit of your soul
B7.
You're gonna drop a lot, though,

When you get the shot
E.
From the feller at the top of the pole.
A.
Then you roll, roll, roll,
B7.
Down the 'money pole', pole, pole,
E.
In the Bottomless Hole.

2.

Yeah, the man at the top
Is called the cock of the walk
And you better not challenge him.
He'll shake the pole
And put you back in the hole
A bouncin' on the bottom again.
You can work and slave and scrimp and save
Till you rise to the rim of the hole,
But then buddy you're beat
When you try to compete
With the feller at the top of the pole.
Then you roll, roll, roll,
Down the money pole, pole, pole
In the bottomless hole.

3.

Now the man upstairs says he really cares
When you go to get the welfare cheque;
And they say the pole is gonna save your soul
And take away your pain in the neck;
They're gonna wash your face
And put you back in the race
With an updated rig-a-maroll,
Where the better you get
Means the bigger your debt,
To the feller at the top of the pole.
Then you roll, roll, roll,
Down the money pole, pole, pole
In the bottomless hole.

Repeat Verse One:

C.D. 19, SNG. 08

POLKA PLAYIN' HENRY.

1.

A.
Come and listen to the music
E7.
Of the Northern land

A.
The hootin', rootin', tootin' Henry Kelnick Band

From the boogie to the oompas
E7.
In the oompa-pa halls
A.
Polka Playin' Henry was the king of them all.

2.

A.
From the picnic to the weddings
E7.
And the big parade

A.
Dancing and romancing to the music he played
E7.
The people and the children all became his fans

And waltzin' down the avenue,
A.
They followed the band.

Chorus...
      D.   A.
With the Twist and the Jig, the town was alive
  E7.   A.
Rockin' and a-Rollin' to the Jitter-Bug Jive
    D.   A.
He played the accordion, the saxophone
   B7.
The fiddle and the trumpet
     E7.
And the slide-trombone. (to 1st verse)

3.

In the cities of the country,
How they took to the sound
The music of the miners up in Timmins town
Where he packed the old pavillion
To the clapping of hands
Of the doctors and the lawyers
And the lumberjack man.

4.

With a magical smile, just as clear as a bell
Mr. Henry Kelnick we'll remember you well
And we'll raise another glass
Up in the Northern land
To Henry and the members
Of a mighty fine band. (to chorus)

C.D. 17, SNG. 03   **PRAIRIE MOON.**   By T.C.Connors

Verse One:
  E.   E7.
Roll along Prairie Moon,
    A.   Gb7.
I'm alone in Saskatoon;
     B7.   E.
Tell me why, tell me why. Baby's gone.
B7. E.   E7.
Maybe you can shed some light
      A.   Gb7.
On the reason she took flight
       B7.   E.
From her true love on the Blue Saskatchewan.

Chorus One:
  E7.   A.
Where the prairie lilies blow,
    E.
She whispered soft and low,
      A.   B7.
You'll be mine and I'll be yours very soon;
     E.   E7.
But if she's found another star,
    A.   Gb7.
Take a note from my guitar,
     B7.   E.
Sing my song and roll along, Prairie Moon.

Verse Two:

Roll along Prairie Moon
Till she knows no other tune
And those rhymes of old times linger on.
Brush her lonely tears away
Till she's right back home to stay
With her true love on the Blue Saskatchewan

Chorus Two:

Where the Prairie Lilies grow
She whispered soft and low
You'll be mine and I'll be yours very soon.
Go to her and if I'm right
Bring my Baby back tonight
If I'm wrong just Roll along, Prairie Moon.
Repeat 1st Verse & Chorus.

C.D. 10, SNG. 01

PRINCE EDWARD ISLAND, HAPPY BIRTHDAY.

CHORUS: (Sing after every verse.)

G.   G7.   C.
Happy Birthday to you, Happy Birthday to you,
D7.   G.
Prince Edward Island, Happy Birthday.

1.
G.   G7.
Well, it ain't so big and bold,
        C.
But it's Heaven to behold,
D7.   G.
Prince Edward Island in the blue;
                G7.
And for One Hundred Years
C.
We're all here to cheer,
D7.   G.
And sing Happy Birthday to you.

2.
It's a time to sing and shout.
We'll bring the lobsters out,
And pass along the bottle to the crew;
Then we'll dance the jamboree
On the Island in the sea,
And sing Happy Birthday to you.

3.
Where the young respect the old
And friends are ahead of gold,
We're happy to be home again with you;
And for those so far away
Who can't be here today,
We'll crack another lobster shell or two.

4.
No it ain't so big and bold
But it's Heaven to behold,
The big mud Bud the Spud came trackin' through;
And for one hundred years
We're all here to cheer,
And sing Happy Birthday to you.

Prince Edward Island, Happy Birthday.

C.D. 16, SNG. 11

REAL CANADIAN GIRL.

CHORUS: (Sing as needed.)

G.
She's a Real Canadian Girl,
          D7.
A Real Canadian Girl;

She's an All-Acadian Northern Lady
           G.
And a Real Canadian Girl.

1.
G.   D7.
She loves the way it feels, driving snowmobiles;

And laughing at her dates,
           G.
When they don't know how to skate.

She knows her Hockey Games
           D7.
And the players of the world;

She's an All-Acadian Northern Lady
           G.
And a Real Canadian Girl.

2.
She's from the Miramichi,
By the old Atlantic Sea;
But like the rolling tide she travels far and wide;
So fond of the great outdoors
With a glowing heart a twirl;
She's an All-Acadian Northern Lady
And a REAL CANADIAN GIRL.

3.

She'll brave the Yukon nights
And dance to the Northern Lights;
Then she's off to ski in the mountains of B.C.
In the Summer she'll play ball,
In the Winter time she'll curl;
She's an All-Acadian Northern Lady
And a REAL CANADIAN GIRL.

4.

From the River of Saint John
To the old Saskatchewan,
Up along the Caribou she'll paddle her canoe;
She loves the bears and birds
And every little squirrel;
She's an All-Acadian Northern Lady
And a REAL CANADIAN GIRL.

5.

And when you see her play
She'll take your breath away;
Bathing in the sun or swimming for the fun;
And if some lucky guy
Should land this precious pearl,
She's an All-Acadian Northern Lady
And a REAL CANADIAN GIRL.

Repeat Verse no. 1. And Chorus:

C.D. 12, SNG. 02
C.D. 21, SNG. 14

RED RIVER JANE.

By T.C.Connors

1.

A.
Here I walk in the Winnipeg rain;
　　　　E7.　　　　　A.
Tryin' to get a bus, tryin' to get a train.
A7.　　　D.
Tryin' to get back to my field of grain
　　　　A.
Away from Portage Ave. and Main,
　　　　E7.　　　　　A.
Where I blew my mind and my money, in vain;
　　　　E7.　　　　　D.
And I blew my past on a fast Red River Jane.

Chorus:
　A7.　　　D.
Red River Jane, that's her name,
　　　　　　　A.
Sixty-nine Rip-Off Lane;
　　　　　　　　　　　　　E7.
I must have been insane to play her game.
　　　　　　　D.
But crazy fools have got to learn,
　　　　　A.
Country boys got to get burned;
　　　　　　E7.　　　　　A.
And I blew my mind and my money, in vain;
　　　　　　E7.　　　　　A.
And I blew my past on a fast Red River Jane.

Repeat as often as needed for time considerations.

C.D. 02, SNG. 10

REESOR CROSSING TRAGEDY.

1.

C.   G7.   C.
Just a little bit west of Kapuskasing,
     G7.   C.
Reesor Crossing, that's the name;
           G7.   C.
Farmers hauled from out of the bushland,
     G7.   C.
Pulpwood for the mill-bound train.
  F.   C.
Twenty farmers met that night
   G7.   C.
To guard their pulp from a Union strike;
  F.   C.
Unaware this night would see
    G7.   C.
The Reesor Crossing Tragedy.

2.

You'll never load this pile of pulpwood
Said the Union men when they came
Though they numbered about five hundred
The twenty farmers took rifle aim,
We've got to get our pulpwood out
Before the muskeg frost comes out
And may God help us all to see
No Reesor Crossing Tragedy.

3.

You'll never touch this pile of pulpwood,
But they came and tragically
Three men died that February
Night in the year of Sixty-three.
Eight more wounded, some beat up,
Tires slashed on the lumber trucks
A night of death and Destiny,
The Reesor Crossing Tragedy.

4.

You'll never touch this pile of pulpwood,
Seven words that spelled out pain
For the widows and their children
And their men who died in vain.
How can anyone forget
The bloodiest labour battle yet
In all Canadian History,
The Reesor Crossing Tragedy.

5.

Just a little bit west of Kapuskasing
They carved a Sculpture beside the tracks
Of the bushman and his family
Who live their lives behind the axe,
It reminds us in the North
Not to bring our tempers forth,
So there may never elsewhere be
A Reesor Crossing Tragedy.

C.D. 15, SNG. 08

RETURN OF THE SEA QUEEN.

1.

  G.
We set sail on a Friday, November, Thirteen;

And there's no superstitions
   Em.
Aboard the Sea Queen.
      G.   C.   G.
But a hell of a 'twister', before we got home.
     C.   G.
Brought the Devil in Hades
    D7.   G. Em.
To the top of the foam.

2.

The sea was in turmoil, the sky it was black
The thunder did rumble
And the lightening did crack
The wind grabbed the Sea Queen
And tossed her up high
Then slapped her down backwards
Like a wet butterfly.

3.

Our weathered old Captain, he lets out a roar
In the name of some God
We ain't heard of before
Our propeller's all tangled, in what I can't tell
But I hope it's a wing
Off that Demon from Hell.

4.

We rocked and we pitched
On the sea without hope
While some tied their waist
To the bulkhead with rope
With bodies half naked
We fought off thc waves
And watched all the rats
Meet their watery graves.

5.

Then all of a sudden, as quick as it came
The wind, she died down,
And the storm, she grew tame
In less than an hour we walked up the shore
And fell in the arms of the ones we adore.

6.

That night as we partied, we drank up the rum
We joked about death
And how close we had come
We spoke of our plan to repair the Sea Queen
We'll meet in the morning
To follow our scheme.

7.

When the sun she came rising
Up Dead Seaman's Hill
We ran to our Captain to follow his will
With marble for muscles and granite for bones
He lets out that beller, we all turn to stone.

8.

Now I've met those people
That say there's no ghosts
They say we're just statues
That stand on the coast
But at night they go dancing
While late fires burn
With the crew of the Sea Queen
That 'never returned'

REPEAT LAST TWO LINES and Finish.

C.D. 03, SNG. 09   **REVERSING FALLS DARLING.**   By T.C.Connors

1.

C.
In Saint John, New Brunswick,
  G7.   C.
A city by the sea,
                           G7.
There is a girl who's longing for me;
      C.   C7.   F.   C.
She waits every day, she's waiting for my call,

'Way up on the hillside
   G7.   C.
By the old Reversing Falls.

2.

Her eyes are like diamonds they sparkle for me
I can see them shining far across the sea
There's a rose in her hair, she's just like a doll
Waiting on the hillside
By the Old Reversing Falls

3.

Listen here you old moon I'm tellin' to you
I'm gettin' sad, so lonesome and blue
I left my sweetheart waiting for my call
Way up on the hillside
By the Old Reversing Falls

4.

My little darlin' is callin' to me
I can hear her song on the lonesome prairie
In dreams I can see reversing waters fall
I'm goin' back to answer my little darling's call.

5.

Goodbye Alberta, I'm going to roam
Back to my darlin', back to my home
I know she'll be lonesome waiting for my call
I'll find her on the hillside
By the Old Reversing Falls
She'll be way up on the hillside
By the Old Reversing Falls,

C.D. 14, SNG. 06 **RIPPED OFF WINKLE.**

1.

D.
When I was young I had an old guitar
                         A7.
And I learned to sing and play

From a book I bought on how to be a "Star",
                              D.
Written in the U.S.A.;

And every movie that I seen
                         D7.   G.
Had a message just for me;
A7.
If you want to be a "Big Country Star"
                                   D.
You go to Nashville, Tennessee.

Chorus: (Sing after each Verse.)
D7.   G.   D.
That's my song, ... That's my song!
A7.
Hey, old Ripped Off Winkle,
          G.   D
Can't you hear the bell go dong?
A7.
Hey, old Ripped Off Winkle,
          G.   D.
Don't you know you slept too long?

2.

Well I had my hopes of being a "Star"
But not for selfish greed,
I' wanted my country to take the credit
For me if I succeed,
And if I don't no one will know,
Except the ones that should,
And no one in some foreign land
Can ever say I was no good.

3.

So I'm a North American, "Second Class"
As some would judge my fate,
But I'll keep singing about what I am
And Nashville, you can wait,
The Canadian National Exhibition
Is where I'd rather be,
But they don't take no "Canadians"
Even at the C.N.E.

4.

I'm forty-one years old today
With a message for the young,
This country has a song to sing
And that song must be sung;
Do a deed that'll make your country great
As a favor to yourself,
And there won't be no greener grass
In a pasture somewhere else.

C.D. 16, SNG. 03 **RITA McNEIL.**
(A Tribute)

1.

D.   D7.   G.
On the banks of Bras D'or, along by the shore,
        D.   A7.
Day has revealed what the night has concealed
                    D.
In Cape Breton once more.
                         D7.   G.
And the automobiles are beginning to wheel
        D.   A7.
Along No. 4, to that little tea store
                    D.
Owned by Rita McNeil.

Chorus:
D.   D7.   G.
Rita McNeil, come in from the field;
                    D.
The world's at your door and they're looking
        A7.
for more

D.
Of that Big Pond appeal.
                    D7.   G.
Oh, Rita McNeil, just sing what you feel;
              D.   A7.
For you are the girl who has captured our world
                    D.
With a song that is real.

2.

So sing all those rhymes of the old Maritimes
Where proudly you speak
Of those men from the deep
Who go down in the mines.
And sing about steel and a heart that won't heal,
And then for the strife
You have known in your life,
Sing of RITA McNEIL.

Repeat Chorus...

C.D. 18, SNG. 03

ROAD TO THUNDER BAY.
(The Ghost)

By T.C.Connors
©1993 CROWN VETCH MUSIC
(SOCAN) All rights reserved.

1.

D.   Gb.   G.
He was standing alone by the highway
  A7.   D.
I stopped and he climbed in the car
                Gb.   G.
When I asked him how far he'd be going
  A7.   D.
He just sang to a small blue guitar.

Chorus: 1

 D7. G.   D.
I'll meet her tonight at the Lake-head
  G.   A7.
I'll tell her I promise to stay
       D.   Gb.   G.
When I've come to the end of my journey
    A7.   D.
Down this long lonely "Road To Thunder Bay,"

2.

While the shadows of night were decending
I could see in the mirror of the car
He had fallen asleep in the back seat
Still holding his small blue guitar.

Chorus: 2

But I still heard the words and the music
They stirred me in some quiet way
As I thought of the girl who was waiting
Down that long lonely "Road To Thunder Bay."

3.

As I came to the crash on the highway
What I saw really gave my mind a jar
When I learned how a young life had ended
For some lad with a small blue guitar.

Chorus: 3

With no need to look in the back seat
I was sure as I drove on my way
This was all just some dream or delusion
Down the long lonely "Road To Thunder Bay."

4.

All at once, to my ear, there was music
It came from the back seat of the car
And there, like a haze, in my mirror
He sang to a small blue guitar.

Chorus: 4

Will you meet her tonight at the Lake-head?
Will you tell her I'll see her some day?
When I've come to the end of my journey
Down this long lonely "Road To Thunder Bay?"

C.D. 05, SNG. 12   **ROCKY MOUNTAIN LOVE.**   **By T.C.Connors**

1.

C.
From the prairies to the mountains

               G7.
You have lured me like a lamb,

Till my lonely heart is crying

     C.
And I don't know where I am.

I can hear you somewhere laughing

            G7.
As you call from up above,

But I'm lost in the foothills of your

              C.
Rocky Mountain Love.

2.

Like a wave of winter breezes
With your high and mighty airs
You have chilled the warmth inside me
Till it seems like you don't care
In your sky there flies an eagle
With his prey, the helpless dove
And I'm lost in the foothills of your
Rocky Mountain love.

3.

I recall the fertile valleys
Where my heart once knew no pain,
Then I looked and saw your shadow
That you cast into my range
When I climbed your hills of promise
I was never dreaming of
Getting lost in the foothills of your
Rocky Mountain Love

4.

Now it's cold and I'm so weary
And my blue skies are all gone
If I dream of you tonight again
I may not live till dawn
For it seems the hand of hope is tired
Searching for its glove
And I'm lost in the foothills of your
Rocky Mountain Love
I'm lost in the foothills of your
Rocky Mountain Love.

C.D. 05, SNG. 05
C.D. 21, SNG. 03   **ROLL ON SASKATCHEWAN.**   **By T.C.Connors**

1.

C.   C7.   F.
Let my heart sing an old river song,
   G7.   C.
As we journey back where I belong;
                 C7.
Where the wind comes to say
     F.
To the river each day,
   G7.   C.
Roll On, Roll On, Saskatchewan.

Chorus:
   G7.   C.
Roll On, Roll On, Saskatchewan,
         G7.   C.
From the wheat fields of my heart;
        C7.   F.
Go find your way to the cool Hudson Bay,
   G7.   C.
And Roll On, Roll On, Saskatchewan.

2.

Old River, go whisper my prayer,
Tell Mother and Dad I still care;
Take this tear that I've cried
To the shore where they bide,
And Roll On, Roll On. Saskatchewan.

Repeat Chorus:

3.

No treasures have I to bring home,
To show for the years I did roam;
Just the song I still know
From the long, long ago;
Roll On, Roll On, Saskatchewan.

Repeat Chorus:

C.D. 14, SNG. 13   **ROSES IN THE SNOW.**   **By T.C.Connors**

1.

C.   C7.
She was his only rose
       F.   C.
Among the sunshine flowers,
             G7.
Till the day she passed away;
    C.   C7.   F.   C.
And when he kissed her in her dying hour,
   G7.   C.
This is what he heard her say.

1st Chorus:
 F.   C.
Flowers die, my love, but not forever,
           G7.
We shall meet again I know;
    C.   C7.   F.   C.
And I'll come back to you in Autumn weather.
   G7.   C.
Watch for Roses In The Snow.

2.

By her grave just like the weeping willow,
Every Sunday he'd be there
And every night upon a dreamless pillow,
God would hear his silent prayer.

2nd chorus.
Flowers die my love but not for ever,
We shall meet again I know,
And you'll come back to me
In Autumn weather,
And I'll see Roses In The snow.

3.

Many years he waited for each Autumn,
While his hair was turning grey,
And he'd remember when the snow was fallin,
These few words from yesterday.

3rd chorus.
Flowers die my love but not for ever,
We shall meet again I know;
And I'll come back to you in Autumn weather,
Watch for Roses In the Snow.

4.

They say he died beside the open window,
While the snow was falling down,
A little girl outside was dropping Roses,
One by one upon the ground.

4th Chorus.
Flowers die my love but not for ever,
We shall meet again I know,
And she came back for him
In Autumn weather,
When he saw Roses In The Snow.

C.D. 09, SNG. 07

ROVING ALL OVER THE LAND.

1.

G.
From the Island of Vancouver
             D7.
To the Isle of Newfoundland,

There's daisies by the wayside
             G.
And the pasture's green again;
             G7.
The blue jay on the fence post
   C.
Has summer in his song,
          G.
While out on the open highway.
     D7.   G.
I thumb my way along.

CHORUS:
  C.   D7.   G.
Roving All Over The Land;
  C.   D7.   G.
Roving All Over The Land.

2.

With a knapsack on my shoulder
And a Flat-top by my side,
I roam the great north country
And I feel so free inside;
There stops an old hay wagon,
I climb up on the load,
Where I munch on a big red apple,
As we jog along the road.

REPEAT CHORUS:

3.

You'll find me by the river,
Where the lively otter plays,
Or asleep beside the meadow,
Where the lazy cattle graze;
You'll find me in the back seat
Of a car that moves along,
To the music of my Flat-top,
On an old Hitch-hiker's song.

REPEAT CHORUS:

4.

Here comes an old truck driver,
I know by the way he smiles:
I'll sing and pick my Flat-top,
For the next two-hundred miles:
And a little voice will tell me
I've made another friend;
I'll share his bacon sandwich,
And I'm on the road again.

Repeat Chorus:
Repeat Verse 1:
Repeat Chorus:

C.D. 03, SNG. 04
C.D. 09, SNG. 12

RUBBERHEAD.
(Goodbye Rubberhead.)

CHORUS:
  E.   B7.   E.
Goodbye Rubberhead, so long Boob,
             B7.
Go and blow your inner tube;

I got a brand new 'sugar cube'.
               E.
So Goodbye Rubberhead, so long Boob.

1.

 E.   B7.
I told my baby nice, please don't flirt around,

And don't give eyes to other guys,

                  E.
It makes my poor heart pound;

And as I told her nice,
               B7.
Please don't make me dread,

She winked her eye at another guy,
                  E.
And when they left here's what she said:

REPEAT CHORUS:

2.

Well, I phoned my baby twice
To say she hurt me bad,
And asked her when she's free again,
To make my poor heart glad.
Oh yes, I phoned her twice,
And as with her I pled
She left me alone on the buzzin' phone
With the memory of what she said:

REPEAT CHORUS:

3.

Well I took some good advice
And I met me another girl,
And just to walk with her one block,
It sets my heart to whirl.
And when we met my ex,
Well, did her face get red,
She must have burned at the way I turned
My nose up in the air and said:

REPEAT CHORUS:

TAG: Goodbye Rubberhead, so long boob,
So long boob, so long boob-ba-ba-boob-
boob, boob-boob.

C.D. 05, SNG. 02　　　　　　**SABLE ISLAND.**　　　By T.C.Connors

1.

A.
About a hundred miles off the coast of my

Nova Scotian home
　　　　　　　　　　　　　　　E7.
There's an island with a tale of woe to tell;
　　　　A.
It's the 'graveyard' of the old Atlantic Ocean
　　E7.　　　　　　　　　　　　　A.
And they say it flies the phantom flag of hell.
　　A7.　　　　D.
There's a demon down below the
　　　　　　　A.
swirling waters
　　　　　　D.
Who has claimed the bones of about ten
　　　　　　　　E7.
thousand men,
　　　　　　D.
Who were ship-wrecked on the shoals of
　　　　A.
Sable Island;
　　　　E7.　　　　　　　　　　　　A.
And he left their dying voices on the wind.

Chorus:
A.　E7.　　　　　　D.　　　A.
So sailor, take warning, and pray every morning,
　　E7.　　　　　　　　　　　　　A.
When it's your luck to sail on a dreary day;
　　E7.　　　　　　D.　　A.
For Sable Island, more than any other island
　　　　　　　　　　　E7.
Has taken more ships and the lives of
　　A.
men away.
　　　　　　　　　　E7.　　A.
It has taken more ships and the lives of men away.

2.

Five hundred wrecks can be found
On the shores of Sable Isle,
With their treasures unrecovered in the sand.
They've been guarded by the 'herd of
hungry horses'
And the ghostly apparitions of the land.

Sable Island that defies a chart position,
Always moving with the North Atlantic tide;
Lies a-waiting for some unsuspecting vessel,
And the sands of hell to turn her on
her side... (To Chorus:)

3.

Many hundred men, through the years,
Have been banished by their kings,
To this 'graveyard' of the Old Atlantic Sea;
Where they killed each other off to keep
on living,
Until death itself could never set them free.

They still walk among the wrecks of
Sable Island,
Forever calling sailors to their doom;
When the fog is thick, "Ahoy", there's a vessel
On it's journey to that land beyond the
tomb... (To Chorus:)

C.D. 21, SNG. 04

SAINT JOHN BLUES.

1.

A.
Way up in King Square,

             E7.
Where the fountain flows

                        A.
I gave my ring there to the Saint John Rose;

               E7.
But all the love I gave, she did refuse;

And now I'm sittin' here

             A.
With the Saint John Blues.

2.

A.   E7.
Way up in King Square, in old Saint John,

             A.
I'm feeding pigeons here upon the lawn.

               E7.
And while I'm sitting here, some pigeon coos

You're not the only one

             A.
With the Saint John Blues.

Chorus...

A.   D.   A.
Way down on Charlotte Street, I used to fly

          E7.   A.
Until my little dove, she said goodbye.

          D.   A.
And now I'm lonely just like you.

        E7.   A.
I've got them old Saint John Blues.

(Repeat whole song if needed.)

C.D. 05, SNG. 09
C.D. 22, SNG. 11

SAM McGEE.
(The Night That I Cremated)

Chorus:

    A.   A7.
Oh, Those old Northern Lights,

        D.
They have seen the queerest sights,

    A.   E7.
But the queerest sight that they did ever see;

    A.   A7.
It was on the moonlit marge

    D.
Of that old Lake LeBarge.

    A.   E7.   A.
On the Night that I Cremated Sam McGee.

1.

Now my pal Sam McGee
Was from old Tennessee
In the land where the cotton blooms and grows
But why Sam left his home
In the deep, deep south to roam
Round the pole way up North God only knows.

2.

In the long search for gold
He was always so cold
How he longed again to roam the southern plain
I would listen to him rave
How he feared an icy grave
And if I die, he said, cremate my last remains.

3.

Well a pal's last need is a thing we have to heed
So I promised and I swore I would not fail
So again we started on
At the first streaks of dawn
But oh God he was lookin' ghastly pale.

4.

He crouched on the sleigh
And he raved away all day
About the warmth of his home in Tennessee
And before the night did fall
I'd a promise to recall
For a corpse was all that was left of
Sam McGee,

5.

Then I came upon the marge
Of that Old lake LeBarge
Where a broken down derelict did lay
She was jammed there in a vice
Of twenty feet of frozen ice
'Twas abandoned and left there to decay.

6.

Some planks I quickly tore
From its old cabin floor
And I gathered up the chunks of
Scattered coal
Soon the blazin' furnace red,
Seemed to know McGee was dead
So I stuffed him in that old crematin' hole.

7.

There sat my buddy Sam
Looking mighty cool and calm
In the heart of those furnace flames aroar

And he wore a great big smile
You could almost see a mile
As he chuckled, "Hurry up and close the door.'

8.

She's a fine place in here but I do gravely fear
You may let in that awful cold and storm
For since I left plum tree
Down in good old Tennessee
She's the first time that I've been really warm

(Repeat Chorus:)

C.D. 20, SNG. 15   **SASQUATCH SONG.**   By T.C.Connors

1.

A.   A7.   D.
One day at midnight the sun was so bright
          E7.   A.
The moon had no light but I could see
              A7.   D.
This big old Sasquatch said he was 'top notch'
          E7.   A.
At playin' hop-scotch 'way up in a tree.

2.

A7.   D.   A.
So I bet my wrist-watch that big old Sasquatch
          E7.   A.
Could never play hop-scotch 'way up in a tree.
              A7.   D.
Now there's a Sasquatch up in a tree-crotch;
          E7.   A.
He's got my wrist-watch and he's laughin' at me.

3.

I told the mounties throughout the counties
To put some bounties all over B.C.
And stop that Sasquatch
From playin' hop-scotch
'Till he gives my wrist-watch right back to me.

4.

Then Corporal Saverin, he found a tavern
In an empty cavern where the sun don't shine.
And he found a Sasquatch drinkin' blue blotch
And wearin' a wrist-watch
Lookin' just like mine.

5.

So he asked the Sasquatch
Where he got the wrist-watch
And that big old Sasquatch, he began to lie.

He said he got the wrist-watch
While playin' hop-scotch
Up in a tree crotch with some stupid old guy.

6.

So the mountie told him
He could never hold him,
But he'd have to scold him for doin' no harm.
So they played some hop-scotch
Until the Sasquatch
Had the mountie's wrist-watch on his other arm.

7.

Now all the mounties throughout the counties
They're placin' bounties all over the land.
And that big old Sasquatch
Wont feel so 'top notch'
When they get their Sasquatch
Like they "get their man".

8.

'Cause if that Sasquatch
Keeps playin' hop-scotch
There won't be a wrist-watch for miles around.
'Cause he'll play hop-scotch
'Till he gets your wrist-watch
Up in that tree-crotch
And he'll never come down.
So don't play hop-scotch near any old tree-crotch
Until that old, watch stealin', big feelin',
Hop-scotchin', Sasquatch is found.

C.D. 18, SNG. 13   **SHAKIN' THE BLUES.**   **By T.C.Connors& G.Lepine**

1.

A.   A7.
Someday, they say,
     D.   E7.   A.
We got to shake this blue, blue world

Somehow, like now,
 B7.   E7.
Love'll come and set your heart in a whirl
         A.   A7.
When you're down, don't frown,
        D.   E7.   A.
You've got to Shake The Blues somehow
          A7.   D.   E7.
So come along Baby, and dance with me
          D.   E7.   A.
And you'll be Shakin' The Blues right now.
 D.   E7.   A.
Shakin' The Blues right now.

2.

A.   A7.
Don't sigh, just fly,
     D.   E7.   A.
With a song called Shakin' The Blues
               B7.
Let's dance, romance, give us a chance
               E7.
To put the 'zip' in your shoes
     A.   A7.
It's our night, so hold tight,
     D.   E7.   A.
We're gonna Shake The Blues somehow
       A7.   D.   E7.
Well, it's all so easy, Baby, can't you see,
     D.   E7.   A.
We're a-Shakin' The Blues right now.
 D.   E7.   A.
Shakin' The Blues right now.

Chorus:
    D.
We're Shakin' The Blues,

So Baby, give me your hand,
 A.
Keep your feet a-movin' to the beat of the band;
 B7.
Blues are only bubbles,

Break 'em on the double,

                                 E7.
Forget about your troubles, Love is so grand.
    A.   A7.
Let's live, let's give,
     D.   E7.   A.
The whole wide world the news;
            A7.   D.   E7.
And while we shake it, all the world will say,
         D.   E7.   A.
They got a sure way of Shakin' The Blues.
 D.   E7.   A.
A sure way of Shakin' The Blues.
              A7.   D.
That's a sure way to shake it, and a sure

way to make it,
     E7.   A.
And a sure way of Shakin The Blues.

3.

O.K., let's sway,
To the new way of shakin' the world
Somehow, right now,
Love'll come and set your heart in a whirl
When you're down, don't frown,
We've got to Shake The Blues somehow
So come and dance everybody,
With my Baby and me
And you'll be Shakin' The Blues right now.
Shakin' The Blues right now.

4.

Don't sigh, just fly,
With a song called Shakin' The Blues
Let's dance, romance, give us a chance
To put the 'zip' in your shoes
It's our night, so hold tight,
We're gonna Shake away the Blues somehow.
So come along my Baby,
Let the whole world see,
We're a-Shakin' The Blues right now.
Shakin' The Blues right now.

Return to CHORUS and Finish..........

C.D. 02, SNG. 03

SHANTY TOWN SHARON.

By T.C.Connors

1.

C.   G7.
There once was a fisherman father,
                 C.
Who lived way down by the sea shore;
                 G7.
He dwelled in a broken down shanty
                 C.
Where planks made a living room floor.
D7.   G.
But he had the prettiest daughter,
D7.   G.   G7.
That ever had lived at the cove;
C.   G7.
The topic of male conversation,
             C.
The seven seas over, by Jove.

2.

And every young man that went fishing,
Way out on the sea waters high,
Can say that she told them she loved them,
They loved her and for her they'd die.
But oh this young queen was a wild one,
She tried to brand every man's heart,
She never would listen to daddy,
So you see how she got a bad start.

3.

Her mother's last words to her father,
When she died ten long years ago,
Be good dear,to your loving daughter,
Don't ever he harsh to her Joe.
But how many times since that parting
has she been led far astray,
And how many nights in a bar room,
Has she drank the wee hours away.

4.

How many drunken men hollered,
And fought for their lives for her smile,
She'd mark a man's face for a lifetime,
With a knife or a fingernail file.
She had as much courage as beauty,
And in her dark eyes there was war,
And if any man doubted her daring,
She'd sail where the wild waters roar.

5.

She became known as Shanty Town Sharon,
Then came the death of her dad,
She'd built her own ship by the sea shore,
And here's the wild notion she had.
She made her way down to the bar room,
To challenge all fishermen bold,
I know that you've all heard the legend,
About the reef only devils do hold

6.

Now if no man will sail to my starboard,
I'll cross that great reef all alone,
Her pretty dark eyes became wilder,
While outside the ocean did groan.
She took her last drink and departed,
To sail where those reef waters roar,
But 'twas tragic how poor Sharon's body,
Next morning washed up on the shore

C.D. 17, SNG. 04

SHE CALLED FROM MONTREAL.

1.

G.   G7. C.
She Called From Montreal
     G.
And darkened all my skies,
D7.   G.
Just when I surmised our love could never die.
    G7. C.
She Called From Montreal
     G.
And darkened all my skies;
D7.   G.
She Called From Montreal to say goodbye.

2.

G.   G7. C.
She Called From Montreal
    G.
And said, "It's all just a lie",
D7.   G.
She was on a 'high' as I was passing by.

       G7. C.
She Called From Montreal
     G.
And said, "It's all just a lie",
D7.   G.
She Called From Montreal to say goodbye.

Chorus:
 C.   G.
I was her 'mistake'. Hearts don't have to break.
 C.   G.   D7.
Can't I ever take a 'joke' without a sigh?
 G.   G7. C.
She Called From Montreal
     G.
And said, "It's all just a lie",
D7.   G.
She Called From Montreal to say goodbye.

Repeat Verses & Chorus as needed.

C.D. 03, SNG. 10

SHE DON'T SPEAK ENGLISH.

1.

C.
Because She Don't Speak English
  G7.
And I don't speak French,
          C.
Our love will be tested but we'll never flinch;
      G7.
For I really love her and that is a cinch;

Though She Don't Speak English
     C.
And I don't speak French.

First Chorus:
C7. F.
No, She Don't Speak English

But she takes my hand,
   C.
And though I don't speak French,
 D7.   G7.
I sure understand.
  F.   C.   Am.
The way that she holds me, I thrill every inch;
   G7.
Though She Don't Speak English
     C.
And I don't speak French.

2.

Now some people say there's a barrier tall
Between French and English
Just like a brick wall,
But with our true love
We have torn down the fence,
Tho' she don't speak English
And I don't speak French.

SECOND CHORUS:

No I don't speak French but I know what I feel
Every time that she's near me,
My world becomes real,
The way that she holds me I thrill ev'ry inch,
Tho' she don't speak English
And I don't speak French.

FIRST CHORUS:

No she don't speak English
But she takes my hand
And though I don't speak French
I sure understand,
The way that she holds me I thrill ev'ry inch,
Tho' she don't speak English
And I don't speak French.

No she don't speak English and I I-I don't
speak French.

C.D. 14, SNG. 11

SINGER, The
(Voice of the People)

1.

G.   D7.   C. G.
You hear every day how they're going away,
           D7.   G.
I guess they just don't understand;
D7. G.   D7.   G.
The Singer is the Voice of the People,
      A7.   D7.
And his song is the soul of our land.
    C.   D7.   C.   G.
So Singer, please stay, and don't go away
          D7.   G.
With so many words to be said.
D7. G.   D7.   C.   G.
For a land without song can't stand very long
           D7.   G.
When the Voice of its People is dead.

2.

O Singer, you must search
For your place on the earth,
While the same for your nation is true;
So lift up the soul of your country

And a place will be found here for you;
Don't go and run till your song has been sung
And the words of your soul have been said;
For a land without song can't stand very long,
When the voice of it's people is dead.

3.

You may pile up your gold
But the pride of your soul,
Is the small bit of hope you bestow;
On the children who come this way tomorrow
In search of the right way to go;
So Singer, sing on like the first ray of dawn,
With your promise of day just ahead;
For the land without song
Can't stand very long,
When the voice of it's people is dead.

REPEAT 1st Verse.

C.D. 08, SNG. 05

SINGING AWAY MY BLUES.

1.

D.
Well, well, my heartaches are all gone,

I feel a song comin' on,
        A7.   D.
I feel like Singing Away My Blues.

I got my fingers in a snap; I got my toes in a tap;
        A7.   D.
I feel like Singing Away My Blues.

Chorus:
  D7.   G.
Not a worry, not a care;
     D.
No regrets and no despair;
    E7.   A7.
I'm recuperatin' fast from a dark and dismal past.
           D.
Well, well, my heartaches are all gone.

I feel a song comin' on,
        A7.   D.
I feel like Singing Away My Blues.

2.

I gave that window blind a tear;
Took a big breath of good fresh air;
I feel like Singing Away My Blues.
I gave my face a water splash;
Threw my troubles in the trash;
I feel like donnin' my dancin' shoes.

Repeat Chorus:

3.

I got my fingers in a snap;
I got my toes in a tap;
I feel like Singing Away My Blues.
I gave my face a water splash;
Threw my troubles in the trash;
I feel like donnin' my dancin' shoes.

Repeat Chorus:

By T.C.Connors
©1988 CROWN VETCH MUSIC
(SOCAN) All rights reserved.

C.D. 15, SNG. 11   **SKINNER'S POND TEAPOT.**

(Recite Verses & Sing Choruses).

1.

A.   E7.   A.
Now, here's one from Prince Edward Island,
                              E7.
Where truth often baffles belief.
              A.   E7.
There's this couple I know,
                    A.   D.
Down the Skinner's Pond Road;
              A.   E7.   A.
Mr. and Mrs. Anthony Keefe.

2.

A.   E7.   A.
And fifty years ago, on the day they were wed,
                                        E7.
There were many fine gifts they had got.
              A.   E7.
But the one they loved most
              A.   D.
Was accompanied by a note,
        A.   E7.   A.
"Hello, I'm your little Teapot."

1st Chorus:
        A.   E7.   A.
Hello, I'm your little old Teapot,
                                        E7.
Said the note with these words written on;
              A.   E7.
For a home I have yearned
              A.   D.
And today I have learned,
        A.   E7.   A.
I now live in old Skinner's Pond.

3.

But some friends of theirs
Also got married that year,
And money for gifts
Was scarce in those days,
And while they thought an awful lot
Of their little Teapot,
They re-wrapped it and gave it away.

4.

But fifty years later
On their Golden Anniversary,
Once again among the presents they got;
To their greatest surprise,
With a note on the side,
Was that very same little Teapot.

2nd. Chorus:
Hello! I'm your little old Teapot,
And for fifty long years I've been gone,
How I've longed and I've yearned
And at last I've returned,
To my home down in old Skinner's Pond.

5.

The note also said,
I've been terribly lonely,
With the years slipping by as they do,
And on that far away shelf
I just wrote by myself,
This letter that I have here for you.

6.

So Happy Anniversary
From an old old friend,
And don't tell me you've gone and forgot,
Why, that very first tear
That you shed the first year,
It's still here in your little Teapot.

3rd Chorus:
So Hello! From your little old Teapot,
For fifty long years I've been gone,
But I've longed and I've yearned
And at last I've returned,
To my home down in old Skinner's Pond.

C.D. 17, SNG. 13 SMILE AWAY YOUR MEMORY.

1.

E.   B7.
Your tide, it was high and rollin' free;
                  E.
You thought you'd roll right over me.
            B7.
But while you live this fantasy,
           E.
I'll Smile Away Your Memory.

2.

I'll Smile Away Your Memory
I'll toss your ring into the sea
And though you've been a storm to me
I'll Smile Away Your Memory.

3.

Too bad love had to end this way
But I couldn't face another day
If all you want is sympathy
I'll Smile Away Your Memory.

4.

I'll Smile Away Your Memory
And leave you with your company
And while you think you're fooling me
I'll Smile Away Your Memory.

5.

Some day, somewhere, another time,
Another love may yet be mine
And when I hear the rolling sea
I'll Smile Away Your Memory.

6.

I'll Smile Away Your Memory
I'll toss your ring into the sea
And though you've been a storm to me
I'll Smile Away Your Memory.

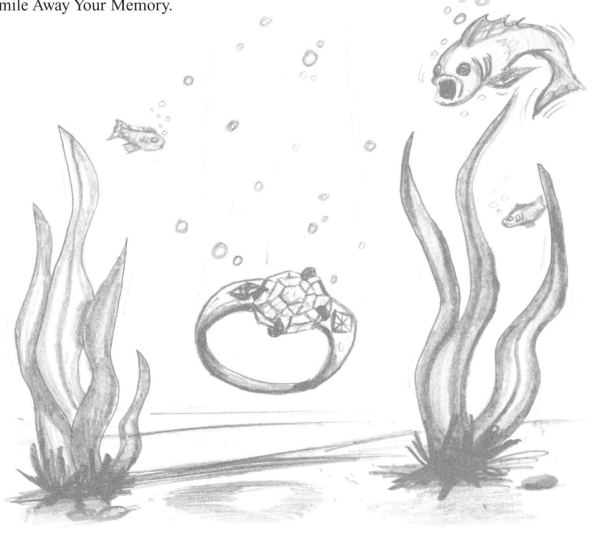

C.D. 07, SNG. 03   **SNOWMOBILE SONG. The**

1.

D.
It's winter time and the weather's fine

With snow on the woods and field
        A7.   D.
When I reveal my Snowmobile.

Thrill by thrill, by gulley and hill,

Baby, it'll make you feel
        A7.   D.
Like an outdoor meal, on a Snowmobile.
 G.   D.
Listen to the sound of the belts go 'round
        A7.   D.
When the winter carnival's here;
 G.   D.
And oh, what fun at the crack of the gun
        E7.   A7.
When the whole gang disappears.
    D.
The race is on from the bush to the pond

And back where the judges feel
        A7.   D.
You've won their seal for the Snowmobile.
        A7.   D.
You've won their seal for the Snowmobile.

2.

Where skiers ski and the skaters be
And snowshoes lend appeal
Like a bogey wheel on a snowmobile.
We tip the glass to the northern lass
For she won't let you kneel
She'd rather squeal on a snowmobile.
You're off to the town
When the word goes 'round
It's winter carnival time.
In goggles, boots, and a snowproof suit
Your sweet heart's on your mind;
You win the race and you see her face
And you know that she must feel
You've got a real good snowmobile,
Yeah, you've got a real good snowmobile.

3.

Now down the street you can hear the beat
And the clickin' of a dancers heel
When the fiddlers peel off a ragtime reel.
You dance and tear with an "I don't care"
And away back home you wheel
Over hill and field on a snowmobile.
Through a golden glow on powdered snow
When the moon comes rollin' along
On the homeward trail you can hear the wail
Of the whole gang singin' a song;
If tomorrow's clear with fishin' gear
We'll head for a lake trout meal
With a rod and a reel and a snowmobile
Life can be real with a snowmobile
There ain't no deal like a snowmobile.

C.D. 02, SNG. 05   **SOMEWHERE, THERE'S SORROW.**

1.

 C.
There's a solemn figure walkin'
            G7.
On some waterfront tonight,
                    C.
There's a woman broken hearted,
        G7.   C.
There's a man not living right.
    C7.   F.
There's a sinner who's repenting,
        C.
A hungry man without a bite,
 G7.
Somewhere, out in this old world,
                C.
There's Sorrow Tonight.

2.

There's a soldier boy dying,
Someone's home is burning down
Or an alcoholic father
Who left a family sorrow-bound,
There's a flood in someone's city,
Some little boy just lost his sight,
Somewhere out in this old world
There's sorrow tonight.

3.

There's a farmer's crop unyielding,
There's a man without a job
There's a wheel chair for some cripple,
There's a jail for those who rob
An awful train wreck in some valley,
Some died and others might,
Somewhere out in this old world
There's sorrow tonight.

(Spoken)

4.

From the casualties of an earthquake
Or from the smashing hurricane,
To the crying heart of a mother who waits
For news now from a crashing plane,
Then there's the man who just killed another
Because his skin was either black or white
Somewhere out in this old world, friends,
There's sorrow tonight.

5.

There will always be some trouble,
A daughter may go astray,
A son may bring you sorrow,
We have to hope and pray,
Don't ever say it couldn't happen
Just thank God that you're all right,
Because somewhere out in this old world
There's sorrow tonight.

C.D. 19, SNG. 12 **SONG BIRD VALLEY.** By T.C.Connors

1.

G.
I got your letter just this morning
    C.   G.
Where you speak of yesterday
    C.   G.
When the mill came to our valley
    D7.   G.
And your old friends moved away.

Chorus:
G.   D7.   G.
And like the song birds on your paper
    C.   G.
That were made in the Songbird Mill
    C.   G.
They're all gone from Song Bird Valley
    D7.   G.
Like the trees from Song Bird Hill.

2.

Now you say you'd like to see me
Where your home sits in the breeze
And amid the smells of devastation
We'll renew old memories.

Chorus:
But like the song birds on your paper
That were made in the Songbird Mill
Your friends are gone from Song Bird Valley
Like the trees from Song Bird Hill.

3.

And I don't care now to remember
Cause I've never been at ease
Since the Mill came to our valley
And destroyed our precious trees.

Chorus:
But like the song birds on your paper
That were made in the Songbird Mill
They're all gone from Song Bird Valley
Like the trees from Song Bird Hill.

Last Chorus:
And the song birds on your paper
That were made in the Songbird Mill
They won't come back to Song Bird Valley
And just like me, they never will.

Tag:
Just like me, old friend,
They never will.

C.D. 07, SNG. 12

SONG OF THE COHOE.

By T.C.Connors & F.Frank
©1971 CROWN VETCH MUSIC
(SOCAN) All rights reserved.

1.

C.   G7.   C.
Oh, I was a game young Cohoe,
               G7.
Swimming in the ocean blue,

With not a worry on my mind
              C.
And not a thing to do;
     G7.   C.
I loved to chase the herring
               G7.
And the shrimp 'way down below,

Till suddenly, as you can see,
             C.
I'm a full grown-up Cohoe.

2.

Oh, I'm a roving Cohoe dashing 'round the bay,
Diving deep where the shell fish creep
And leaping o'er the spray,
And when this Cohoe "cutie"
Came swimming up to me,
I flipped and sighed, Will you be my bride?"
And she said "Yes siree".

3.

Now we're two happy Cohoes
Splashing up the stream,
And we're gonna puff our way on up
To the rivers of our dreams,
Back to the rocky shallows
Where the tempting spinners shine,
But I'd like to know what dumb Cohoe
Would fall for that old "line".

4.

So, come now we must go-ho
And leap for the canyon wall,
Over the rocks and leap for the top
Of the highest water-falls,
Then back to the snow-capped mountains
In the land of the wild hawthorn,
We'll build our nest and a place to rest
In the pool where I was born.

5.

Then, I'll be the daddy Cohoe,
And you'll be the Cohoe mom,
With a little "roe" of babies-o
Until our days are done,
And they'll grow up and travel
Down to the Western sea,
And go to "school" to learn this "rule"
And sing this melody.

REPEAT FIRST VERSE:

C.D. 07, SNG. 08

SONG OF THE IRISH MOSS.

By T.C.Connors
©1971 CROWN VETCH MUSIC
(SOCAN) All rights reserved.

1.

C.   G7.   C.
Down on old Prince Edward Island,
            G7.   C.
When the winds are on the blow,
            G7.   C.
And the ocean water's rollin'
            D7.   G7.
Through the reefs and rocks below;
      C.   G7.   C.
And the Irish Moss comes driftin'
C7.   F.   C.
Where the white-cap waters roar;
                 G7.
With my scoop and my fork
           C.   F.
And my wagon and my horse
      C.   G7.   C.
I'll be headin' on down the shore.

2.

On old Prince Edward Island,
Where the Irish Moss is found,
With bags and ropes and baskets
They come from miles around
Thrashin' though the water,
Bein' careful not to fall
Cause one good dash and a hell-of-a-splash
You could lose your overalls.

3.

There's horses in the water
And horses on the road
And here comes old Russell Aylward
And he's haulin' up another big load
And the party lines are ringin',
And the word keeps passin' on
You can hear them roar from the Tignish shore
"There's moss in Skinner's Pond."

4.

On old Prince Edward Island,
There's one big hullaballoo
The boys and the girls and the old folks,
They're gonna make a few bucks too.
Getting wet to the neck in the ocean,
Where the waves all turn and toss
But it's a free for all, and they're havin' a ball
They're bringin' in the Irish Moss.

5.

Now the moss plant boys are waitin',
To pay so much a pound
And there goes a guy on horseback
And they both look damn near drowned
But all those smiling faces,
Just mean one thing to me
For every man with a calloused hand
There's a blessing from the sea.

6.

There's an Islander somewhere lonesome
'Cause he can't be home today
To get a little sip of the moonshine
And haul another load away
In the "Land of the Great Potato"
Where the lobster feeds are wild
We thank the Boss for the Irish Moss
Down on old Prince Edward Isle.

C.D. 07, SNG. 09   # SONG OF THE PEDDLER.   By T.C.Connors

1.

C.   G7.   C.
Oh, Come hear the Song of the Peddler
  G7.   C.
Who died with a sad broken heart;
        G7.   C.
He loved the fairest young maiden
        G7.   C.
That ever bought wares from his cart.
  D7.   G7.
He met her one dark rainy morning;
                 C.
She begged him a fish for to eat;
        G7.   C.
He whispered as she stood there crying
  G7.   C.
From cold in her poor naked feet.

CHORUS:
  C.   G7.
I'd wheel my wheel barrow
         C.   G7.
Through streets broad and narrow
  C.   G7.   C.   G7.
Day time and night time to make you a home;
    C.   G7.
I'd wheel my wheel barrow
         C.   G7.
Through streets broad and narrow
  C.   G7.   C.
Day time and night time if you'd be my own.

2.

She told him that she'd be his darling,
He kissed her and called her his own
Their hearts beat together as one heart
Not knowing 'Fate seeds had been sown;
'Twas only one month from that morning,
A man came to buy from the cart;
With riches he stole from the peddlar
His darling and broke his poor heart.

REPEAT CHORUS:

3.

Oh come hear the song of the peddler
Who thought he would marry today;
But wedding bells ring for his darling
And the rich man who stole her away;
They found his wheel-barrow this morning,
And this very sad message they read;
"Go whisper these words to my sweetheart,
But don't tell my darling I'm dead."

REPEAT CHORUS:

C.D. 20, SNG. 02

SONGWRITER'S WIFE, The

1.

A.
Said the Songwriter's Wife
A7.   D.
I'm wasting my life
A.   E7.
While you hope to write some 'big hit song'.
A.
But not a dime have I seen
A7.   D.
From your grandiose dreams
E7.   A.
And I'm leaving tonight right or wrong.

2.

A.
Then she packed up her things
A7.   D.
And she tossed him her ring
A.   E7.
Without saying Goodbye or So Long.
A.
And that very same night
A7.   D.
She was gone from his sight
E7.   A.
He was writing her name in a song.

Chorus no: 1.
D.   A.
And he sang all her words in a song.
                             E7.
And the song was recorded before very long.
A.
And as it rose on the charts
A7.   D.
Her own words broke her heart
E7.   A.
While the Radio played them in his song.

3.

Then one day in the Spring
She went back for her ring;
Softly saying, "I've missed you for so long".
But he just drove out of sight
From her pleading that night
While the Radio played his 'big hit song'.

Chorus no: 2.
And the Radio played his 'big hit song'.
And the song keeps haunting her dreams
All night long.
And though her love now is gone
All those Words linger on
When the Radio plays them in his song.

REPEAT CHORUS NO: 2. WITH THE
FOLLOWING 1ST LINE...
And the Radio plays them in his song... etc.

C.D. 16, SNG. 07

SAINT ANNE'S SONG AND REEL.

1.

D.
I was livin' in the city

Where you never get to know
G.   D.
Why they never play a fiddle on the radio;

Then one day I met a country girl,
G.   A7.   D.
And now I'm livin' in another world.

CHORUS ONE:
D.   D7.   G.
Up to the barn dance we did go,
A7.   D.
Swing your honey and you 'do-see-do';

            D7.   G.
Fiddle up a little bit of Saint Anne's Reel,
A7.   D.
Promenade her home and you click your heels.

2.

A little sip of cider wouldn't do her any harm
When you take her for a Hayride on the farm
Make that Country Girl your wife
And you'll be happy all your life.

CHORUS TWO:
Pick a little guitar; sing a little song;
Gran' Ma got the old man steppin' right along
Do a little kissin' if you get a little chance
When you do a little swingin' at the
Old Barn Dance. Yeeahoo (Fiddle Break)

3.
The little dog chewin' on the old man's pipe
And the old man chewin at the dog all night
Where did the Caller's hair-piece go?
It's hangin' on the end of the fiddler's bow.

CHORUS THREE:
Have another corn-cob; yellow and big
Clap your hands now and do a little jig
Swing your honey all around the hall
Promenade her home now and that'll be all.
Yeeahoo (Fiddle Break & END).

NOTE:
Fiddle plays Saint Anne's Reel throughout.

C.D. 21, SNG. 13   **STOMPIN' TOM FAN TANGLE.**   By T.C.Connors

1.
A.   A7.   D.   A.
It was early in May of two-thousand-and-one;
                                      E7.
I'm reading my paper, the Vancouver Sun.
     A.   D.   A.
Just flipping some pages and what did I see?
                          E7.   A.
Some feller named Sandler was mentioning me.

2.
He said that the Mounties arrested some man
For being too much of a Stompin' Tom fan.
Some neighbour complained
How his records would blare
And now he's in jail for poluting the air.

3.
It happened in Langley, 'way out in B .C.
Clelland and Begg were the R.C.M.P.
John Michael Haffenden was the man's name
And for playin' "The Stomper",
It brought him to shame.

4.
This man over sixty, they raided his place.
They took him by force
And they sprayed him with mace.
And if you never heard
Such a thing in your life,
Why, they even came back
And arrested his wife.

5.
She had called the reporters
And there on the, phone
They could hear the commotion
Outside of her home.
They broke through the door
And they dragged her away,
Then they hung up the phone
And said, "Have a nice day".

6.
Now everything's quiet in this neighbourhood,
With Bach and Beethoven, their music is good.
They're oiling their mowers
And washing machines,
Cause if they get noisey
Those Mounties get mean.

7.
And if you have a neighbour
That's bothering you
By playing that "Stomper",
Then here's what to do:
Just call the police and create an uproar
And you won't have to hear
Stompin' Tom any more.

Just call up the Mounties
And they will make sure
You won't have to hear
Stompin' Tom any more.

STOP ME.

By T.C.Connors

1.

G.   D7.
Stop Me: If you've heard these words before

G.
Stop Me: I won't say them any more

C.
Stop Me: From wanting all of you

D7.
'Cause I'll be yours tonight for sure

G.
If you don't Stop Me.

2.

G.   D7.
Stop Me: If you have another love

G.
Stop Me: For the things I'm dreaming of

C.
Stop Me: From doing what I do

D7.
Or I'll be too in love with you

G.
If you don't Stop Me.

CHORUS:

G7. C.
If you don't Stop Me now

G.
I know I can't return

C.
To where (how) I was without you

G.   D7.
Letting old desires burn.

3.

G.   D7.
Stop Me: Or show me that you'll be mine

G.
Stop Me: While your heart beats out of time

C.
Stop Me: Or tell me when you knew

D7.
It was too late for me to wait

G.
For you to Stop Me.

STORY OF JESUS.

By T.C.Connors

1.

C.   G7. C.
In a land so far away, so long ago,

G7.
Lived a boy with his parents, meek and low;

C.   C7.   F.
By miraculous birth He came to this earth,

G7.   C.
The Savior of this wicked world of woe.

2.

Now His mother was a pure and shining dove
And Joseph showed the boy his tender love
For an angel of light had appeared on that night
Proclaiming Him the Son of God above.

3.

Now the first of many wonders to behold,
Was when Mary couldn't find her twelve year old.
In the temple He was found
Teaching wise men all around;
As they marvelled at the wisdom that he told.

4.

Soon the people from both near and far away
Came to hear the precious words he had to say,
And when thousands wanted food
He fed the multitude
With five loaves and seven fishes on that day.

5.

Now He brought the dead to life in Galilee,
Where the deaf could hear
And all the blind could see
And when all the dumb could talk
He taught the lame to walk;
Saying "Now pick up your Cross
and follow me."

6.

Now it wasn't long before the final test
Betrayed by one of twelve he loved the best
And for 30 pence we're told,
The Son of God was sold
And upon the cross they put this man to death.

7.

As he died he told the world
They shouldn't grieve,
And He later showed them why
They should believe,
For He died to save our sin
And came back to life again
And we think of Jesus every Christmas Eve.

STREAKER'S DREAM.

1.

C.   C7. F.   C.
I woke up this mornin' and let out a scream

(a h h h)
                D7.   G7.
Then I remembered, I had a dream;
C.   C7. F.   C.
People were shriekin' all over town,

While millions of Streakers
    Cm.   C.
Just ran up and down.

2.

You should of seen them, Frannies and Freds,
All of them just wearin'
Them bags on their heads;
Streakin' down Yonge Street, runnin' like deer,
I ain't had a nightmare like this in years.

3.

Oh what a clang-bang all through the night,
Streakers went beep-beep,
While shriekers took flight,
Some played the bag-pipes, some rang a bell,
I took my blankets and tore them all to pieces.

4.

Streakers in sneakers that's how they knew,
All of the "bears" Don't come from the zoo.
That's how the mounties picked up the trail,
And stroked all them streakers
Straight off to jail.

5.

When I awoke there was fog in my head,
I wasn't long now gettin' out of bed;
Without even thinkin' I threw on my boots,
And streaked off to work in my birthday suit.

6.

I heard the judge say, "Bring on that freak,
Ten days for causin' people to shriek,
With your kind of face no wonder they fled,
Next time you streak wear a bag on your head."

STREETS OF TORONTO.

1.

C.   G7.
Tonight I'm far away but I'm dreamin'
                      C.
Of home and my darlin' so true;
                        G7.
Tonight I'm far away but I'm dreamin'
                      C.
Of my Home in Toronto and you.

FIRST CHORUS:
    C.   G7.   C.
We were kids on the Streets of Toronto;
  G7.   C.
In school, we were sweethearts, so true;
                       G7.
I might be far away but I'm dreamin'
                      C.
Of my Home in Toronto and you.
  G7.   C.
My Home in Toronto and you.

2.

Tonight I'm far away but I'm dreamin'
Simple dreams of the places we knew.
If I could only live what I'm dreamin'
I'd be home in Toronto with you.

SECOND CHORUS:

Where we strolled down the streets of Toronto,
In days when our true love was new.
Tonight I'm far away but I'm dreamin'
Of my home in Toronto and you,
My home in Toronto, my home in Toronto,
My home in Toronto and you.

C.D. 01, SNG. 13
C.D. 03, SNG. 12
C.D. 06, SNG. 09

SUDBURY SATURDAY NIGHT.

By T.C.Connors
©1970 CROWN VETCH MUSIC
(SOCAN) All rights reserved.

Chorus:

  A.   A7.
Oh, The girls are out to Bingo
      D.
And the boys are gettin' 'stinko';
   A.
We think no more of INCO
              E7.
On a Sudbury Saturday Night.
    A.   A7.
The glasses, they will tinkle,
       D.
When our eyes begin to twinkle,
              A.
And we think no more of INCO
  E7.   A.
On a Sudbury Saturday Night.

1.

  A.   A7.
With Irish Jim O'Connell there
      D.
And Scotty Jack MacDonald,
    A.   E7.
There's Honkey Frederick Hurgel gettin' tight,

but that's all right;
      A.   A7.
There's Happy German Fritzy there
      D.
With Frenchy gettin' tipsy,
          A.
And even Joe the Gypsy knows
   E7.   A.
It's Saturday tonight.

2.

Now when Mary Ann and Mabel
Come to join us at the table,
And tell us how the Bingo went tonight,
We'll look a fright;
But if they won the money,
We'll be lappin' up the honey, boys,
'Cause everything is funny, for
It's Saturday tonight.

Repeat Chorus:

3.

We'll drink the loot we borrowed
And recuperate tomorrow,
'Cause everything is wonderful tonight,
We had a good fight;
We ate the Dilly Pickle
And we forgot about the Nickel,
And everybody's tickled, for
It's Saturday tonight.

4.

The songs that we'll he singing,
They might be wrong, but they'll he ringing,
When all the lights of town are shinin' bright,
and we're all tight;
We'll get to work on Monday,
But tomorrow's only Sunday,
And we're out to have a fun day for
It's Saturday tonight.

Repeat Chorus:

C.D. 17, SNG. 09 **SUNSHINE & TEARDROPS.** By T.C.Connors

Chorus:
D7.
Rain drops, just like my tears,
                          G.
Won't let me watch the kids play;
        D7.
But Sunshine, dries up the sidewalks,
                          G.
And wipes all my Teardrops away.

Recite Verses: 1.
  G.   D7.
I wheel my wheel-chair to the window and stare
        G.   D7.
At the rain as it falls on the street;

  G.   D7.
I wish, in the gloom of my dark little room,
        G.   D7.   G.
That a ray from the Sunshine would peep....

Because...... Repeat Chorus:

2.
It's so good to see children like me,
Playing games on the street when it's dried;
They laugh and have fun,
They skip and they run,
And they make me feel happy inside....
But...... Repeat CHORUS.

3.
Sometimes when I smile at the kids for awhile
They come up to my window to see;
My funny wheel-chair
And my legs that aren't there,
And they often pick flowers for me....
Until...... Repeat CHORUS.

4.
Tomorrow I know, I don't want to go
With that lady who comes in the van;
She'll take me away where children won't play
Near my Sun-shiny window again....
And the...... Repeat CHORUS.

Finish last Chorus with:
Oh Sunshine, dry up the sidewalks
And wipe all my teardrops away.

C.D. 18, SNG. 11

SUZANNE DE LAFAYETTE.
aka (Girl from Lafayette).

1.

A.
I travelled south to Baton Rouge,
E7.
'Way down in Louisianna;

I met a girl with eyes of blue,
A.
La Plus Belle Suzanna.

She said, "I live not far away,
A7.   D.
A few miles to the west;
A.
I'm Bayou born and raised,
E7.   A.
I'm Suzanne De Lafayette."

2.

A.
J'ai voyage vers Baton Rouge,
E7.
Dans la Louisianna;

J'ai rencontre ma belle amour,
A.
Nomme la p'tite Suzanna.

Elle ma dit, "Je vien pres dici,
A7.   D.
Dans un conte de l'ouest;
A.
C'est mon chez-nous, car Je suis
E7.   A.
La Fille De Lafayette."

Chorus No.1
A7. D.
We danced away till the break of day
A.
And I learned the Cajun Two-Step
E7.
While fiddles played, I was swayed
A.
By the Girl From Lafayette.

3.

I held her as I spoke about
My home 'way up in Canada;
She said, "Oh my, that's far away
From old Louisianna."
I asked her on that very day
If new plans could be set;
If she could love and always be
My Girl From Lafayette.

4.

On a parlez de mon chez-nous,
Mon bon pays, mon Canada;
On a parlez de son amour pour la Louisianna.
Voici la bague pour l'epouse,
Je l'aime et Je repette;
Je demeur pour la marier La Fille De Lafayette.

Chorus No.2
She said, "O.K." as we danced away,
All night to the Cajun Two-Step
While fiddles played and I was swayed
By The Girl From Lafayette.

5.

I placed a call to old Quebec,
Away up north in Canada;
I told them all about the girl
From old Louisianna.
And when my folks had heard the news
And the wedding was all set,
They all came down to see me wed
Suzanne De Lafayette.

6.

J'appelere ma chere maman,
Mes freres, au Canada
Pour annonce un grand moment
dans la Louisianna.
Elle ma dit, "Oui", Je la marie
la Suzanne, la Plus Belle;
Je m'etablis pour marier
La Fille De Lafayette.

Chorus No. 3
We danced away all the night and day,
and we did the Cajun Two-Step
While fiddles played and I was swayed by
The Girl From Lafayette.

Chorus No. 4
We danced away all the night and day
And we pranced to the Cajun Two-Step
While fiddles played, I was swayed
By The Girl From Lafayette.

C.D. 12, SNG. 11

TAKE ME DOWN THE RIVER.

1.

A.
There's a flivver on the river
E7.
Where the moon hangs low;

There's an old barn dance
A.
To where we used to go.
A7.   D.   A.
Where my childhood sweetheart used to say
B7.   E7.
In her cute little devilish way,
A.
"Hey, Take Me Down The River

In your birch canoe;
E7.   A.
Take Me Down The River with you".

2.

Her papa used to tell me,
"Don't you take Louise",
But I was hearing music on the evening breeze,
When my childhood sweetheart used to say

In her cute little devilish way,
"Hey, Take me down the river
In your birch canoe,
Take me down the river with you.

3.

Beneath a starry-eyed heaven
When the sun goes down,
There's an old mill river just a mile from town.
Where my childhood sweetheart used to say
In her cute little devilish way,
"Hey, Take me down the river
In your birch canoe,
Take me down the river with you."

4.

Now that we are older
And we've gone our ways,
I often get to thinkin' of the bygone days;
When my childhood sweetheart used to say
In her cute little devilish way,
"Hey, Take me down the river
In your birch canoe,
Take me down the river with you."

C.D. 21, SNG. 05

TEARDROPS ON MY PILLOW.

1.

A.
The other night dear

Through the window
D.
Of my bedroom
A.
I heard the wind blow.
D.
As it whispered
A.
I love you so
E7.
There were Teardrops
D.   A.
On My Pillow.

Chorus...
A.   D.
There were Teardrops
A.
On My Pillow
D.
As I cried out
A.
I love you so.
D.
Just remember

A.
Wherever you go
E7.
There'll be Teardrops
D. A.
On My Pillow.

2.

And tonight dear
Through the window
Of my bedroom
I see the moon glow.
And it whispers
You love me so,
But there's Teardrops
On My Pillow.

Second Chorus.

There are Teardrops
On My Pillow
As I cry out
I love you so.
Just remember
Wherever you go,
There'll be Teardrops
On My Pillow.

C.D. 07, SNG. 06   **TILLSONBURG.**   **By T.C.Connors**

1.

D.   A7.
While away down Southern Ontario,
           D.
I never had a nickel or a dime to show;
           A7.
A fella 'beeped up' in an automobile;

He said, "D'ya wanna work in the
  D.   D7.
tobacco fields?"
  G.   D.
Of Tillsonburg, Tillsonburg;
  A7.   G.   D.
My back still aches when I hear that word.

2.

He said "I'll only give you seven bucks a day,
But if you're any good you get a raise in pay,
Your bed's all ready on the bunkhouse floor,
If it gets a little chilly you can close the door."
Tillsonburg, Tillsonburg;
My back still aches when I hear that word.

3.

I was feelin' in the morning anything but fine,
The farmer said I'm gonna teach you
how to "prime",
He said you gotta don a pair of oilskin pants,
If you wanna work in the tobacco plants
Of Tillsonburg, Tillsonburg;
My back still aches when I hear that word.

4.

We landed in a field that was long and wide,
With one old horse and five more guys,
I asked him where to find the cigarette trees,
When he said bend over I was ready to leave.
Tillsonburg, Tillsonburg;
My back still aches when I hear that word.

5.

He said to pick just the bottom leaves,
And don't start crawlin' on your
hands and knees;
Prime your row 'cause you'll get no pay,
For standin' there pickin' at your nose
all day 'round
Tillsonburg, Tillsonburg;
My back still aches when I hear that word.

6.

With a broken back from bendin' over there,
I was wet right through to the underwear,
And it was stuck to my skin like glue,
From the nicotine tar in the morning dew
Of Tillsonburg, Tillsonburg;
My back still aches when I hear that word,

7.

Now the nearest river was two miles from
The place they were waitin' for a "boat" to come;
When I heard some talk about makin' the kiln,
I was down the highway and over the hill
From Tillsonburg, Tillsonburg;
My back still aches when I hear that word.

8.

Now there's one thing you can always bet,
If I never smoke another cigarette,
I might get 'taken' In a lot o' deals,
But I won't go workin the tobacco fields
Of Tillsonburg, Tillsonburg;
My back still aches when I hear that word.

C.D. 10, SNG. 02

TO IT AND AT IT.

1.

A.
There's a rainbow in Toronto
      E7.
Where the Maritimers are bold;
 A.
They always get a 'potfull',
      E7. A.
But they never get a Pot of Gold.

But they're...

CHORUS:
 A.
To It And At It, and At It And To It,
        E7.
You gotta 'tune your attitude in';
  A. A7. D.
If you don't get At It when you get To It
 E7.   A.
You won't get To It to get At It again...

Repeat This Line.

2.

A guy from old New Brunswick,
He couldn't even pay his rent,
We don't know how he travelled,
But we all know where he went. He was

REPEAT CHORUS:

3.

A girl from old Spud Island, old potato lips;
She married a Newfoundlander,
And they lived on fish and chips.
But they were

REPEAT CHORUS:

4.

A Guy from Nova Scotia,
He can't afford the train,
He's sittin' on the streetcar,
But he's eastbound just the same.
'Cause he's

REPEAT CHORUS:

5.

A Frenchman from the Gaspe,
Said frogs don't like smog;
So he hopped in a swamp of lillies,
Where he lives in a hollow log.
'Cause he's

REPEAT CHORUS:

6.

A guy from old Cape Breton,
So lonesome he got stoned;
He crawled into a suitcase and somebody
mailed him home... He was... etc.

REPEAT CHORUS TWICE:

C.D. 02, SNG. 01

TRAGEDY TRAIL.

Chorus:
 G.   G7.
Tragedy Trail; Tragedy Trail;
      C.   G.
You taught the wind how to whimper and wail.
     D7.
You taught me to cry, now teach me to die,
  G.
Tragedy Trail.

1.

 G7. C.   G.   G7.
When the moon sails by on the ocean of the sky,
 C.   G.
I wonder why her beams of love are pale,
 D7.
so pale;

 G.   G7.
All alone I wander on,
    C.
Knowing love has come and gone,
      G.   D7.
And every night you'll find me here
    G.
On Tragedy Trail.

Repeat Chorus:

Then Repeat Verse and Chorus and End.

C.D. 07, SNG. 07

TRIBUTE TO WILF CARTER.

1.

D.
In the year nineteen-o-four
     G.   D.
Upon a cold December morn,

In Port Hilford, Nova Scotia,
     E7.   A7.
Wilf Carter, he was born;
       D.   D7.
Went to work for the local farmers
     G.   D.
At a very tender age,

Till the bush camps of New Brunswick
     A7.   D.
Hired Wilf for a better pay.

Chorus One:
     G.
And Wilf began to yo-del-ee-del-ay-ee
     D.
In the backwoods of N.B.,

With his yo-del-ee-del-ay-ee,
     A7.   D.
dee-yo-del-ee-del-ay-ee-hee.

2.

From the Maritimes to Boston,
Now the wheat fields of the west;
And the plains of old Alberta,
They just seemed to suit him best.
Punchin' cows and breakin' horses
Was the life he loved to lead;
And you'd always see Wilf Carter
At the Calgary stampede.

Chorus Two:
And Wilf would always yod-el-eed-el-ay-ee
On the streets of Calgary,
With his yod-el-eed-el-ay-ee,
dee yod-el-eed-el-ay-ee hee.

3.

When he sang he played the guitar,
Tellin stories that were true;
For the songs he wrote were always
About people that he knew,
And he took his compositions
Down to Montreal by train
Where he made his first recording
And was on his way to fame.

Chorus Three:
And Wilf began to yod-el-eed-el-ay-ee
On the radio C.B.C.
With his yod-el-eed-el-ay-ee,
dee yod-el-eed-el-ay-ee hee.

4.

Just a plain and simple cowboy
With that old familiar grin,
To the U.S.A. Wilf Carter was now "Montana Slim".
From the hungry hobo jungles
To the top recording star;
And the people came by thousands
When he strummed his old guitar.

Chorus Four:
And Wilf would always yod-el-eed-el-ay-ee
With a voice so young and free,
With a yod-el-eed-el-ay-ee
dee-yod-el-eed-el-ay-ee hee.

5.

Now the message of my story
Won't be hard to understand;
And I think I speak for every
Hard core country music fan.
Though the modern record players
Have replaced the gramophone,
I still love to hear Wilf Carter
Sing and play the cowboy songs.

Chorus Five:
And Wilf can always
yod-el-eed-el-ay-ee
Any time he wants for me,
With a yod-el-eed-el-ay-ee,
dee yod-el-eed-el-ay-ee hee.

Yeah, Wilf can always yod-el-eed-el-ay-ee
Any time he wants for me,
With his yod-el-eed-el-ay-ee,
dee yod-el-eed-el-ay-ee,
dee yod-el-eed-el-ay-ee hee.
Yod-el-eed-el-ay-ee,
dee yod-el-eed-el-ay-ee hee.

C.D. 08, SNG. 10

TRUE, TRUE LOVE.

1.

C.
It's a dark and stormy night,
G7.   C.
As my heart takes weary flight;
C7.   F.
Oh, my God, in heaven, please
C.   G7.   C.
Send my True, True Love back to me.

2.

Many dreams away from here,
Take me back to yester-year;
Lose my soul in memory,
Or send my True,
True Love back to me.

3.

Through the shadows of the dark,
Sorrow seeks my aching heart;
Just a lie not meant to be,
Brought this cold dark storm over me.

Repeat 1st & 2nd Verses and finish.

C.D. 03, SNG. 13

T.T.C. SKIDADDLER.

CHORUS:
A7.   D.   A.
I'm a T.T.C. Skidaddler;
E7.   A.
Gotta sock it to my big Red Rattler.
E7.   A.
Gotta sock it to my big Red Rattler.

1.

A.   E7.
I've been a streetcar driver now
A.   E7.
About eleven years
A.   E7.   A.
And I know the old Toronto city well.
A7.
There's a whole lot of people
D.
Who wait along the track
E7.   A.
For the signal from my clangin' trolley bell.

REPEAT CHORUS:

2.

Put the pole upon the wire now
And open up the switch,
It's time to get old rattler sparkin' through,
She's red around the bottom
And she's yellow on the top,
And I drive her like a driver ought to do.

REPEAT CHORUS:

3.

I love my little wife at home,
I love my coupla kids,
They often take the trolley to the park,
They know their daddy's driving
The people here and there
But I'll be back again to pick them up at dark.

REPEAT CHORUS:

4.

Now don't forget your ticket
When I open up the door
Kindly make your way along the aisle.
I'll drive you down to work
And I'll safely bring you back
And I'll try to render service with a smile.

REPEAT CHORUS:

REPEAT FIRST VERSE:

REPEAT CHORUS:

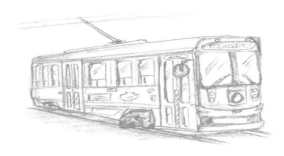

C.D. 09, SNG. 10

TWICE AS BLUE.

1.

A.   E7.
When life gets rough and the goin's tough
A.
And you don't know what you'll do;
E7.   A.
Think of me 'cause I've been Twice As Blue.

2.

A.   E7.
When you fight for sleep at night
A.
And you cry the hours through;
E7.   A.
Think of me 'cause I've been Twice As Blue.

CHORUS:
A7.   D.
Remember how you said you loved me
A.
And then you said goodbye;
B7.   E7.
Remember how you caused my heart to cry;
A.   E7.
When all you gave becomes a wave

A.
The sea rolls back on you,
E7.   A.
Think of me 'cause I've been Twice As Blue.

3.

When you look back upon the track
And the past is in revue
Think of me cause I've been twice as blue.

4.

When it's your time to tow the line
Down Sorrow's Avenue
Think of me cause I've been twice as blue.

CHORUS:

Remember how you said you loved me
And then you said goodbye
Remember how you caused my heart to cry
When every day is just a way
To break your heart anew
Think of me cause I've been twice as blue.

C.D. 11, SNG. 05

UNFAITHFUL HEART.

1.

C.   C7.
Your Unfaithful Heart goes and finds
F.
someone new,
C.   G7.
Just when I start re-loving you;
C.   C7.   F.
Just when I'm finally taking your part,
C.   G7.   C.
You satisfy your Unfaithful Heart.

1st Chorus:
F.   C.
If there's no use in forgiving,
D7.   G7.
Please let my heart go on living.
C.   C7.   F.
Rather than being just half-way apart,
C.   G7.   C.
Please set me free from your Unfaithful Heart.

2.

Your Unfaithful Heart goes and laughs
me to shame,
Each time I try to shoulder the blame.
Just when I'm finding some light in the dark,
You walk away with your Unfaithful Heart.

2nd Chorus:

When you don't want my forgiving,
Please let my heart go on living.
Rather than being just half-way apart,
Please set me free from your Unfaithful Heart.

(Repeating 2nd Chorus Optional).

C.D. 12, SNG. 07

UNITY.

Chorus: (Sing as required)
A.   A7.   D.   A.
Unity for you is Unity for me;
                         E7.
Unity for all means all for Unity.
A.   A7.   D.   A.
Together we shall rise, forever to recall,

That the Maple Tree is Unity
      E7.   A.
And our flag will never fall.

1.

A.   A7.   D.   A.
When I was just a lad, I had a wondrous dream;

I travelled through a land
                   E7.
Where freedom was supreme;
A.   A7.   D.   A.
Rising in the North and stretching sea to sea,

Where the voices rang and people sang
    E7.   A.
a song of Unity.

2.

Someone said to come and took me by the hand,
And opened up my eyes
To the blessings of this land,
Nature was in bloom
With abundance ev'rywhere;
And again I heard those magic words
Come ringing through the air.

3.

Then I saw the flag, a maple leaf unfurled,
Standing on a tower, the highest in the world.
And as I watched it wave,
Its colours came in view;
The red was sacred brotherhood
And the white was pure and true.

4.

One small red maple leaf
Was pinned on my lapel,
Then my dream did end,
But I still remember well
The voice that said to write
And sing of what shall be,
There's a promised land for those who stand
in Canada's unity.

C.D. 21, SNG. 07

VALENTINE SONG.
(My One And Only Valentine)

1.

A.   E7.
You are My One And Only Valentine
                       A.
You are my love and true sweetheart of mine
                   E7.
In the Spring, Summer, Fall and Winter time
             A.
You are My One And Only Valentine.

2.

A.   E7.
You are my pal, my soul-mate, sherry wine
                   A.
With open arms I'm yours and you are mine.
                 E7.
When we kiss, you can make it oh so fine.
               A.
You are my One And Only Valentine.

Chorus...
A. A7. D.   A.
I'm never lonely, I'm never blue
      E7.   A.
I'm never sorry you are you
         D.   A.
And like it says right here, on this card of mine
       E7.   A.
You are My One And Only Valentine.

3.

You are My One And Only Valentine
You are my love and true sweetheart of mine
Every day, every night and morning time
You are My One And Only Valentine.

4.

You are my pal, my soul-mate, sherry wine;
With open arms I'm yours and you are mine.
If I go out, I'll leave a little note behind;
You Are My One And Only Valentine.

REPEAT CHORUS AND FINISH.

C.D. 20, SNG. 16   # WALTZING MATLIDA.   **By T.C.Connors (Trad. Arr.)**

1.

G.   D7.
Once a jolly swag-man
G.   C.
Was camping by the billabong
G.   D7.
Under the shade of the coolie-bah tree
G.   D7.
And he sang as he watched
G.   C.
And he waited while his billy boiled
G.   D7.   G.
You'll Come A-Waltzing Matilda With Me.

Chorus: (Sing after each verse.)
G.   C.
Waltzing Matilda, Waltzing Matilda,
G.   D7.
You'll Come A-Waltzing Matilda with me
G.   D7.   G.   C.
(- Sing the 4th & 5th line of each verse -)......
G.   D7.   G.
You'll Come A-Waltzing Matilda With Me.

2.

Down came a jumbuck to drink beside
The billabong. And up jumped
The swag-man to capture him with glee
And hc sang as he shoved
The jolly jumbuck in his tucker-bag
You'll Come A-Waltzing Matilda With Me.

3.

Down came the trooper,
He was mounted on his thorough-bred
He saw the 'squatter' counting, one, two, three
And to the swag-man he said,
If there's a jumbuck in your tucker-bag
You'll Come A-Waltzing Matilda With Me.

4.

But the swag-man jumped
And he sprang into the billabong
You'll never catch me alive, said he;
And his ghost may still be heard
Singing by the billabong
You'll Come A-Waltzing Matilda With Me.

C.D. 14, SNG. 09   # WE DOUBT EACH OTHER'S LOVE.   **By T.C.Connors**

1.

C.   G7.
I'm gonna scratch your name right off my slate,
                            C.
I'm gonna scram before it gets too late;
                            G7.
I'll say goodbye and stop our little game,

'Cause something tells me
                    C.
That you plan the same.

Chorus:
C.   G7.   C. G7.
And if you say goodbye before I do,
D7.   G.   D7.
I'll be left to cry and I'll be so blue;

C.
And if my guess is right,
                                G7.
I know just what you're thinking of;

Just like me you tell yourself,
                            C.
We Doubt Each Other's Love.

2.

Yes I doubt your love and you doubt mine,
We accuse each other all the time,
You say I cheat and you tell me you are true,
When all the time I think the same of you.

Chorus.
So I'm gonna leave you to your sorrow,
Cause you might do the same on me tomorrow,
And if my guess is right,
I know just what you're thinkin' of,
Just like me, you tell yourself,
We Doubt Each Other's Love.

3.

I gonna move tonight, I'm gonna go,
I won't be sad for you because I know,
You want to be the first to say goodbye,
You want to be the first, but so do I.

Chorus.
And if you say goodbye before I do,
I'll be left to cry and I'll be so blue,
And if my guess is right,
I know just what you're thinkin' of,
Just like me, you tell yourself,
We Doubt Each Other's Love.

REPEAT second verse and Chorus.

C.D. 11, SNG. 07

WE'RE TRADING HEARTS.
(OUR WEDDING DAY SONG)

1.

A.   A7.   D.
We're Trading Hearts today,
    A.
We're going all the way;
      E7.
Changing from yesterday,
    A.
Two people apart.
A.   A7.   D.
I'll love you, come what may;
    A.
This holy vow we say,
    E7.
On this, our wedding day;
    A.
We're Trading Hearts.

2.

We're trading hearts today,
Knowing the world's O.K.,
Walking the same highway,
Never to part.
And if the sky be grey,
I'll take your hand and say,
Will you be mine today,
We're trading hearts.

REPEAT FIRST AND LAST VERSE:

C.D. 22, SNG. 02   **WHALE AND THE REX-N-DALE. The**   **By T.C.Connors**

1.

C.   C7.
Come 'ere, me b'ys, I'll tell the tale
  F.
About the night the awesome whale
  G7.
Sank the Schooner, REX-N-DALE
                              C.
'Way down in Newfoundland.

                              C7.
We're sailin' around the Labrador;
  F.
The whale began to 'blow and roar';
  G7.
"And thar's the one we'll take for sure"
                        C.
The Captain did demand.

2.

So when, beside, we threw the spear
All the b'ys began to cheer;
We thought we had our 'souvenir'
Just like the Captain planned.
But all at once she flipped 'er tail
Across the bow and over the sail,
And that was the end of the REX-N-DALE,
The Pride of Newfoundland.

3.

While jumpin' off the sinkin' boat,
We'll find a piece of wood, we hope;
Somethin' that will help us float
And take us to the strand.
But what do we find a-floatin' here,
Bobbin' up and down, me dear,
A half a barrel o' Dominion beer,
The best in Newfoundland.

4.

Upon the barrel we makes a grip
While each o' the b'ys was takin' a sip.
You'd think we were havin' a 'pleasure trip'
Until we hit the sand.
And there we had to stand in awe,
The largest whale we ever saw
Was splashin' around the Bay, Ha Ha,
And totally in command.

5.

And then the whale, as if to say,
"I hope ya learned a lot today;
The barrel, I pushed it into your way,
And I hope the beer was grand".
She said "Goodbye" and flipped 'er tail
And showed us where she wore the sail
That bore the name of the REX-N-DALE,
The Pride of Newfoundland.

TAG.
And now me b'ys, you've heard the tale
About the WHALE AND THE REX-N-DALE,
And how she came to wear that sail,
'Way down in Newfoundland.

WHEN SNOW FLURRIES FALL. By T.C.Connors

Chorus 1.
C.   C7.
Well, it's too late to hurry
F.   C.
When Snow Flurries Fall;
                        D7.   G7.
And it's too late to worry if you don't ever call.
C.   C7.
You'd better love me right away,
F.   C.
Or don't love me at all;
                    G7.   C.
It's too late to hurry When Snow Flurries Fall.

Verse 1.
C.   C7.
Tell me that you want me
F.   C.
And that your love is real,

Just don't keep me hangin'
D7.   G7.
So you can play the field.
C.   C7.
I don't need a snow storm
F.   C.
Of winter with the blues
                    G7.   C.
To know I can't recover any summer love I lose.

Chorus 2.
And it's too late to hurry
When snow flurries fall,
And I might have a number I might like to call.
You'd better love me right away,
Or don't love me at all
It's too late to hurry when snow flurries fall.

Verse 2.
Tell me that you need me
And that your love is true,
Just don't keep me waitin'
If you want someone new
I don't need a heart ache
For every day you're gone,
Hopin' you'll remember winter's comin' on.

Chorus 3.
And, it's too late to hurry
When snow flurries fall,
And it's too late to worry if you don't ever call.
You'd better love me right away,
Or don't love me at all
It's too late to hurry when snow flurries fall.

**WHEN THE ICE WORM
NESTS AGAIN.** Revised By T.C.Connors

1.
E.   A.
There's a husky dusky maiden in the Arctic
B7.   E.
In her igloo she'll wonder where I've been.
                                A.
I guess I'll put my mukluks on and ask her
B7.
If she'll wed me When The Ice
            E.
Worm Nests Again.

Chorus: (Repeat after each verse.)
E.
In the land of the pale blue snow
        A.   F#7.
Where it's 99 below
        B7.   E7.
And the polar bears are roaming o'er the plain.

In the shadow of the Pole
        A.   F#7.
I will clasp her to my soul,
        B7.
We'll be happy When The Ice
            E.
Worm Nests Again.

2.
The wedding feast will be seal oil and flippers;
In our kyaks we'll roam the boundless main.
How the walruses will turn their
necks to rubber;
We'll be happy When The Ice Worm
Nests Again.

3.
We could honeymoon down south
But we'll take Nunavut,
And we'll have a whale of a time
Before we're through.
We'll rub noses in the town of Iqaluit
When we trade the huskies in for a new Skidoo.

4.
And when all those northern icebergs
Bound around us
She'll present me with a bouncin' baby boy.
How the polar bears will dance
The rumba round us
And the walruses will click their teeth with joy.

C.D. 13, SNG. 02
WHERE THE CHINOOKS BLOW.

Chorus:
G.   G7.   C.
Where The Chinooks Blow,
          G.
And the sun sinks low,
          D7.   G
I'm goin' back again to Vancouver Island;
          G7.   C.   G.
Where the moonlight seems to throw her beams
          D7.
On a sea of dreams for you and me,
          G.
my little darling.

G.   1.
I was gonna write every other night;
          D7.
I was gonna telephone.

But I can't stay away, not another day,
                              G.
And be without my baby, back home.

And here's another fact; I'm already packed,
          G7.   C.
Riding on 'silver wings';
                    G.
Over the blue, thinking of you;
          D7.   G.
Thinking of my everything.

Repeat Chorus:
(Then sing Verse again and end with Chorus).

C.D. 08, SNG. 09
WHERE WOULD I BE?
(The Entry Island Song)

1.
A.
Where Would I Be if I told you
          E7.
I'm standing on a hill,

Lookin' at the ocean all around
                    A.
To give my heart a thrill.

Away up high, near the sky,
          E7.
If I look down and see,

That little nook called Kitty's Brook,
                    A.
Can you tell me where I'd be?

1st Chorus:
A7.   D.   A.
Where Would I Be? Where Would I Be?
E7.
If I see boats and buoy floats,

Horse-drawn carts and friendly folks;
                    D.
Capes of red that shed the rolling sea;
E7.   A.
Where Would I be? You tell me.

2.
Where would I be if I told you
There's only thirteen family names;
Dixon, Patton, Josey, Morrison,
Aikins and MacLean,

Goodwin, Clark, Shinell and Quinn,
Collins and Cassidy,
And if Peter Welsh was here himself,
He could tell you where I'd be.

2nd Chorus:
Where would I be, where would I be?
If I see mackerel fishing tackle,
Big red lobsters shells a crackle,
People singing shanties of the sea,
Where would I be, you tell me.

3.
Where would I be if I told you,
I see old No Bottom Pond'.
In Mosey's hollow by the hill
The old light house is on,
Where cattle grazing on the braes
low so peacefully,
It's seven miles around this Isle
Now tell me where I'd be.

3rd Chorus:
Where would I be, where would I be?
If I could be somebody's neighbour,
Do someone some kindly favour,
Nestled in yon billows by the sea,
Where would I be, you tell me,
Where would I be, you tell me.

C.D. 20, SNG. 09 **WILDWOOD FLOWER.**

1.

A.   E7. A.
She is waiting for me in a rose covered bower

And her eyes are like the violets are
  E7. A.
Right after the shower
   A7.
She dreams pretty dreams
    D.   A.
Through the long summer hours

My sweetheart, my own,
    E7.   A.
She's my frail Wildwood Flower.

2.

All the wild forest creatures are under her spell
On her shoulder, the dove,
His love secrets do tell
And the shy, dapple fawn
Comes to lie at the feet
Of my frail Wildwood Flower
So gentle and so sweet.

3.

I will pick tender blossoms to twine in her hair
Blushing roses so red and the lillies so fair
Lovely myrtle so bright
With its emerald coloured hue
Modest butter-cups so yellow
And forget-me-nots blue.

4.

Hand in hand through the wild wood
together we'll stray
She will sing, she will dance,
And my heart she will sway
Her laughter will echo like ripples at their play
Till my cares like my heart
She has stolen them away.

5.

There's no artist who can paint her,
No poet who can write
How she warms up my heart
Like the sun beams so bright
I will love and protect her and never will I part
From that frail Wildwood Flower
That twines around my heart.

C.D. 11, SNG. 11 **WISHFUL HUMMIN'**

Chorus:
 C. F.   C.
Hmm hmm,... hmm hmm,...
  G7.   C.
hmm hmm, ... hmm hmm.

1.

 C.   G7.
That's what I'll do; that's what I'll mention;
        C.
That's how I'll get all her attention.
        G7.
She'll come to me just like I planned;
          C.
I'll have her heart, heart, heart right in my hand.

REPEAT CHORUS:

2.

Well, here she comes, I'm gonna do it,
I'll tell her now, there's nothin' to it.
No sir, I'm not, one bit afraid,
I've got my plan, plan, plan, already made.

REPEAT CHORUS:

3.

Well, here I go, watch me say it
I've got the card, watch me play it.
This is the place and now's the time,
She's gonna beg, beg, beg, to be all mine.

REPEAT CHORUS:

4.

That's what I'll do, that's what I'll mention
That's how I'll get, all her attention.
She'll crawl to me, just like I planned
If she ever gets that close again.

REPEAT CHORUS:

Hum hum, Hum hum; Hum hum, Hum hum;
Hum hum, Hum hum, if she ever
gets that close again
I'm really gonna tell her.

REPEAT CHORUS:

C.D. 07, SNG. 04   **WOP MAY.**   **By T.C.Connors**

1.

A.
From out of all the heroes of the land
                   E7.
There comes a mighty Manitoba man;

He left his home in Carberry

For Edmonton, Alberta,

Where he went to school
               A.
And soon became a man.

Now, Orville and Wilbur Wright

Had come to fame,
                     E7.
And every night he dreamt about their names;

And when for men there came a cry,

He bid the folks at home, goodbye,
            A.
To join the war to fly an aeroplane.

CHORUS ONE:
D.   A.
Wop May, Wop May.
B7.   E7.
He met the old 'Red Baron' far away.
D.   A.   E7.
Wop May, Wop May. The Top Canadian Pilot
        A.
of the day; Wop May,
     E7.   A.
The Top Canadian Pilot of the day.

2.
He played the old Red Baron for a clown,
Until the German chased him all around;
Loop for loop and dive for dive,
The Baron was so occupied
He never saw the plane that shot him down.
Of all the German planes that ever flew;
The "Wop" had chopped a dozen or
more in two;
And when they fin'ly won the war,
Said the British Flying Corps,
"The Flying Cross we now present to you."

CHORUS TWO:
Wop May, Wop May,
He won the Flying Cross and took it away.
Wop May, Wop May, the top Canadian pilot
of the day, Wop May,
You're the top Canadian pilot of the day.

3.
When home again to Edmonton he came,
He set the hearts all over the land a-flame;
To Fort Vermillion he was bound
To stop the plague and save the town
With medicine he flew in by aeroplane.
Then up along the old McKenzie Trail,
To Aklavik he flew the Northern Mail;
And when he helped the Mounties track
The man they thought they'd never catch,
Why even the King of England heard the tales.

CHORUS THREE:
Wop May, Wop May, Got a medal from the
King and heard him say,
Wop May, Wop May, You're the top Canadian
pilot of the day, Wop May,
The top Canadian pilot of the day.

4.
Now when the second war it did arrive,
From nineteen Thirty-Nine to Forty-Five;
He showed the pilots, ev'ry one,
The proper way to man the gun
And he taught them how to fly and stay alive.
And when the States were losing many planes,
Far across the Northland Terrain,
They all came out from Washington,
To see the man from Edmonton
Form the famous 'Search and Rescue' team.

CHORUS FOUR:
Wop May, Wop May;
Received a medal from the U.S.A.;
Wop May, Wop May; You're the top
Canadian pilot of the day,
Wop May, You're the top Canadian pilot
of the day.

C.D. 01, SNG. 01

WORLD GOES ROUND. The

By T.C.Connors
©1967 CROWN VETCH MUSIC
(SOCAN) All rights reserved.

FIRST CHORUS:

C.   G7.
The World Goes Round with a happy sound

And the children sing the song
                              C.
Of the way the World Goes Round.
                                    G7.
The World Goes Round, not up and down;

And the children sing the song
                              C.
Of the way the World Goes Round.

1.

F.
Bells are ringin', birds are singin'

Flutes are playin' too;
C.
Horns are a-tootin', guns salutin',
D7.   G7.
Whistles blowin', woo!
C.
Drums are boomin', rockets zoomin',
        C7.   F.
All the world will say;
                    C.
Tap your feet to the birthday beat
     G7.   C.
For Expo's under way.
F.   C.
Tap your feet to the birthday beat for
  G7.   C.
Expo's under way.

REPEAT 1st CHORUS:

2.
Mountain climbers, Maritimers,
Indians galore,
Cowboys, singers, go-go swingers,
Clowns that make you roar;
With candy bars and soda pop,
And all the world will say,
Prepare the halls in Montreal
Where Expo's underway,
Prepare the halls in Montreal
Where Expo's underway.

SECOND CHORUS:

And the world goes round,
With a happy sound,
And the children sing the song
Of the way the world goes round,
The world goes round, in every town,
All the children sing the song
Of the way the world goes round.

3.
The Occidentals, Orientals,
Meet them at the fair;
Chefs are cookin', the strangest lookin'
Foods from everywhere,
Hands are shakin' through the nation
All the world will say,
Pack your grip and take the trip
For Expo's underway,
Pack your grip and take the trip
For Expo's underway.

REPEAT FIRST CHORUS;

TAG:
The world goes round in every town,
While the children sing the song
Of the way the world goes round.

C.D. 15, SNG. 15

WRECK OF THE TAMMY ANNE.

Chorus:
E7.   A.
They went down; they went down with the
      E.
Tammy Anne;
  A.   E.
They never saw those island shores again.
    A.
It was way out on 'the hook', boys,
 E.
She tossed up in the sand;
   B7.
And five young people lost their lives
               E.
In the WRECK OF THE TAMMY ANNE.

1.

 E.
We'll remember '87. on November, twenty-one;
  B7.   E.
It was storming on the Isles of Magdalene.
                  E7.
While the wind blew through the riggin'
  A.   E.
Of the little Tammy Anne,
  B7.   E.
She was loaded with ten barrels of gasoline.
     B7.
There were 5 young men and women;
    E.
Darla Hickey and Tracey Clark,
 B7.   E.
Kimberley Patton, Delbert and Lorne MacLean.

                      E7.
And when they left the Grindstone Harbour,
      A.   E.
They were bound for Entry Isle,
   B7.   E.
But they never saw those island shores again.

Chorus:

2.
When the Tammy Anne went missing
And the Coast Guard came to search
There were fishing boats already on the scene;
And when the bright lights hit the channel
From the liner Lucy Maude
They could see those drifting drums of gasoline.

3.
And when they later found the cabin
Tossing out there in the dark,
All hopes of the rescue fled with the
freezing wind;
And those brave young men and women
Who were bound for Entry Isle,
They never saw their island home again.

Repeat Chorus:

C.D., SNG.
To Be Recorded

YESTERDAY'S DREAM.

1.
A.   A7. D.   B7.
Yesterday's Dream never comes true;
E7.   A.
You're not with me, and I'm not with you.
     A7. D.   B7.
Sad as it seems, I must dream anew;
E7.   A.
Yesterday's Dream just never came true.

2.
  A.   A7. D.   B7.
Yesterday's Dream never comes true;
E7   A.
Wish as I may, I may never have you.

      A7. D.   B7.
Look at the rain, everything's blue;
E7.   A.
Yesterday's Dream just never came true.

Chorus:
E7   A.
Yesterday's Dream has gone with the tide;
E7.   A.
Castle of sand, oh, why have I cried?
     A7. D.   B7.
All is in vain, what else can I do?
E7.   A.
Yesterday's Dream just never came true.

C.D. 08, SNG. 12   **YOUR LOVING SMILE.**
By T.C.Connors
©1972 CROWN VETCH MUSIC
(SOCAN) All rights reserved.

Chorus: (Same melody as Verses)
C.   G7.
All the way from Thunder Bay,
C.   G7.   C.
Across the prairie wide;
                        G7.
I rode a train through hail and rain
C.   G7.   C.
To be here by your side.
          F.   C.
On a Mountain pass, smooth as glass,
            G7.   C.
I covered the icy miles;

Came over the 'moat' in a motor boat
  G7.   C.
To reach Vancouver Isle;
  G7.   C.
To see Your Loving Smile.

1.

I took it that you were kinda blue,
The way your letter read,
So I came out to clear the doubt,
From out of your pretty head,
From car to car beneath the stars,
I thumbed a thousand miles
 To bring the kiss you said you missed,
To old Vancouver Isle,
To see your loving smile.

2.

I've been over the muck in the back of a truck,
While bummin' and thumbin' along;
At thirty below and covered with snow,
I sang to keep me warm.
A couple of eggs, in a couple of days,
A biscuit once in a while,
Who gives a damn cause here I am
On old Vancouver Isle,
To see your loving smile.

3.

So open your arms and give me the charms,
That you've been longing to give;
Cause it's your lot to get what I got,
For ever as long as you live.
My heart for you has kept so true,
My love from over the miles,
All the way from Thunder Bay
To old Vancouver Isle,
To see your loving smile.

REPEAT CHORUS:

I know it's all worthwhile.

C.D. 18, SNG. 04   **YOUR SOMEONE LONESOME.**
By T.C.Connors & G.Lepine
©1993 CROWN VETCH MUSIC
(SOCAN) All rights reserved.

1.

  G7.   C.   D7.   G.
When Your Someone Lonesome loves you
  G7.   C.   D7.   G.
And you're someone lonesome too,
  G7.   C.   D7.   G. G7. C.
All your nights are filled with love-light
                        D7.   G.
And your lonesome days are through.
  G7.   C.   D7.   G.
When Your Someone Lonesome loves you
  G7.   C.   D7.   G.
And you're someone lonesome too,
  G7.   C.   D7.   G. G7. C.
All your nights are filled with love-light
              G.   D7.   G.
And your lonesome days are through.

YOU STRUCK ME OUT.

1.
VER:

D.   D7.   G.
You Struck Me Out before you got to know me
           A7.   D.
You broke my heart by throwing me a curve
              D7.   G.
I guess my life will always be a failure
        A7.   D.
And your love is more than I deserve.

2.
CHOR:

D7.   G.   D.
I should have told you everything about me
D7.   G.   A7.
But I guess I didn't have the nerve
          D.   D7.   G.
Your love is gone and though I'm out of prison
        A7.   D.
It's just another sentence I will serve.

3.
VER:

I meant to show you that I could be faithful
And with your help I could have kept my word
But you have flown because I didn't tell you
And I'm alone because of what you heard.

4.
CHOR:

You Struck Me Out before you got to know me
You broke my heart by throwing me a curve
I guess my life will always be a failure
And your love is more than I deserve.

5.
VER.

I should have told you everything about me
But I guess I didn't have the nerve
Your love is gone and though I'm out of prison
It's just another sentence I will serve.

6.
CHOR:

You Struck Me Out before you got to know me
You broke my heart by throwing me a curve
I guess my life will always be a failure
And your love is more than I deserve.

ZAKUSKA POLKA.

Chorus:

A.   E7.
Up, up, up, up. Papa; Up, up, up, up;
                        A.
Come up and dance, Mama, Up, up, up, up.
      A7.   D.
Samohonka, put some in cup;
      E7.   A.
Up, up, up, up; Up, up, up, up;
      E7.   A.
Up, up, up, up; Up, up, up, up.

1.
A7.   D.
Come up and dance and when you wish,
      A.
You could eat one pickled fish;
A7.   D.
Maybe cabbage roll, pyrogy, kobassa;
B7.   E7.
Maybe bowl of borscht, then polka.

2.
A.   E7.
Zakuska Polka, she's very fine;
                     A.
Sometime we dance, sometime we dine;
                       E7.
Sometime we drink, (hic), too much wine;
                A.
But Zakuska's good any time.

Repeat Chorus:

Now Repeat 1st & 2nd Verses
and End with Chorus

Final TAG-LINE:
Up. up, up, up; Up, up, up, up.
(Then Shout) ZAKUSKA!

C.D. 13, SNG. 03

By T.C.Connors
©1975 CROWN VETCH MUSIC
(SOCAN) All rights reserved.

ZEPHYRS IN THE MAPLE.

1.

C.   C7.
Oh, the holidays are back
   F.   C.
And we got the trailer packed,
           G7.
We're headin' for the country, don't you know;
     C.   C7.
Where the lazy days are long
    F.   C.
And the nights are full of song
        G7.   C.
And the Zephyrs in the Maple whisper low.

Chorus:
 C7.   F.   C.
Where the Zephyrs in the Maple whisper low,
          G7.
To a little country cabin we will go;
     C.   C7.
We'll put every care away
    F.   C.
And be happy every day,
         G7.   C.
Where the Zephyrs in the Maple whisper low.

2.

Where the trout jumps free
And says you'll not be catching me,
Up and down the river we will row;
When we catch him on the line,
He'll be good at suppertime,
When the Zephyrs in the Maple whisper low.

Chorus:

3.

You can hear the cricket sing
To the birds upon the wing,
And the furry creatures hurry to and fro;
And the kids are finding out
Here what nature's all about,
Where the Zephyrs in the Maple whisper low.

Chorus:

4.

Oh, to go forever more
To the cabin by the shore
And sit beside the little fire glow
Where the lazy days are long
And the nights are full of song
And the Zephyrs in the Maple whisper low,

Chorus:
And the Zephyrs in the Maple whisper low.

ACKNOWLEDGEMENT

While the purpose for compiling this book was to deal only with the recorded songs that I have personally written, co-written or traditionally arranged, the reader will no doubt discover that within the 22 album discography at the back of this book, there are songs which, although I recorded, I certainly did not write. The following is a list of these songs with an Album Number and a Song Number by which they can be located in the discography. Along with the songs I also wish to acknowledge and thank the following songwriters:

01. **ALCAN RUN.** By J. Simpson. Alb. 10, Song 10.
02. **COME WHERE WE'RE AT.** By D. Nolan. Alb. 06, Song 03.
03. **DOMINOES & DICE.** By Wood & Dobbs. Alb. 20, Song 12.
04. **GHOST OF BRAS D'OR.** BY C. MacKinnon. Alb. 13, Song 09.
05. **GREEN GRASS OF HOME #2.** (Not Known). Alb. 06, Song 04.
06. **HAPPY ROVIN' COWBOY.** (Unknown). Alb. 06, Song 01.
07. **I'VE BEEN EVERYWHERE.** By G. Mack. (Added Verses by T.C.) Alb. 06, Song 08.
08. **ISLE OF NEWFOUNDLAND.** By B. Cuff. Alb. 14, Song 12.
09. **LAST FATAL DUEL.** By F. Dixon. Alb. 08, Song 02.
10. **LOG TRAIN.** By S.J. Foote. Alb. 05, Song 04.
11. **MUK TUK ANNIE.** By B. Ruzicka. Alb. 11, Song 06.
12. **MULESKINNER BLUES.** By J. Rodgers. (Modified by T.C.) Alb. 06, Song 06.
13. **MY HOME BY THE FRASER.** By K. Reagan. Alb. 11, Song 02.
14. **MY OLD CANADIAN HOME.** By W. Carter. Alb. 11, Song 13.
15. **PADDLE WHEELER.** By A. Oster. Alb. 11, Song 04.
16. **POOR, POOR FARMER.** By K. Reagan. Alb. 05, Song 10.
17. **RENFREW VALLEY.** (Not Known). Alb. 11, Song 12.
18. **SAMMY MORGAN'S GIN.** By C.E. Snow. Alb. 20, Song 11.
19. **SILVER SEA.** By Evans & Wainwright. Alb. 20, Song 08.
20. **SPIN, SPIN.** By G. Lightfoot. Alb. 06, Song 05.
21. **THAT "AWFUL" THING.** (aka The Thing). By Greane. Alb. 22, Song 13.
22. **THE FRENCH SONG.** By Pease & Vincent. Alb. 15, Song 04.
23. **THE CANADIAN LUMBERJACK.** By R. Miron. (Translation by T.C.) Alb. 03, Song 11.

DISCOGRAPHY
(The Number of Song and the Page it's on.)

NORTHLAND'S ZONE.
Album (CD) No: 01.
Song No:

	Pg. No:
01. World Goes Round.	167
02. Maritime Waltz.	93
03. Northern Gentleman.	113
04. Movin' On To Rouyn.	101
05. May, The Millwright's Daughter.	95
06. Algoma Central No.69	9
07. Emily, The Maple Leaf.	42
08. Goin' Back Up North.	50
09. Streets Of Toronto.	149
10. My Home Cradled Out In The Waves.	106
11. Peterborough Postman.	120
12. Carolyne.	30
13. Sudbury Saturday Night.	150
14. Little Wawa.	84
15. My Swisha Miss.	110
16. Flyin' C.P.R.	48

ON TRAGEDY TRAIL.
Album (CD) No: 02.
Song No:

	Pg. No:
01. Tragedy Trail.	155
02. How The Mountain Came Down.	62
03. Shanty Town Sharon.	137
04. Fire In The Mine.	46
05. Somewhere There's Sorrow.	142
06. Don Valley Jail.	40
07. Benny The Bum.	16
08. Black Donnelly's Massacre.	20
09. Battle Of Despair.	14
10. Reesor Crossing Tragedy.	126
11. Little Boy's Prayer.	83
12. Around The Bay And Back Again.	12

BUD THE SPUD.
Album (CD) No: 03.
Song No:

	Pg. No:
01. Bud The Spud.	27
02. Ketchup Song.	77
03. Ben, In The Pen.	15
04. Rubberhead.	132
05. Luke's Guitar.	88
06. My Brother Paul.	104
07. Old Atlantic Shore.	117
08. My Little Eskimo.	108
09. Reversing Falls Darling.	127
10. She Don't Speak English.	138
11. Canadian Lumberjack.	172
12. Sudbury Saturday Night.	150
13. T.T.C. Skidaddler.	157
14. Gone With The Wind.	51

MERRY CHRISTMAS EVERYBODY.
Album (CD) No: 04.
Song No:

	Pg. No:
01. Merry Christmas Everybody.	97
02. Merry Bells.	96
03. Christmas Angel.	31
04. Down On Christmas.	42
05. Jingle Jangled Aeroplane.	72
06. Kiss Me The New Year In.	78
07. Mr. Snowflake.	103
08. Story Of Jesus.	148
09. An Orphan's Christmas.	11
10. One Blue Light.	118
11. Gloria.	50
12. Our Father.	119

DISCOGRAPHY

(The Number of Song and the Page it's on.)

DISCOGRAPHY
(The Number of Song and the Page it's on.)

DISCOGRAPHY

(The Number of Song and the Page it's on.)

UNPOPULAR STOMPIN' TOM. Album (CD) No: 13. Song No:	Pg. No:
01. Good Morning Mr. Sunshine.	52
02. Where The Chinooks Blow.	164
03. Zephyrs In The Maple.	171
04. My Door's Always Open To You.	105
05. Blue Misery.	22
06. Pole And The Hole, The	122
07. Muckin' Slushers. (Damn Good Song,)	37
08. Cowboy, Johnny Ware.	35
09. Ghost Of Bras D'Or.	172
10. Don Valley Jail.	40
11. Big And Friendly Waiter John.	17
12. Olympic Song, The	118

GUMBOOT CLOGGEROO. Album (CD) No: 14. Song No:	Pg. No:
01. Legend Of Marty And Joe.	81
02. Jacqueline.	71
03. Handy-Man Blues.	53
04. Man From The Land.	90
05. Farewell To Nova Scotia.	45
06. Ripped Off Winkle.	128
07. Gumboot Cloggeroo.	52
08. Happy Hooker, The	54
09. We Doubt Each Other's Love.	160
10. Little Old Forgetful Me.	83
11. Singer, The	139
12. Isle Of Newfoundland.	172
13. Roses In The Snow.	131
14. Home On The Island.	57

FIDDLE AND SONG. Album (CD) No: 15. Song No:	Pg. No:
01. Lady. K.D. Lang.	80
02. Fiddler's Folly.	46
03. It's All Over Now, Anyhow.	69
04. French Song, The (With Lena)	172
05. I Never Want To See The World Again.	67
06. Hillside Hay-Ride.(instrumental)*	N/A
07. Morning & Evening & Always.	99
08. Return Of The Sea Queen.	126
09. Canada Day, Up Canada Way.	29
10. Jolly Joe MacFarland.	74
11. Skinner's Pond Tea Pot,	140
12. Teardrop Waltz. (instrumental)*	N/A
13. Entry Island Home, My	43
14. I Am The Wind.	63
15. Wreck Of The Tammy Anne.	168

STOMPIN TOM PHENOMENON. Album (CD) No: 16. Song No:	Pg. No:
01. Margo's Cargo.	92
02. Flyin' C.P.R.	48
03. Rita MacNeil. (A Tribute)	128
04. Brown Eyes For The Blues.	26
05. J.R.'s Bar.	75
06. Loser's Island.	86
07. St. Anne's Song & Reel.	146
08. Made In The Shade.	89
09. Love's Not The Only Thing.	87
10. Land Of The Maple Tree.	80
11. Real Canadian Girl, A	124
12. Okanagan Okee.	116
13. No Canadian Dream.	111
14. Gone With The Wind.	51

━━ DISCOGRAPHY ━━
(The Number of Song and the Page it's on.)

DISCOGRAPHY
(The Number of Song and the Page it's on.)

NOTE:

* The two instrumentals found on album **NO: 15. FIDDLE & SONG,**
namely Hillside Hayride and Teardrop Waltz
were written respectively by T.C.Connors and T.C.Connors with G.Lepine.
Both songs ©1986 by Crown-Vetch Music (SOCAN) All Rights Reserved.

** **For all information and availability of all Stompin' Tom books,
songs, recordings, ETC., please visit: W W W . S T O M P I N T O M . C O M
or write to: A-C-T Records Ltd. Box 129 Georgetown, Ontario, Canada L7G 4T1.**

HANDY RHYMES AND MEMORY AIDS
(WITH RHYMING WORDS UNDERLINED.)

1. Always Remember, whatever you <u>do</u>; That Pi is 3.14<u>2</u>

2. And don't you know, it's been <u>declared</u>, The Area of a Circle is Pi <u>R^2</u>.   (^{2} = squared)

3. The Circumference of a Circle is Certain to <u>be</u> Twice Pi Radius or Once Pi <u>D</u>.   (D = diameter)

4. The Surface Area of a Sphere is <u>sure</u> To be Pi R^2, Multiplied by <u>4</u>.

5. The Volume of a Sphere is Pi <u>R^c</u>, If you 4 Times that and Divide by <u>3</u>. (^{c} = cubed)

6. The Surface Area of a Cone is <u>Pi</u> Times the Radius Squared, Plus Pi R <u>Side</u>.

7. The Volume of a Cone will always <u>be</u> Pi R^2 Times Height-Over-<u>Three</u>.

8. The Surface Area of a Cylinder <u>equates</u> With Twice Pi R^2 Plus 2 Pi R <u>H</u>.

9. The Volume of a Cylinder will always be <u>right</u> When you Multiply the Area of the Base by the <u>Height</u>.

10. The Volume of a Pyramid? You Multiply <u>these</u>: Length, Width, Height; and Divide by <u>3</u>.

11. The Area of any Triangle; "P, D, <u>Q</u>." Is Base Times Height and Divide by <u>2</u>.

12. The Square of the Hypotenuse of a "Right-Ang.-<u>Tri</u>'.' Equals the Sum of the Squares of the Other 2 <u>Sides</u>.

13. To make the Circle's Diameter <u>known</u> When only a Section of Arc is <u>shown</u>,
    Square Half the Length of the Base of the Arc, Then Add the Square of its <u>Height</u>:
    If you then Divide by the Height of the Arc The Diameter comes to <u>light</u>.

EXPLANATION of Above Terms and Abbreviations:

Rhyme No. 2	R = Radius = 1/2 Diameter. R^2 = R x R.
Rhyme No. 3	Twice Pi Radius = 2 x Pi x R. Once Pi D = 1 x Pi x Diameter.
Rhyme No. 4	Pi R^2 = Pi x R^2. (3.142 x R x R). Then Multiply by 4.
Rhyme No. 5	R^c = Radius Cubed or R x R x R. (Pi R^c = Pi x R^c.)
Rhyme No. 6	The Formula here is: Pi x R^2 + Pi x R x Length of the Side.
Rhyme No. 7	Height-Over-Three = Height (H) Divided by 3.
Rhyme No. 8	The Formula here is: 2 x Pi x R^2 + 2 x Pi x R x Height (H).
Rhyme No. 9	The Area of the Base = Pi R^2. (See Rhyme No. 2).
Rhyme No. 11	P,D & Q = Each of the 3 Sides. Base = Floor of the Triangle.
Rhyme No. 12	"Right-Ang.-Tri" = Right Angle Triangle.

NOTE: If one were to take 2 weeks and memorize just one of these Rhymes per day, he or she could utilize these very important formulas anywhere and at any time throughout life without searching for that always elusive reference book which contains them.

By Tom C. Connors

━━ STOMPIN TOM'S 3000 YEAR CALENDAR ━━

To **MY READERS** who may be interested in perpetual calendars, I now print here, free of charge, a calendar I invented that is truly perpetual and complete with instructions for immediate use. In reality, what you get here is exactly what I once advertised in the National Enquirer and is totally accurate for all practical day and date calculations. But as extensive as it may seem, it is merely a very small segment of my much larger "Everdate Perpetual Calendar" which calculates millions of years. This little one is only operative from the time of Christ to A.D. 3200, but quite adequate for the needs of most people. The larger one is more adapted to archaeologists and people with like interests.

First off, in calculating any dates, it's always important to remember how many days there are in each month of the year. So here is a simple poem I've composed that will tell you just that. It is an adaptation of a much older poem which was considerably harder to memorize.

DAYS IN A MONTH POEM

30 days in September, April, June and November;
The rest have 31 like January.
But the month with the fate of only having 28,
And in Leap Year, 29, is February

DAY CHART C

DAY CODE	Sn	M	T	W	T	F	S	Sn	M	T	W	T	F	S	Sn	M	T	W	T	F	S	Sn	M	T	W	T	F	S	Sn	M	T	W	T	F	S	Sn	M
J-7							1	2	3	4	5	6	7	8	9	10	11	12	13	14	15	16	17	18	19	20	21	22	23	24	25	26	27	28	29	30	31
K-6						1	2	3	4	5	6	7	8	9	10	11	12	13	14	15	16	17	18	19	20	21	22	23	24	25	26	27	28	29	30	31	
V-5					1	2	3	4	5	6	7	8	9	10	11	12	13	14	15	16	17	18	19	20	21	22	23	24	25	26	27	28	29	30	31		
R-4				1	2	3	4	5	6	7	8	9	10	11	12	13	14	15	16	17	18	19	20	21	22	23	24	25	26	27	28	29	30	31			
M-3			1	2	3	4	5	6	7	8	9	10	11	12	13	14	15	16	17	18	19	20	21	22	23	24	25	26	27	28	29	30	31				
S-2		1	2	3	4	5	6	7	8	9	10	11	12	13	14	15	16	17	18	19	20	21	22	23	24	25	26	27	28	29	30	31					
T-1	1	2	3	4	5	6	7	8	9	10	11	12	13	14	15	16	17	18	19	20	21	22	23	24	25	26	27	28	29	30	31						

STOMPIN' TOM'S 3000 YEAR CALENDAR

EVERDATE © 1978
BY T.C. CONNORS
ALL RIGHTS RESERVED

MONTH — CHART B

Ja	Fb	Mr	Ap	My	Jn	Jl	Au	Sp	Oc	Nv	Dc
J	M	R	J	S	V	J	M	K	T	R	K
K	S	M	K	T	R	K	S	V	J	M	V
V	T	S	V	J	M	V	T	R	K	S	R
R	J	T	R	K	S	R	J	M	V	T	M
M	K	J	M	V	T	M	K	S	R	J	S
S	V	K	S	R	J	S	V	T	M	K	T
T	R	V	T	M	K	T	R	J	S	V	J

Ja	Fb	Mr	Ap	My	Jn	Jl	Au	Sp	Oc	Nv	Dc
7	3	3	6	1	4	6	2	5	7	3	5
6	2	2	5	7	3	5	1	4	6	2	4
5	1	1	4	6	2	4	7	3	5	1	3
4	7	7	3	5	1	3	6	2	4	7	2
3	6	6	2	4	7	2	5	1	3	6	1
2	5	5	1	3	6	1	4	7	2	5	7
1	4	4	7	2	5	7	3	6	1	4	6

CENTURY BOX

CENTURY BOX	00
0 4 8 12 16 20 24 28	J
1 5 9 13 17 21 25 29	6
2 6 10 14 18 22 26 30	4
3 7 11 15 19 23 27 31	2

YEARS CHART A

01	02	03	04	05	06	07	08	09	10	11	12	13	14	15
16	17	18	19	20	21	22	23	24	25	26	27	28	29	30
31	32	33	34	35	36	37	38	39	40	41	42	43		
44	45	46	47	48	49	50	51	52	53	54	55	56	57	58
59	60	61	62	63	64	65	66	67	68	69	70	71		
72	73	74	75	76	77	78	79	80	81	82	83	84	85	86
87	88	89	90	91	92	93	94	95	96	97	98	99		

Code grid (century codes J, 6, 4, 2):

LY	*			LY				LY				LY			LY												
K	1	2	3	R	6	7	1	S	4	5	6	J	2	3	4	V	7	1	2	M	5	6	7	T	3	4	5
R	6	7	1	S	4	5	6	J	2	3	4	V	7	1	2	M	5	6	7	T	3	4	5	K	1	2	3
S	4	5	6	J	2	3	4	V	7	1	2	M	5	6	7	T	3	4	5	K	1	2	3	R	6	7	1
J	2	3	4	V	7	1	2	M	5	6	7	T	3	4	5	K	1	2	3	R	6	7	1	S	4	5	6

*LY—Stands for Leap Year

3000 YEAR CALENDAR INSTRUCTIONS

To find the name of the day any given date falls on, you must first, of course, have a date. So let's pick the year of 1895, on July 22. The number of centuries that have gone by is 18, and the number of years is 95. Now look for 18 in the Century Box on the calendar and move to the right along the row it's situated on, until you come to the column in which the 95 is situated in the Years Chart A. Your finger should now be resting on a "3" which is your key number for going to the next chart, called the Month Chart B.

You will now notice that Chart B has a left side composed of all letters which represent Leap Years, and a right side composed of all numbers which represent Regular Years.

We now look for your key number "3" in the January Column of Regular Years in Chart B and from the "3" we follow the row to the right until we come to the column which contains July, and here we find a "2."

The "2" now is your key number for going to the Day Chart C and there on the far left we find a column of letters and numbers called the Day Code.

We now find your key number "2" in the Day Code and we move along this row to the right until we come to the number 22. And there at the top of the column which contains the number 22 is "M" for Monday.

We have just found out that July 22 of 1895 was a Monday. Now, that wasn't too hard, was it? So let's find out now what day Christmas fell on in the year 1976.

First we take the 19 from the 1976 and go to the Century Box. With our finger on the 19 we follow the row to the right until we stop at the bottom of the column which contains the number 76 in the Years Chart A. This time our finger has stopped on the letter "V" instead of a number. This means that 1976 was a Leap Year as indicated by the letters LY in the middle of the column.

We now take our key letter "V" and go to the January Column on the Leap Year side of the Month Chart B and from the "V" we follow the row to the right until we come to the last column under December and our finger should now be resting on an "R."

We now look for the "R" in the Day Code Column at the far left of the Day Chart C. And if we follow the row to the right which contains the "R" we pass all the days in December until we stop at 25, which is Christmas Day, and at the top of the column we see that Christmas, on the twenty-fifth of December in 1976, Fell on a Saturday.

Now, there's only one more thing you need to know. If you look at the Years Chart A you will see that the numbers only go from 01 to 99. So what happened to all the years that end in 00, such as 1400, 1900, 2000, 2300, etc.? Well, just to the immediate right of the Century Box you will see a small column with two zeros (00) on the top. So if you wanted to find out what day March 1 fell on in the year 2000, you would go to the 20 in the Century Box and follow this row to the right and immediately stop at the small column directly under the two zeros (00), and there you would find a "J." And because "J" is a letter and not a number you know the year 2000 is a Leap Year.

You now go to the January Column on the Leap Year side of the Month Chart B and in the row that starts with "J" you go across to the March Column and find that your finger now rests on an "R." Now, in the Day Code Column of the Day Chart C you will find that "R" will lead you directly to the number one (1) right under the "W" for Wednesday. So March 1 in the year 2000 was a Wednesday.

Always remember that Key Letters represent Leap Years and you go to the left side of the Month Chart B, and Key Numbers represent Regular Years and you go to the right side of the Month Chart B. And one more little thing that you'll no doubt find out for yourself: once you have found your Key Letter or Key Number in the Years Chart A and the date you're looking for is in January of any year, you can bypass the Month Chart B altogether, and go directly to the Day Code in the Day Chart C. (This quick method is only good for January and no other months.)

Well, there it is. And with a little bit of practice you will be able to operate the calendar at a glance. And here's a few names of some famous people, along with their birthdates and the day of the week on which they were born, so you can look them up and check your accuracy. This will give you enough practice to go ahead and reveal to all your friends the actual day they were born on. Happy Dating.

Neil Armstrong was born August 5, 1930, on a Tuesday.
Albert Einstein was born March 14, 1879, on a Friday.
Martin Luther King was born January 15, 1929, on a Tuesday.
Sophia Loren was born September 20, 1934, on a Thursday.
Pierre Trudeau was born October 18, 1919, on a Saturday.
Wayne Gretzky was born January 26, 1961, on a Thursday.
George Washington was born February 22, 1732, on a Friday.
Stompin' Tom Connors was born February 9, 1936, on a   ?

GUITAR CHORDS

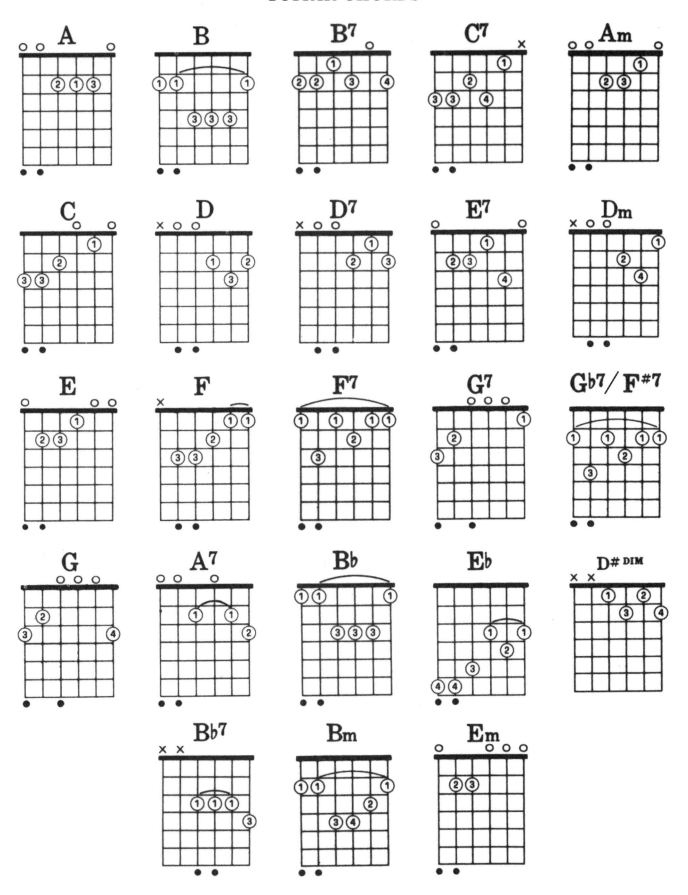

Black dots under charts indicate alternate bass notes.

NOTES

NOTES

NOTES

NOTES